MW01194805

CAREER
COUNSELING

AN ANTHOLOGY OF RELEVANT
CAREER COUNSELING RESEARCH

CAREER COUNSELING

AN ANTHOLOGY OF RELEVANT CAREER COUNSELING RESEARCH

FIRST EDITION

Edited by David A. Scott, Ph.D. and Chadwick W. Royal, Ph.D.

cognella® | ACADEMIC PUBLISHING

Bassim Hamadeh, CEO and Publisher
Kassie Graves, Vice President of Editorial
Jamie Giganti, Director of Academic Publishing
Jackie Bignotti, Production Artist
Jennifer McCarthy, Field Acquisitions Editor
Michelle Piehl, Senior Project Editor
Stephanie Kohl, Licensing Coordinator
Casey Hands, Associate Production Editor

Copyright © 2019 by Cognella, Inc. All rights reserved. No part of this publication may be reprinted, reproduced, transmitted, or utilized in any form or by any electronic, mechanical, or other means, now known or hereafter invented, including photocopying, microfilming, and recording, or in any information retrieval system without the written permission of Cognella, Inc.

Trademark Notice: Product or corporate names may be trademarks or registered trademarks, and are used only for identification and explanation without intent to infringe.

Copyright © 2010 Depositphotos/Joingate.

Printed in the United States of America

ISBN: 978-1-5165-3161-5 (pbk) / 978-1-5165-3162-2 (br)

cognella® | ACADEMIC PUBLISHING

CONTENTS

CHAPTER 7 CAREER COUNSELING RESOURCES 176

CHAPTER 8 CAREER CHOICES ACROSS THE LIFESPAN 200

CHAPTER 9 CAREER COUNSELING SETTINGS   224

ACKNOWLEDGMENTS

We would like to thank Jennifer McCarthy, Kassie Graves, Michelle Piehl, and the editorial team at Cognella for the support and guidance. We would also like to thank our families for their support and encouragement throughout the project.

INTRODUCTION

Think back to when you were a child. Do you remember what you wanted to be when you grew up? Many times, our first career thoughts are generated by the people around us. We see our family and teachers engaged in occupations that seem like options. As we grow older and enter high school, we are posed with one of the toughest questions we will ever try to answer: "What do you want to do as your career?" How are we supposed to decide what our career will be for the next 50 years? How much money will I make, how long do I need to stay in school, where will I need to live, will my parents be happy with my decision, and will I be happy with my decision are just a few questions that could take years and several career changes to determine. Some people take career exploration lightly or don't value career counseling in general. Did you know that we will spend roughly one third or our lives at work? Now, does it seem like a trivial decision?

One of the goals of the career counseling class is to help students understand the importance of career counseling and how it can impact almost every part of a person's life. Many of our future clients will come in for counseling due to something career related. Our goal as counselor educators is to provide students with information related to career counseling theories by working with diverse clients and using assessments and interest inventories, career resources, and settings where career counseling can take place. While most of the primary career counseling texts provide an overview of these topics, we believe that adding these outside readings provide a much-needed perspective that can complement traditional textbooks. These readings and discussion questions hopefully encourage the exploration of career-related issues relevant to today's career professional. We have also included key terms and suggestions for further reading.

Through the information we have provided in these chapters, we hope you will come to appreciate the need for competent career practitioners, engage in discussions that will lead to something exciting, and understand the role you will play in the field of career counseling.

CAREER CHOICE

EXTERNAL AND INTERNAL FACTORS

INTRODUCTION

I am sure that we all can think back to some first memories of career exploration. Many times, we wanted to grow up to work in fields that had the most impact and influence in our lives. When I talk to young children, I hear careers such as teachers (they spend most of their days with teachers), veterinarians (many kids love animals) or a job similar to a parent or family member's. I hear so many stories about college students being *encouraged* by family members to pick majors that will enable them to pay their bills. Who said we have to define career success by how much we earn at a job? When you think of how you finally decided on a career path, what or who helped you make this critical decision?

Whether we know it or not, there are numerous internal and external factors that contribute to our career decisions. This chapter contains articles that examine the external and internal factors that impact our career decisions. As you read this chapter, think about some of the external and internal factors that helped shape your career decisions.

Beyond the Self
External Influences in the Career Development Process

RYAN D. DUFFY AND BRYAN J. DIK

The purpose of this article is to explore the wide spectrum of external influences that affect career decision making across the life span and, in particular, how these factors may directly or indirectly alter one's career trajectory and the extent of one's work volition. Career development practitioners are encouraged to respect externally oriented frameworks, explore the social influence of career choice alternatives faced by clients, encourage clients to voice their emotional responses to external constraints, and use career decision-making strategies that seek an optimal balance of internal and external influences.

Within the field of vocational psychology, several major theories have emerged to explain the process by which individuals make career choices. According to some of these theories, person-environment fit is most critical, whereby an individual's unique interests, values, and skills are ideally matched with a certain job setting (Dawis & Lofquist, 1984; Holland, 1997). Other theories view individuals as being in a constant state of development, in which the optimal career is one that best facilitates

Ryan D. Duffy and Bryan J. Dik, "Beyond the Self: External Influences in the Career Development Process," *The Career Development Quarterly*, vol. 58, no. 1, pp. 29-43. Copyright © 2009 by National Career Development Association. Reprinted with permission. Provided by ProQuest LLC. All rights reserved.

the implementation of a person's current self-concept (Savickas, 2002; Super, 1990). Theories that emphasize social learning and cognition have also been advanced. According to these theories, an individual's learning experiences about work and perceived ability to perform particular tasks necessary to succeed in a certain career are vital to decision making (Krumboltz, 1996; Lent, Brown, & Hackett, 1994). Although these theories differ in substantive ways, all focus primarily on the influence of an individual's internal goals, needs, and pursuit of satisfaction in career decision making. This commonality carries an implicit assumption that individuals making career decisions have the volition to do so and are primarily seeking their own satisfaction. However, recent work throughout the social sciences has demonstrated that these assumptions may be unfounded, because decisions are often made with limited options or in a collectivist context (e.g., Blustein, McWhirter, & Perry, 2005; Jackson, Colquitt, Wesson, & Zapata-Phelan, 2006; Oyserman, Coon, & Kemmelmeier, 2002).

Recently, the conceptual and theoretical work of Blustein and colleagues (e.g., Blustein, 2006; Blustein et al., 2005) has highlighted the need to better understand the role of volition in the career development process, with a particular focus on the negative influence of an individual's life circumstances on freedom of choice. The concept of volition is not new to the field of psychology, and most commonly refers to an individual's ability to have freedom in life choices (Lazarick, Fishbein, & Loiello, 1988). In a counseling context, research has demonstrated that therapists tend to view clients as having free will to make their own decisions (Chen, 2006; Slife & Fisher, 2000) and often view shifting the responsibility of choice away from clients as harmful (Kernes & McWhirter, 2001). However, although viewing individuals as absolute agents may be convenient, it is evident that life experiences and circumstances can significantly affect the degree to which each decision is volitional.

From a career development perspective, *work volition* refers to an individual's ability to freely make career choices, including the initial job choice when first entering the work world and any subsequent career decisions. Although volition has primarily been an underlying assumption of career choice theories, rather than a variable that has been investigated empirically, research has found that employed individuals who feel freedom in their job tasks report more positive work outcomes, including job satisfaction, meaning, and involvement (Bond & Bunce, 2003; Henderson, 2000; Muhonen & Torkelson, 2004; von Rosenstiel, Kehr, & Maier, 2000). This same principle could likely be extended to the career choice process, in which a higher degree of satisfaction may be found with individuals who believe they have high levels of control over their career paths. For example, one study found individuals with greater perceived control of their decision making reported lower anxiety in making decisions (Weinstein, Healy, & Ender, 2002).

Despite the common assumption of personal control and a focus on internal satisfaction embedded in most psychological theories of career choice and development, some theorists have placed a greater emphasis on certain aspects of external and nonvolitional components. For example, the theory of work adjustment (Dawis & Lofquist, 1984) postulates that changes in work environments often require changes on the part of the employee to maintain an acceptable degree of fit. However, the theory focuses little on external influences outside of the immediate work environment. Gottfredson's (1981, 2005) theory of circumscription and compromise delineates the influence of external influences related to gender stereotypes and prestige. However, Gottfredson's (1981, 2005) treatment of external influences is noncomprehensive, and empirical support for its tenets has been called into question (e.g., Swanson & Gore, 2000).

Social cognitive career theory (Lent et al., 1994; Lent, Brown, & Hackett, 2000) perhaps does the best job of postulating a critical role for external factors by suggesting resources and barriers influence career decision making indirectly through their effects on the acquisition of self-efficacy and outcome expectations and directly through their effects on choice goals and choice actions. However, internal influences (e.g., self-efficacy, outcome expectations) have been the dominant focus of this theory's researchers, and of the studies that have been completed focusing on barriers and resources, few have surveyed working adults. As such, empirical efforts to examine the role of external influences are needed to balance the knowledge base.

Other theorists have questioned the utility of volition-based approaches for many workers and proposed holistic models that place a greater emphasis on external factors, such as the changing economy, the changing world of work, and the connection of an individual's multiple life roles to the individual's career choices (Hansen, 1997). Similarly, sociological research (Hotchkiss & Borow, 1996; Johnson & Mortimer, 2002) has explored societal-level external influences (e.g., education structure and quality, local market conditions) on career behavior. However, this work tends to lack a unified theoretical framework useful for practitioners and is limited in scope to variables of primary interest to sociologists. To build on this previous theory and research, the present article addresses several factors across the spectrum of external influences that may limit or enhance a person's career decision-making process and examines how counselors might work effectively with clients for whom external influences are particularly salient.

Defining the major constructs used throughout this article is important. First, when the term *career* is used as a qualifier (e.g., career decision making, career choice), it refers to any process related to work or working, whereas when the term is used as a noun (e.g., the course of an individual's career), it refers generally to a series of paid or unpaid occupations a person holds throughout his or her life (Sears, 1982). Second, throughout this article, the terms *internal* and *external* are used to describe different sources of influence on career decision making, when at a given time an individual could be simultaneously influenced by both types of sources. An *internal* source is defined as originating within the individual, whereby individual satisfaction represents the primary motivation. In contrast, an *external* source is defined as originating from someone or something outside the individual, whereby the satisfaction of some external factor or criteria represents the primary motivation. Examples of these sources of influence, which will be discussed at length, include external factors that individuals have freely chosen to guide their choice processes (i.e., motivators such as responding to a set of needs in society) as well as largely uncontrollable factors that develop from life circumstances (i.e., constraints such as prejudice because of racism or sexism).

The line between what serves as a motivator or a constraint is not always clear, and a particular factor may serve as a motivator, a constraint, or both, depending on individual circumstances. Additionally, external factors (both positive and negative) serve to shape the development of internal interests, values, and skills among all individuals. For example, individuals raised in particular environments and subjected to particular socialization experiences will develop unique sets of career beliefs and expectations; research and theory examining these factors for groups of children, adolescents, and college students is robust (Fouad, 2007). The current article focuses on the influences that are salient immediately before a person's decision point, rather than on the more distal developmental processes that shape many of those influences over time.

Finally, an argument can be made that an individual who chooses to place weight on an external factor in making a career decision is doing so using internal mechanisms, thus confounding any attribution of an influence as external. Space constraints preclude delving into the philosophical debates that this point has incited over the centuries (e.g., free will vs. determinism). Rather, for purposes of the present article, we consider an influence to be external if it is perceived by the individual to have originated beyond the self. The assumption is that all clients appeal to some combination of internal and external factors in their decision making and the ratio of importance placed on each category will greatly vary. However, given their status as both critically important and understudied, the focus of this article is on external influences and the types of individuals especially inclined to view them as primary.

We focus specifically on four categories of external influences; family expectations and needs, life circumstances, spiritual, and religious factors, and social service motivation. Each of these categories represents factors outside the individuals that are hypothesized to constrain or motivate an individual's choice behavior. We also assume that each of these categories of external factors interacts with internal factors to varying degrees when they influence an individual's choice-making process. For example, social service motivation may become a salient influence on career choice when a person experiences a pull from a particular social need, such as reversing the detrimental effects of climate change (an external influence), that converges with a push from the individual's own altruistic values (an internal influence). Thus, the separation of external from internal influences is a matter of convenience to facilitate discussion and is not intended to suggest that the influences operate independently. By no means are these four categories meant to exhaust the expanse of external factors, many of which have been reviewed at length elsewhere (e.g., institutional racism). However, these factors have received comparatively less attention in the literature, yet are arguably among the most salient for populations seeking career counseling.

FAMILY EXPECTATIONS AND NEEDS

Perhaps the most significant category of external factors affecting most individuals' career development entails the expectations and needs of family (Greenhaus & Powell, 2006; Halpern, 2005; Schultheiss, 2006). Even in an American culture that often values individualism over collectivism (Williams, 2003), an individual's family can affect the development of internal values, interests, and skills and a person's stability in the working world. A review by Whiston and Keller (2004) explored family-of-origin influences as they relate to the career development process across the life span. On the basis of 77 studies, these authors concluded that family-of-origin characteristics significantly relate to people's aspirations, interests, feelings of support, self-efficacy, and choice; these relationships also seem to vary on the basis of gender and race. Although a family can be viewed as external to the individual, the values and expectations a family imposes are likely among the many factors influencing the development of internal interests, values, and skills. Beyond their indirect effects, however, family expectations and needs can play a dramatic role in making here-and-now career choices, and these factors may often supersede internalized processes (Halpern, 2005).

Family expectations and needs can affect individuals at all stages of career decision making, from the adolescent seeking a first job to the seasoned worker looking for new employment (Phillips, Christopher-Sisk, & Gravino, 2001). Research has found that for many adolescents, particularly those from collectivist cultures, parents may already have a career path planned for the child, such as taking over the family business, or parents may inflict shame and guilt if a specific career path is not followed (Miller & Brown, 2005; Young et al., 2001). This influence may be especially poignant for individuals from families whose cultures or local economies require specific work tasks and responsibilities, such as those raised on an American Indian reservation or in an Amish community (Juntunen et al., 2001). For adults in the working world, the influence of having children, having to make career decisions that affect both oneself and a partner, the need to care for older family members, family relocation, and juggling economic pressures are just several of the many factors that can significantly undermine career choice volition (Greenhaus, Parasuraman, & Collins, 2001; Halpern, 2005). Although the value underlying most theories of career development is that finding a career in line with an individual's values, interests, and skills would be best, expecting single parents supporting their families to make career choices solely on the basis of the dominant internal factors in these theories would be unreasonable. Similarly, expecting adolescents to completely deny the expectations and needs of their families, should these expectations and needs go against their own desires, would be imposing a subjective, individualist view on the career choice process.

The power and influence of one's family on initial career decisions and subsequent job choices is critical to consider for all clients with career concerns, especially those for whom family expectations and needs conflict with internal aspirations. Although the constraining components of a family, which are infrequently discussed in the literature, have been mentioned, a great deal of research exists that also describes the supportive role a family can provide in an individual's career process. This may come in the form of financial and emotional support, networking, and social resources (Pearson & Bieschke, 2001; Schultheiss, 2003; Young et al., 2001).

LIFE CIRCUMSTANCES

The phrase *life circumstances* can convey a variety of meanings; here, it refers to all of the uncontrollable situations, events, and conditions that occur at an individual and societal level that may constrain career decision making. Often these circumstances are positive and produce beneficial career outcomes for an individual, such as serendipitous events that lead to better employment or experiences that illuminate a type of job-related task that is particularly enjoyable. Mitchell, Levin, and Krumboltz (1999) discussed this notion with the idea of career-related planned happenstance, in which they acknowledge the large role of seemingly random events in clients' career processes and provide strategies for clients to create and capitalize on serendipitous occurrences.

Often, however, life events may not be easily used as learning or growth experiences and can have significant detrimental effects on work volition. For example, situational variables such as poverty, marginalization, and stigmatization have been found to hamper the career aspirations and career achievements of children, adolescents, and adults (Arnold & Doctoroff, 2003; Blustein et al., 2002). As in the case of Maslow's (1943) need hierarchy, if physiological, safety, and belonging needs are not met, expecting an individual to view work as anything more than a means to meet these needs may be unrealistic. On an even broader scale, changes in economic and market conditions that may be caused by historical events and environmental constraints such as natural disasters can ripple through the work world and affect job opportunities and resources (Hotchkiss & Borow, 1996; Johnson & Mortimer, 2002). A clear example of this phenomenon is the Hurricane Katrina disaster, in which the career paths of more than 200,000 people were suddenly and dramatically altered.

On a smaller scale, specific life events can trigger shifts in an individual's career path that are antithetical to internalized objectives. These events may include job loss, injury, or a sudden change in an individual's financial situation. When these types of events occur, the ideal career needs of the individual will likely be subjugated to meet these more pressing and immediate demands caused by such life circumstances. Also, the degree to which a person's career choices are volitional may be heavily influenced by an individual's physical and mental conditions. Taken from 2000 Census data, estimates show that approximately 1 in 5 Americans have some type of disability and 1 in 10 have a severe disability (Waldrop & Stern, 2003). Clearly, a physical or mental disability can limit career opportunities; individuals with disabilities may be forced to choose jobs and careers that best fit with their disabilities rather than with their personalities or goals (Beveridge, Craddock, & Liesener, 2002; Enright, Conyers, & Szymanski, 1996). Although some theories of career decision making emphasize the role of person inputs, such as a disability, in the development of learning experiences (Lent et al., 1994), the role of these factors as they relate directly to choice tends to be understudied in terms of significance and the degree to which they may limit work volition. In sum, the unpredictability of life circumstances may have both positive and negative effects on an individual's career development from childhood to retirement. The circumstances that place a limit on the volition of career choice may be particularly powerful, although the degree to which these external factors are salient can be understood only on an individual client level.

SPIRITUAL AND RELIGIOUS FACTORS

Whereas family expectations and needs and life circumstances are often viewed as largely or wholly uncontrollable, spiritual and religious factors can, depending on the individual, be viewed as both volitional and determined. Research on the role of spirituality and religion in career development, although limited in scope, has suggested that such factors relate positively to desirable career development outcomes such as career decision self-efficacy, career maturity, and job satisfaction (Duffy, 2006; Duffy

& Blustein, 2005; Duffy & Lent, 2008). For many individuals with spiritual or religious commitments, faith plays a critical role in the career decision-making process. This may be especially true for those with intrinsic religious orientations (Allport, 1950; Allport & Ross, 1967), in which faith is approached as an end in itself rather than a means to some other end. Such individuals may express belief in a Divine will or plan for their lives, or specifically for their careers (e.g., Constantine, Miville, Warren, Gainor, & Lewis-Coles, 2006), and may view career decision making as an extension of a general process of trying to discern God's will.

For some, this discernment process may entail having (or wanting) an experience in which a particular career path is shown to them through Divine inspiration or revelation, akin to well-known examples from the Abrahamic religious traditions (e.g., Noah, Abraham, Moses, and others; Colozzi & Colozzi, 2000) and other world religions (e.g., Siddhartha Gautama's experience of the four heavenly messengers at the advent of Buddhism). Perhaps more commonly, individuals with religious beliefs may view Divine directives as mediated through life experiences or circumstances or through their own interests, abilities, and personality characteristics. Regardless, once a particular career path is identified as consistent with God's will or plan, individuals may orient their activities in pursuing that path as a way in which they might honor God or a Higher Power. This approach to the work role is prototypic of what Dik and Duffy (2009) referred to as a *calling*, defined as an orientation toward a particular life domain, such as work, containing three dimensions: the experience of a transcendent summons originating beyond the self, the pursuit of activity within the work role as a source or extension of an individual's overall sense of purpose and meaningfulness in life, and viewing other-oriented values and goals as primary sources of motivation. This conceptualization of calling does not limit its application to spiritual or religious individuals, although it may be particularly salient for such individuals. Previous research on calling, although limited, has shown that participants who approach work as a calling tend to report higher levels of both general and work-specific well-being outcomes, in comparison with the levels reported by individuals with other approaches to work (e.g., Davidson & Caddell, 1994; Duffy & Sedlacek, 2007, in press; Treadgold, 1999; Wrzesniewski, McCauley, Rozin, & Schwartz, 1997).

Other mechanisms also exist through which an individual's spirituality and religion may influence career decision making, such as when spiritual or religious teachings require particular career decisions (e.g., young men in the Latter-Day Saints church are asked to devote 2 years to fulltime missions; Ulrich, Richards, & Bergin, 2000). Additionally, external influences may interact with internal influences to affect career decision making. For example, adolescents expressing interest in pursuing careers in ministry may receive considerable encouragement and mentoring to support this path from members of their religious communities.

SOCIAL SERVICE MOTIVATION

The final factor discussed, and arguably the most volitional, concerns the pull to use work for the primary purpose of bettering the external world. In the United States, the pervasive values of economic freedom and the American dream, combined with the secularization of the West, has arguably placed current emphasis on work as a path to individual well-being. Indeed, career development professionals frequently describe the goal of career counseling as helping clients attain optimal levels of job satisfaction and job performance, with the implicit goal of promoting personal fulfillment (Brown & Krane, 2000). Yet, for some individuals, such as those pursuing work as a calling or vocation, the desire to serve others may take precedence over other aspects of personal fulfillment. For example, some areas of job satisfaction (e.g., pay, comfort, social status) may be sacrificed when they are perceived to conflict with the value of making a difference in society (Hardy, 1990). Recently, the resurrection of the concept of *social fit*, or fit between an individual's work personality and a particular set of social needs, as a potentially important parameter to incorporate into career counseling has been suggested (Dik, Duffy, & Eldridge, in press).

Many individuals who pursue meaningful work with the goal of contributing to the common good choose their career paths for internal or self-motivated reasons. Thus, they may be characterized by the second and third dimensions of calling (i.e., the pursuit of activity within the work role as a source or extension of an individual's overall sense of purpose and meaningfulness in life and viewing other-oriented values and goals as primary sources of motivation); this approach to work is identified as a *vocation* according to Dik and Duffy's (2009) conceptualization. However, the first dimension of the calling construct (i.e., the experience of a transcendent summons originating beyond the self) is also relevant for some individuals, such as those for whom critical life events serve as a call to address certain social needs through their careers. This critical life event may be something the individual experiences directly (e.g., enduring a custody battle as a child) or may entail indirect exposure to a certain social need (e.g., watching a documentary on the AIDS epidemic). As another example, after highly visible disasters such as the September 11 attacks and Hurricane Katrina, news reports abounded of people who left their jobs to come to the aid of those affected, often for indefinite periods.

Anecdotal evidence has suggested that this social-need-as-calling phenomenon is not limited to those in social service occupations. For example, when doing volunteer work in Grand Forks, North Dakota, after the Red River flood in the late 1990s, the second author encountered a forklift operator providing services for a Salvation Army food distribution center. The operator indicated that he had previously been managing several warehouses in a neighboring state, but when he saw news coverage of the disaster, he immediately left his job and drove to Grand Forks to help, even living out of his car until he found housing. The external pull an individual feels to do work for the betterment of others will likely coincide with the individual's internal career influences whereby, as in this example, the individual might pursue a different job that requires similar skills but produces far more proximal societal benefits. However, only on an individual client level may a counselor understand if, how, and why societal factors serve as important influences.

IMPLICATIONS FOR THEORY AND RESEARCH

Unfortunately, because the majority of research in vocational psychology has been completed with populations for whom external influences may be the least salient (i.e., late adolescent, single, wealthy, White, precareer college students; Fitzgerald & Betz, 1994), the potential influence of external influences has been widely overlooked and represents a research domain in desperate need of catching up with practice. External influences are believed to be particularly salient constructs for individuals who are currently employed and attempting to balance work, family, and difficult life circumstances. Additionally, the expectation is that for underrepresented groups (e.g., people of color, women, intrinsically religious individuals), the pervasive influence of external constraints will be especially strong.

Whereas qualitative research has begun to highlight these factors (e.g., Blustein et al., 2002; Blustein, Phillips, Jobin-Davis, Finkelberg, & Roarke, 1997), researchers should attempt to quantitatively measure external influences and their effects on important career-related and psychological variables. Perhaps the most important step in this process is the development of instruments to measure work volition, or the degree to which individuals feel control over their work lives. Ideally, such instruments would assess the wide range of variables that constrain an individual's decision making. Scores on these instruments could then be correlated with such variables as job satisfaction and well-being. Individuals who experience greater levels of work volition are hypothesized to also experience more favorable career-related and psychological outcomes. Additionally, instruments to measure constraints should be complemented by those measuring external motivators, especially those related to the perception of a calling, vocation, or motivation to serve others. Whereas initial evidence has suggested the positive effect of a calling and service motivation on career-related variables, no psychometrically sound instruments have been developed to date that would assess these constructs (Dik & Duffy, 2009; Duffy, 2007; Duffy & Sedlacek, 2007).

Theorists are also encouraged to qualify theories in ways that more explicitly highlight the role of external influences, particularly as they apply to currently employed workers. Rather than conceptualizing external influences as simply barriers or resources, viewing them as moderator variables that affect the extent to which internal influences relate to outcomes might be more appropriate. It might be hypothesized that the degree to which variables such as self-efficacy and vocational interests predict career choice is moderated by the degree to which individuals have volition in their choices, suggesting that the lower the level of volition, the less strongly these variables might correlate with criterion variables. This same principle could be extended to external motivators, whereby variables such as person-environment fit might differentially relate to job satisfaction for workers who believe they have a calling. Each of these examples is meant to illustrate the hypothesized importance of external influences in career choice and satisfaction, and theorists are encouraged to view these factors as central components of any model. Clearly, however, the role of external influences in career development processes is ultimately an empirical question.

IMPLICATIONS FOR COUNSELING PRACTICE

Despite the relatively limited emphasis on external influences in many career development theories, most career counselors are likely acutely aware of how pervasive external factors can be on the decision-making processes of clients. Perhaps most evident is that all clients seeking career counseling are guided to some degree by external influences. External influences may take the shape of factors that are chosen as guiding mechanisms for career behavior, such as placing the needs of society or religious directives above the individual's own needs. For these types of clients, counselors are encouraged to explicitly assess the relevance of external factors among the range of influences a person perceives as salient when making a career choice. Counselors might also initiate exploration of how these sources of motivation relate to clients' internal interests, values, and skills, and ultimately assist clients in identifying career options that may encompass as many of these factors as possible. Similarly, when working with all clients, counselors are encouraged to ask about the prosocial components of clients' career choices and explore the extent to which these considerations influence their decision making (Dik et al., in press). Although the research in this area is limited, a few studies have shown that when a career is viewed as something that meets more than just an individual's desires, it tends to be more satisfying and fulfilling (e.g., Garcia-Zamor, 2003; Lips-Wiersma, 2002; Milliman, Czaplewski, & Ferguson, 2003; Wrzesniewski et al., 1997).

For perhaps most clients, external influences are constraining, are out of the individual's control, and can significantly alter a given career path. Several counseling approaches have been proposed for working with client populations that disproportionately experience such constraints (Blustein et al., 2005; Caporoso & Kiselica, 2004; Hershenson, 2005; Pope, 2003; Tang, 2003). For many lower- to middle-class working Americans, for example, external factors related to life circumstances and family needs are likely the primary form of motivation, and thus traditional career theories may be insufficient in explaining career choice behavior. For counselors working with these types of clients, the first recommendation is to assist clients in voicing any frustration and anger that may exist concerning the relinquishing of their personal goals to meet external needs. In the United States, a pervasive cultural message is that, with hard work and dedication, people can do whatever they choose; realizing that this may not be the case can be disheartening and painful for clients.

Counselors are also encouraged to examine the extent to which factors beyond clients' control may constrain their desired career paths. For some clients, these limitations may be inconvenient but relatively easily navigated obstacles, such as for a high school teacher looking for a new position because of his wife's job transfer to another part of the country. Although this client may have to leave a good work environment, with the right help, proper effort, and patience, he will likely find another job that resembles his previous employment. Other clients may experience major external limitations that can have both sudden and lifelong effects on their career choices. For example, clients who develop unexpected physical disabilities and work in environments that require complex or demanding physical skills will likely have to completely reevaluate their careers. The spectrum of uncontrollable external factors that may influence a client's career path is wide ranging and unique; thus, counselors are reminded to take the time to understand the idiosyncratic scope of these limitations on an individual client level.

Once the nature and extent of clients' external influences are understood, counselors are encouraged to help clients construct their own unique career decision-making models that take into account both internal and external factors. Here, the counselor would explore with clients how much weight they put on specific internal factors (e.g., skills, interests, values) versus specific external factors (e.g., family needs). One simple and practical method is to have clients list all the factors they believe are affecting their eventual career choice, and then rank these from most important to least important. On the basis of this ranking, the counselor could then proceed to help find specific career choices that match these needs. In sum, counselors are encouraged to respect and honor clients' external influences and not relinquish the importance of finding careers in line with clients' internal desires; balancing these two components may be critical for clients' eventual work satisfaction.

CONCLUSION

The discussion of external factors outlined in this article is by no means exhaustive; instead, it is intended to highlight the importance that such influences may play in the career choice process of many clients. Although the traditional career models are believed to be excellent in capturing the how and why of decision making for a privileged number of individuals, they do not sufficiently meet the needs of the more typical clients who, either by choice or circumstance, place factors outside themselves as critical and often primary in their career paths. For clients, each of the four factors discussed (family expectations and needs, life circumstances, spiritual and religious factors, and social service motivation) could be considered constraints or motivators, depending on the particulars of the situation or circumstance. Theorists, researchers, and counselors are greatly encouraged to appreciate these factors and better understand their power in the career development process.

REFERENCES

Allport, G. W. (1950). *The individual and his religion, a psychological interpretation.* New York: Macmillan.

Allport, G. W., & Ross, J. M. (1967). Personal religious orientation and prejudice. *Journal of Personality and Social Psychology, 5,* 432–443.

Arnold, D. H., & Doctoroff, G. L. (2003). The early education of socioeconomically disadvantaged children. *Annual Review of Psychology, 54,* 517–545.

Beveridge, S., Craddock, S. H., & Liesener, J. (2002). INCOME: A framework for co-ceptualizing the career development of persons with disabilities. *Rehabilitation Counseling Bulletin, 45,* 195–206.

Blustein, D. L. (2006). *The psychology of working: A new perspective for career development, counseling, and public policy.* Mahwah, NJ: Erlbaum.

Blustein, D. L., Chaves, A. P., Diemer, M. A., Gallagher, L.A., Marshall, K. G., Sirin, S., & Bhati, K. S. (2002). Voices of the forgotten half: The role of social class in the school-to-work transition. *Journal of Counseling Psychology, 49,* 311–323.

Blustein, D. L., McWhirter, E. H., & Perry, J.C. (2005). An emancipatory communitarian approach to vocational development theory, research, and practice. *Counseling Psychologist, 33,* 141–179.

Blustein, D. L., Phillips, S. D., Jobin-Davis. K., Finkdberg, S. L., & Roarke, A. E. (1997). A theory-building investigation of the school-to-work transition. *Counseling Psychologist, 25,* 364–402.

Bond, F. W., & Bunce, D. (2003). The role of acceptance and job control in mental health, job satisfaction, and work performance. *Journal of Applied Psychology, 88*, 1057–1067.

Brown, S. D., & Krane, N. E. R. (2000). Four (or five) sessions and a cloud of dust: Old assumptions and new observations about career counseling. In S. D. Brown & R. W. Lent (Eds.), *Handbook of counseling psychology* (3rd ed., pp. 740–766). New York: Wiley.

Caporoso, R. A., & Kiselica, M. S. (2004). Career counseling with clients who have a severe mental illness. *The Career Development Quarterly, 52*, 235–245.

Chen, C. P. (2006). Strengthening career human agency. *Journal of Counseling & Development, 84*, 131–138.

Colozzi, E. A., & Colozzi, L. C. (2000). College students' callings and careers: An integrated values-oriented perspective. In D. A. Luzzo (Ed.), *Career counseling of college students: An empirical guide to strategies that work* (pp. 63–91). Washington, DC: American Psychological Association.

Constantine, M. G., Miville, M. L., Warren, A. K., Gainor, K. A., & Lewis-Coles, M. E. L. (2006). Religion, spirituality, and career development in African American college students: A qualitative inquiry. *The Career Development Quarterly, 54*, 227–241.

Davidson, J.C., & Caddell, D. P. (1994). Religion and the meaning of work. *Journal for the Scientific Study of Religion, 33*, 135–147.

Dawis, R. V., & Lofquist, L. H. (1984). *A psychological theory of work adjustment: An individual-differences model and its applications.* Minneapolis: University of Minnesota Press.

Dik, B. J., & Duffy, R. D. (2009). Calling and vocation at work; Definitions and prospects for research and practice. *Counseling Psychologist, 37*, 424–450.

Dik, B. J., Duffy, R. D., & Eldridge, B. (in press). Calling and vocation in career counseling: Recommendations for promoting meaningful work. *Professional Psychology: Research and Practice.*

Duffy, R. D. (2006). Spirituality; religion, and career development: Current status and future directions. *The Career Development Quarterly, 55*, 52–63.

Duffy, R. D. (2007, May). *A focus on other: Motivation to serve and career development.* Poster session presented at the conference of the Society for Vocational Psychology, Akron, OH.

Duffy, R. D., & Blustein, D. L. (2005). The relationship between spirituality, religiousness, and career adaptability. *Journal of Vocational Behavior, 67*, 429–440.

Duffy, R. D., & Lent, R. W. (2008). Relation religious support to career decision self-efficacy in college students. *Journal of Career Assessment; 16*, 360–369.

Duffy, R. D., & Sedlacek, W. E. (2007). The presence of and search for a calling: Connections to career development. *Journal of Vocational Behavior, 70*, 590–601.

Duffy, R. D., & Sedlacek., W. E. (in press). The salience of a career calling among college students: Exploring group differences and links to religiousness, life meaning, and life satisfaction. *The Career Development Quarterly.*

Enright, M. S., Conyers, L. M., & Szymanski, E. M. (1996). Career and career-related educational concerns of college students with disabilities. *Journal of Counseling & Development, 75*, 103–114.

Fitzgerald, L. F., & Betz, N. E. (1994). Career development in cultural context: The role of gender, race, class, and sexual orientation. In M. L. Savickas & R. W; Lent (Eds.), *Convergence in career development theories: Implications for science and practice* (pp. 103–117). Palo Alto, CA: CPP Books.

Fouad, N. A. (2007). Work and vocational psychology: Theory, research, and applications. *Annual Review of Psychology, 58*, 543–564.

Garcia-Zamor, J.-C. (2003). Workplace spirituality and organizational performance. *Public Administration Review, 63*, 355–363.

Gottfredson, L. S. (1981). Circumscription and compromise: A developmental theory of occupational aspirations. *Journal of Counseling Psychology, 28,* 545–579.

Gottfredson, L. S. (2005). Applying Gottfredson's theory of circumscription and compromise in career guidance and counseling. In S. D. Brown & R. W. Lent (Eds.), *Career development and counseling: Putting theory and research to work* (pp. 71–100). Hoboken, NJ: Wiley.

Greenhaus, J. H., Parasuraman, S., & Collins, K. M. (2001). Career involvement and family involvement as moderators of relationships between work-family conflict and withdrawal from a profession. *Journal of Occupational Health Psychology, 6,* 91–100.

Greenhaus, J. H., & Powell, G. N. (2006). When work and family are allies: A theory or work-family enrichment. *Academy of Management Review, 31,* 72–92.

Halpern, D. F. (2005). Psychology at the intersection of work and family: Recommendations for employers, working families, and policymakers. *American Psychologist, 60,* 397–409.

Hansen, L. S. (1997). *Integrative life planning: Critical tasks for career development and changing life patterns.* San Francisco: Jossey-Bass.

Hardy, L. (1990). *The fabric of this world: Inquiries into calling, career choice, and the design of human work.* Grand Rapids, MI: Eerdmans.

Henderson, S. J. (2000). "Follow your bliss": A process for career happiness. *Journal of Counseling & Development, 78,* 305–315.

Hershenson, D. B. (2005). INCOME: A culturally inclusive and disability-sensitive framework for organizing career development concepts and interventions. *The Career Development Quarterly, 54,* 150–161.

Holland, J. L. (1997). *Making vocational choices: A theory of Vocational Personalities and work environments* (3rd ed.). Odessa, FL: Psychological Assessment Resources.

Hotchkiss, L., & Borow, H. (1996). Sociological perspectives on work and career development. In D. Brown, L. Brooks, & Associates (Eds.), *Career choice and development* (3rd ed., pp. 281–334). San Francisco: Jossey-Bass.

Jackson, C. L., Colquitt, J. A., Wesson, M. J., & Zapata-Phelan, C. P. (2006). Psychological collectivism: A measurement validation and linkage to group member performance. *Journal of Applied Psychology, 91,* 884–899.

Johnson, M. K., & Mortimer, J. T. (2002). Career choice and development from a sociological perspective. In D. Brown & Associates (Eds.), *Career choice and development* (4th ed., pp. 37–81). San Francisco: Jossey-Bass.

Juntunen, C. L., Barraclough, D. J., Broneck, C. L., Seibel, G. A., Winrow, S. A., & Morin, P. M. (2001). American Indian perspectives on the career journey, *Journal of Counseling Psychology, 48,* 274–285.

Kernes, J. L., & McWhiter, J. J. (2001). Counselors' attribution of responsibility, etiology, and counseling strategy, *Journal of Counseling & Development, 79,* 304–313.

Krumboltz, J. D. (1996). A learning theory of career counseling. In M. L. Savickas & W. B. Walsh (Eds.), *Handbook of career counseling theory and practice* (pp. 55–80). Palo Alto, CA: Davies-Black.

Lazarick, D. L., Fishbein, S.S., & Loiello, M.A. (1988). Practical investigations of volition. *Journal of Counseling Psychology, 35,* 15–26.

Lent, R. W., Brown, S. D., & Hackett, G. (1994). Toward a unifying social cognitive theory of career and academic interest, choice, and performance. *Journal of Vocational Behavior, 45,* 79–122.

Lent, R. W., Brown, S. D., & Hackett, G. (2000). Contextual supports and barriers to career choice: A social cognitive analysis. *Journal of Counseling Psychology, 47,* 36–49.

Lips-Wiersma, M. (2002). The influence of spiritual "meaning making" on career behavior. *Journal of Management Development, 21,* 497–520.

Maslow, A. H. (l943). A theory of human motivation. *Psychological Review, 50,* 370–396.

Miller, M. J., & Brown, S. D. (2005). Counseling for career choice: Implications for improving interventions and working with diverse populations. In S. D. Brown & R. W. Lent (Eds.), *Career development and counseling: Putting theory and research to work* (pp. 441–465). Hoboken, NJ: Wiley.

Milliman, J., Czaplewski, A. J., & Ferguson, J. (2003). Workplace spirituality and employee work attitudes: An exploratory empirical assessment. *Journal of Organizational Change Management, 16,* 426–447.

Mitchell, K. E., Levin, A. S., & Krumboltz, J. D. (1999). Planned happenstance: Constructing unexpected career opportunities. *Journal of Counseling & Development, 77,* 115–124.

Muhonen, T., & Torkelson, E. (2004). Work locus of control and its relationship to health and job satisfaction from a gender perspective. *Stress and. Health: Journal of the International Society for the Investigation of Stress, 20,* 21–28.

Oyserman, D., Coon, H. M., & Kemmelmeier, M. (2002). Rethinking individualism and collectivism: Evaluation of theoretical assumptions and meta-analyses. *Psychological Bulletin, 128,* 3–72.

Pearson, S. M., & Bieschke, K. J. (2001). Succeeding against the odds: An examination of familial influences on the career development of professional African American women. *Journal of Counseling Psychology, 48,* 301–309.

Phillips, S. D., Christopher-Sisk, E. K., & Gravino, K. L. (2001). Making career decisions in a relational context. *Counseling Psychologist, 29,* 193–213.

Pope, M. (2003). Career counseling in the twenty-first century: Beyond cultural encapsulation. *The Career Development Quarterly, 52,* 54–60.

Savickas, M. L. (2002). Career construction: A developmental theory of vocational behavior. In D. Brown & Associates (Eds.), *Career choice and. development* (4th ed., pp. 149–205). San Francisco: Jossey-Bass.

Schultheiss, D. E. P. (2003). A relational approach to career counseling: Theoretical integration and practical application. *Journal of Counseling & Development, 81,* 301–310.

Schultheiss, D. E. P. (2006). The interface of work and family life. *Professional Psychology: Research and Practice, 37,* 334–341.

Sears, S. (1982). A definition of career guidance terms: A National Vocational Guidance Association perspective. *Vocational Guidance Quarterly, 31,* 137–143.

Slife, B. D., & Fisher, A. M. (2000). Modern and postmodern approaches to the: free will/determinism dilemma in psychotherapy. *Journal of Humanistic Psychology, 40,* 80–107.

Super, D. E. (1990). A life-span, life-space approach to career development. In D. Brown, L. Brooks, & Associates (Eds.), *Career choice and development: Applying contemporary theories to practice* (2nd ed., pp. 197–261). San Francisco: Jossey-Bass.

Swanson, J. L., & Gore, P. A., Jr. (2000). Advances in vocational psychology theory and research. In S. D. Brown & R. W. Lent (Eds.), *Handbook of counseling psychology* (3rd ed., pp. 233–269). New York: Wiley.

Tang, M. (2003). Career counseling in the future: Constructing, collaborating, advocating. *The Career Development Quarterly, 52,* 61–69.

Treadgold, R. (1999). Transcendent vocations: Their relationship to stress, depression, and clarity of self-concept. *Journal of Humanistic Psychology, 39,* 81–105.

Ulrich, W. L., Richards, P. S., & Bergin, A. E. (2000). Psychotherapy with Latter-Day Saints. In P. S. Richards & A. E. Bergin (Eds.), *Handbook of psychotherapy and religious diversity* (pp. 185–209). Washington, DC: American Psychological Association.

von Rosenstiel, L., Kehr, H. M., & Maier, G. W. (2000). Motivation and volition in pursuing personal work goals. In J. Heckhauscn (Ed.), *Motivation and psychology of human development: Developing motivation and motivating development* (pp. 287–305). New York: Elsevier Science.

Waldrop, J., & Stem, S. M. (2003). *Disability status: 2000* (Census 2000 Brief No. C2KBR-17). Retrieved May 19, 2009, from U.S. Census Bureau Web site: http://www.census.gov/prod/2003pubs/c2kbr-l7.pdf

Weinstein, F. M., Healy, C. C., & Ender, P. B. (2002). Career choice anxiety, coping, and perceived control. *The Career Development Quarterly, 50,* 339–349.

Whiston, S. C., & Keller, B. K. (2004). The influences of the family of origin on career development: A review and analysis. *Counseling Psychologist, 32,* 493–568.

Williams, B. (2003). The world view dimensions of individualism and collectivism: Implications for counseling. *Journal of Counseling & Development, 81,* 370–374.

Wrzesniewski, A., McCauley, C., Rozin, P., & Schwartz, B. (1997). Jobs, careers, and callings: People's relations to their work. *Journal of Research in Personality, 31,* 21–33.

Young, R. A., Valach, L., Ball, J., Paseluikho, M. A., Wong, Y. S., DeVries, R. J., et al. (2001). Career development in adolescence as a family project. *Journal of Counseling Psychology, 48,* 190–202.

The Role of Values in Career Choice and Development

JOANN HARRIS-BOWLSBEY

THEORETICAL PERSPECTIVES

From the beginning of career choice theory, attributed to Frank Parsons (1909), it has been assumed that there is an identifiable relationship between the attributes of individuals and the characteristics of occupations or jobs. Some theorists in the sequence of development of career theory have stressed the influence of needs (Roe, 1956), interests and personality traits (Briggs-Myers & Myers, 1980; Holland, 1973) values (Brown, 2002a; Katz, 1969), and still others the combination of all of these. Perhaps the most comprehensive picture of the combination and interaction of personal attributes and environmental influences on an individual's career was proposed by Super (1992) in his *Arch of Determinants*.

In that graphic he proposed that individual career choice is influenced by needs, values, interests, intelligence, aptitudes, and personality. All of these contribute to the formation of a self-concept in general and a vocational self-concept in particular. In turn, Super (1992) proposed that this vocational self-concept seeks to be translated into a career choice. Related specifically to values, Super wrote

JoAnn Harris-Bowlsbey, "The Role of Values in Career Choice and Development," *The Role of Values in Careers*, ed. Mark Pope, Lisa Y. Flores and Patrick J. Rottinghaus, pp. 37-47. Copyright © 2014 by Information Age Publishing. Reprinted with permission.

> Often referred to as the Onion Model, the theory proposes that just
> as biological basis of personality may be viewed as a core surround-
> ed by needs which are the internal result of interaction with the
> environment, values may be viewed as another, surrounding layer,
> with interests an outer layer of personality. (p. 38)

Super's work contributed to our understanding that values are one important piece in the puzzle of career choice, though our understanding still does not include how significant that influence is related to others or what the factors are that may modify values and their influence over time.

Holland (1973) proposed that there are six definable personality types and six definable work environments. Further, he found that all individuals can be described as a combination of the six personality types, whose definitions are a combination of interests, skills, and values held by those who belong to that type. In the sequence of development of these personality types (described by a two- or three-letter code) he indicated that interests are formed first, perhaps beginning in the middle school years, due to the positive reinforcement that parents, significant others, and the environment provide for specific activities in which young people engage. Once interests are developed, he then suggested that those possessing those interests seek to develop skills that support them. Finally, in late adolescence or early adulthood, people assume a set of values that pervade the work environment in which their interests and skills place them. In his own words, he explained

> A child's special biology and experience first lead to preferences
> for some kinds of activities and aversions to others. Later, these
> preferences become well-defined interests from which the person
> gains satisfaction as well as reward from others. Still later, the pursuit
> of these interests leads to the development of more specialized
> competencies as well as to the neglect of other potential compe-
> tencies. At the same time, a person's differentiation of interests with
> age is accompanied by a crystallization of correlated values. (p. 16)

For example, individuals whose interests and skills have led them to work in the Social environment adopt values such as the importance of helping others and having good face-to-face communication skills which are common in that environment.

Martin Katz (1969) proposed a theory of career choice based on values. The basic tenet of his theory was that people expect to attain values through work and that occupations can be rated on the degree to which they reflect these values. He asserted that individuals can identify their values from a clear description of the various options and that the use of values to identify career options is more effective than the use of interests.

Dawis and Lofquist (1984) proposed a theory of work adjustment that states that individuals are likely to experience job satisfaction when they can maintain correspondence between their needs and values (combining these as one kind of attribute) and the rewards that a given work environment can provide. Further, their theory, much like that of Holland, predicted job tenure and productivity when there is this balance, or correspondence, between the needs/values of the individual and the properties of the work environment.

Brown (2002a, 2002b) proposed a theory of value-based career choice. He stated that "highly prioritized work values are the most important determinants of career choice for people with an individualism social value (i.e., the individual is the most important unit) if their work values are crystallized and prioritized" (p. 49). Within his theory the availability of values-based information (i.e., what a given work environment can provide) is essential as well as an appropriate amount of self-efficacy in the decider. Further, he proposed that, in order to have impact on career choice, an individual's values must be selected freely, from among alternatives, after careful thought, with happiness, and with commitment to a degree that individuals are willing to affirm their values publicly and use them repeatedly in the making of life choices.

Other theorists have expressed propositions related to the role of values in career decision making, but the theorists cited here appear to be the leading ones in this specialty. From their statements, we can infer the following:

- The values held by individuals are the sole criterion or at least one important criterion for making informed career choices.
- The values of individuals are influenced by or interact with a number of other variables, including culture, self-efficacy, needs, interests, and stage of development (i.e., crystallization of the values).
- It is possible to relate values to specific occupations and work environments.
- It is possible to make individuals aware of their values and to assist them to prioritize them.

THE UNIVERSE OF VALUES

Three of the theoretical positions cited above—Super, Dawis and Lofquist, and Katz—have engaged in extensive research designed to identify and define the universe of values that affect career choice. Super (1970), using his Work Values Inventory defined and measured 15 values, namely altruism, esthetics, creativity, intellectual stimulation, achievement, independence, prestige, management, economic returns, security, surroundings, supervisory relations, associates, way of life, and variety. He used the expert panel approach to analyze the work tasks and typical work settings of hundreds of occupations to rate each on its potential to satisfy each of these 15 values.

Dawis and Lofquist, in their research at the University of Minnesota, defined 20 work needs, namely ability utilization, achievement, activity, advancement, authority, company policies, compensation, coworkers, creativity, independence, moral values, recognition, responsibility, security, social service, social status, supervision-human relations, supervision-technical, variety, and working conditions. The level of an individual's need/value in each of these areas can be measured by the Minnesota Importance Questionnaire (Rounds, Henly, Dawis, Lofquist, & Weiss, 1981). These values have been organized under six categories as follows: achievement, comfort, status, altruism, safety, and autonomy. The potential of an occupation to satisfy an individual's needs/values has been researched for 185 occupations. The National Center for O*Net Development (http://www.onetcenter.org/content.html/1.B.2#cm_1.B.2) has grouped these same values into six slightly different categories as follows: achievement, working conditions, recognition, relationships, support, and independence and provides an online assessment called the *Work Importance Profiler* to link a user's values with those assigned to the occupations in the O*Net database. In 2008 the 909 occupations in O*Net were rated by an expert panel on their potential to satisfy the values contained in these six categories. Those ratings are provided in O*Net Online at (www.onetonline.org).

At Educational Testing Service, Katz and his team engaged in extensive research to identify 10 values, namely high income, prestige, early entry, security, leadership, helping others, variety, independence, leisure, and interest field. Then they developed a computer-based delivery system called the *System for Interactive Guidance Information (SIGI)* and a process whereby these values would be used to lead users to select occupations for exploration. In this system, there was an explicit algorithm for winnowing a user's list of occupations based on a two-step process. In the first step, the definitions of the ten values were provided and users were led through a process of comparison of values and prioritization that resulted in the rank ordering of these values. In the second step of the process, users were helped to consider the probability of their being able to accomplish the education needed to enter the occupations identified by the system user's highest-ranked values. Probability of accomplishing needed education was measured by a combination of achievement scores and current grade point average in related subjects. In his more recent theory, Blustein (2006) proposed that the work on values done to date has focused on that segment of the population that has the luxury of choosing which values to implement in work. He stated that most career development theory has not placed sufficient emphasis on understanding how the lives of people in diverse situations influence which core work functions are of greatest importance. He simplifies the array of work values by stating that individuals work for one of three reasons: (1) for survival and power, (2) for social connection, and (3) as a means of self-determination. It is likely that all of the values proposed by the theorists reviewed above could be organized under these three categories.

PRACTICAL APPLICATIONS

Given the review provided here, it appears that values may be used (1) as a sole search criterion for occupations, (2) in conjunction with other personal attributes (such as interests, abilities, skills, or personality type) to identify occupations, or (3) as indicators of the kinds of activities that individuals may pursue in different life roles as they distribute their values across roles. The assessment of values may be accomplished through either informal assessments or formal assessments.

In the area of informal assessments, there is a variety of informal approaches, both in print version and online such as checklists (see http://career.asu.edu/S/careerplan/selfdiscovery/ValuesAssessment.htm and http://www.selfcounseling.com/help/personalsuccess/personalvalues.html), real or virtual card sorts like the one shown below in Figure 1.1, and online inventories (see http://people.usd.edu/~bwjames/tut/time/workinv.html).

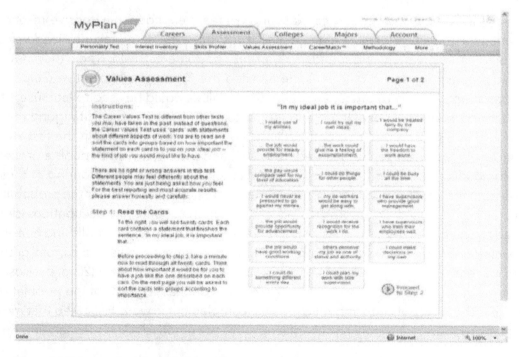

Figure 1.1 Values card sort from MyPlan.com

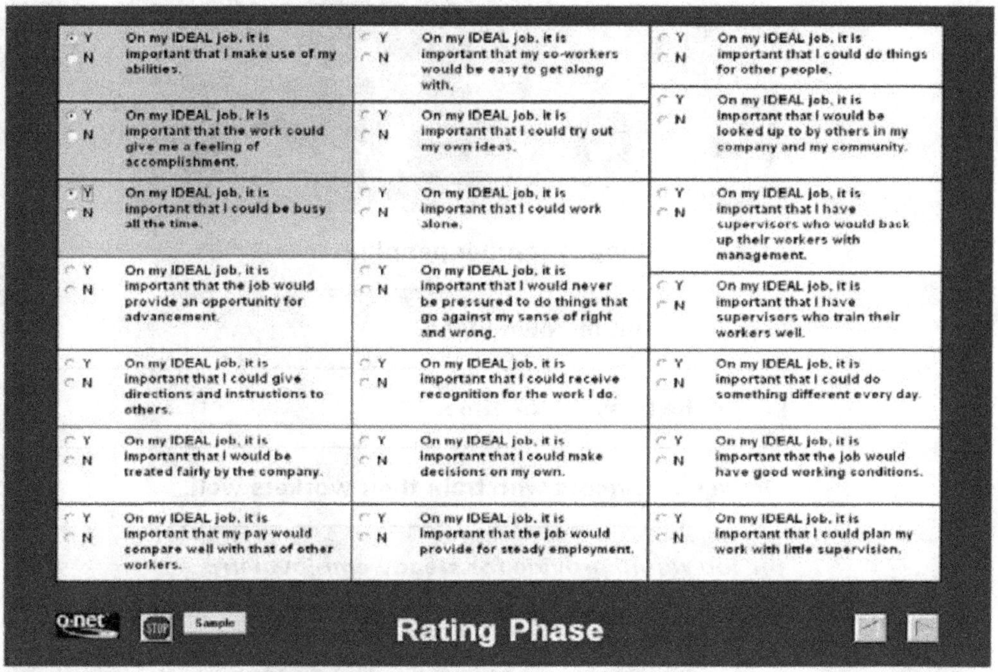

Figure 1.2 Rating of values on the *O*Net Work Importance Profiler*.

In addition, there are formal assessments of work values, such as the *O*Net Work Importance Profiler* (O*Net Resource Center, 1999), the *Super Work Values Inventory-Revised* (Zytowski, 2004), and the *Values Scale* (Super & Nevill, 1985). In contrast, the formal assessments have been subjected to scientific rigor which assures the quality of items, reliability, validity, and norms. The *O*Net Work Importance Profiler* can be downloaded from the O*Net Online site (www.onlineonet.org) either in print version or software version free of charge. The online assessment asks users to rate values items as either important or not important (Figure 1.2) and then place sets of work statements in priority order as shown in Figure 1.3. There are 21 sets of 5 statements each in which many different items (values) have to be prioritized.

After these two steps individuals receive a score report like that shown in Figure 1.4. Following receipt of the results of the Profiler, the user selects one of the five O*Net Job Zones (levels of future education) and receives a list of occupations at that education level that have potential to assist the user to attain his or her highest values, in this example, Achievement and Independence.

Kuder's *Super Work Values Inventory-revised* (Zytowski, 2004) is only available in online form from Kuder, Inc. as an integral part of its standard *Navigator* or *Journey* products or its customized ones. In those systems, the 72-item assessment is administered as shown in Figure 1.5.

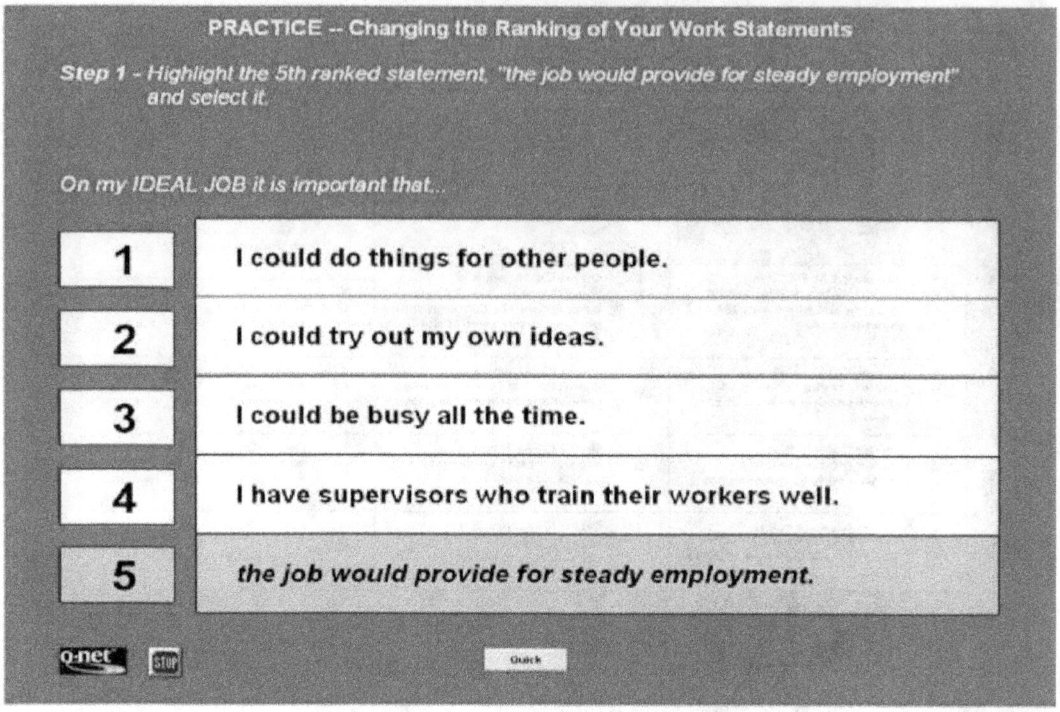

PRACTICE -- Changing the Ranking of Your Work Statements
Step 1 - Highlight the 5th ranked statement, "the job would provide for steady employment" and select it.
On my IDEAL JOB it is important that...
1
I could do things for other people.
2
I could try out my own ideas.
3
I could be busy all the time.
4
I have supervisors who train their workers well.
5
the job would provide for steady employment.
o-net
STOP

Figure 1.3 Ranking of work values on the *O*Net Work Importance.*

Your Work Importance Profiler Results!
Your top two work values in order of importance are:
Achievement
Independence
Your other work values in order of importance are:
Relationships
Working Conditions
Support
Recognition
You can think about your work values as the aspects of work that are important to you.
Knowing your work values can help you decide what kinds of jobs and careers you might want to explore.
The more a job agrees with your work values, the more likely you are to be satisfied with that job.
o-net
STOP

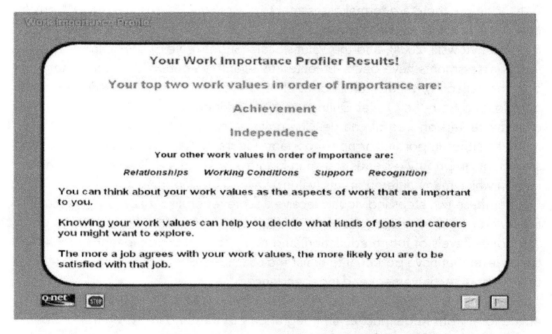

Figure 1.4 Results of the *O*Net Work Importance Profiler.*

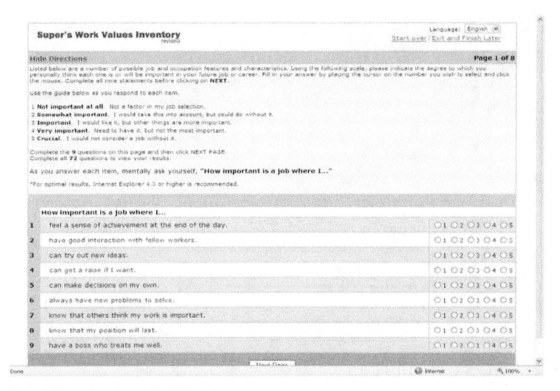

Figure 1.5 Items from Super's Work Values Inventory.

Upon completion of the 72 items, the user's profile is displayed as shown in Figure 1.6, showing the values in rank order by percentile, compared to a large national sample. Users also have the opportunity to identify real adults (called Person Matches) in a large pool of workers who have taken the inventory and have similar results to those of the user, as shown in Figure 1.7. Further, a list of occupations with potential to allow the user to attain his or her highest three values at the educational level selected by the user is displayed.

The Minnesota Importance Questionnaire (Gay, Weiss, Hendel, Dawis, & Lofquist 1971) is another formal assessment that could be used as an illustration. In all three illustrations the list of occupations that is suggested has been generated based on the expert judgment of those who have rated the O*Net occupations by their potential to satisfy the needs/values identified by Lofquist and Dawis.

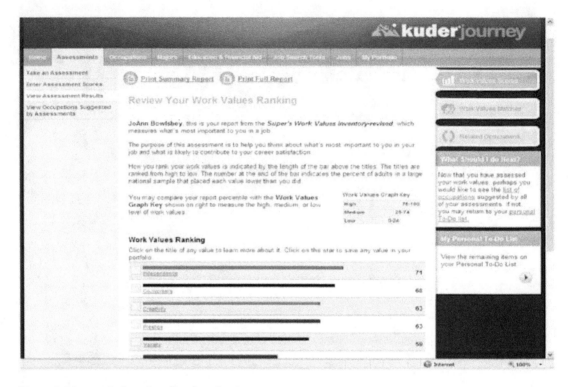

Figure 1.6 Percentile-based profile of user's values.

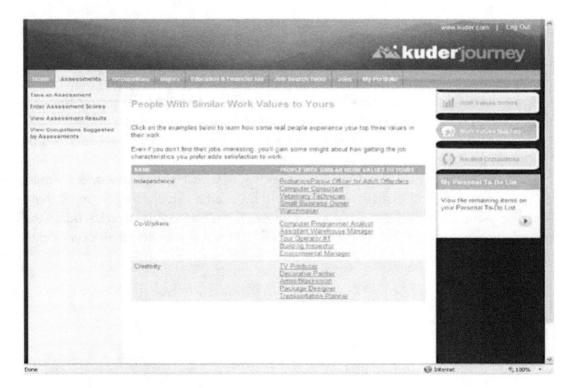

Figure 1.7 List of real people with similar scores.

In summary, as we examine the practical applications that are being made by career practitioners, websites, and web-based systems, some conclusions can be drawn:

1   Values serve as one useful approach to identifying occupations for exploration, but should not be the only way. It is likely that they would be more useful as a filter for a long list of occupations generated by interests or skills/abilities.

2   There is little overlap across occupations suggested by interests, skills, and values. Where such overlap exists, it is probably quite meaningful.

3   The linkages made between values and occupations are fuzzy. First, agreement is lacking across theorists about values domains—that is, their titles, how many there are, and what their definitions are. Second, the relationships of the values to specific occupational titles has been done by different expert panels for different projects and systems, and doubtless there is lack of uniformity in these judgments. Third, the values that can be attained in occupations vary across the environments in which those occupations are practiced, meaning that universal uniformity of the potential satisfactions of any occupations cannot be achieved.

REFERENCES

Blustein, D. L. (2006). *The psychology of working: A new perspective for career development, counseling, and public policy.* Mahwah, NJ: Lawrence Erlbaum Associates.

Briggs-Myers, I., & Myers, P. B. (1980). *Gifts differing: Understanding personality type.* Palo Alto, CA: Davies-Black.

Brown, D. (2002a). The role of work values and cultural values in occupational choice, satisfaction and success: A theoretical statement. In D. Brown & Associates (Eds.), *Career choice and development* (4th ed., pp. 465–509). San Francisco, CA: Jossey-Bass.

Brown, D. (2002b). The role of work values and cultural values in occupational choice, satisfaction, and success: A theoretical statement. *Journal of Counseling & Development, 80,* 48–56.

Dawis, R. V., & Lofquist, L. H. (1984). *A psychological theory of work adjustment.* Minneapolis, MN: University of Minnesota Press.

Gay, E. G., Weiss, D .J., Hendel, D. D., Dawis, R. V., & Lofquist, L. H. (1971). *Minnesota Importance Questionnaire.* Minneapolis, MN: University of Minnesota Press.

Holland, J. L. (1973) *Making vocational choices: A theory of careers.* Upper Saddle River, NJ: Prentice-Hall.

Katz, M. (1969). Theoretical foundations of guidance. *Review of vocational research, 39,* 127–140.

O*NET Resource Center. (1999). Work importance locator. Retrieved from http://www.onetcenter.org/WIP.html

Parsons, F. (1909). *Choosing a vocation.* Boston, MA: Houghton-Mifflin.

Roe, A. (1956). *The psychology of occupations.* New York, NY: Wiley.

Rounds, J. B., Henly, G. A., Dawis, R. V., Lofquist, L. H., & Weiss, D. J. (1981). *Manual for the Minnesota Importance Questionnaire*. Minneapolis, MN: University of Minnesota Department of Psychology.

Super, D. E. (1970). *Manual: The work values inventory*. Chicago, IL: Riverside.

Super, D. E., & Nevill, D. (1985). *The values scale*. Palo Alto, CA: Consulting Psychologists Press.

Super, D. E. (1992). The arch of career determinants. In D. H. Montross & C. J. Shinkman (Eds.), *Career development: Theory and practice*. Springfield, IL: Charles C. Thomas.

Zytowski, D. G. (2004). Super work values inventory-revised: User manual. Retrieved from http.//www.kuder.com/downloads/SWV-tech-manual.pdf.

DISCUSSION QUESTIONS

1   How much of a role did your parents/family have in determining your career decision?

2   What kind of an impact can a job have on your self-esteem?

3   Do you know people who define themselves by their jobs? What would happen if they lost their job? What happens when they retire?

4   What are some of your values that may help determine your career path?

CONCLUSION

After reading the articles, we hope that you have a better appreciation of the multiple factors that can go into your career decision. It is not as easy as opening the classifieds and selecting your next career. These articles provide a glimpse of some factors that you may not have been aware of that can play a critical role in your career decisions. Keep in mind that internal and external factors are just pieces of the overall decision-making process. The more you know, the better prepared you will be in making career choices.

INDEX OF KEY TERMS

- career values
- external variables
- internal variables

SUGGESTED PUBLICATIONS FOR FURTHER READING

Kinjerski, V., & Skrypnek, B. J. (2008). Four paths to spirit at work: Journeys of personal meaning, fulfillment, well-being, and transcendence through work. *Career Development Quarterly, 56*(4), 319–329. doi:10.1002/j.2161–0045.2008.tb00097.x

Rivera, L. (2016). Breaking glass ceilings in corporate careers: The case of elite hiring. *Qualitative Organizational Research, 3*, 265–280.

HISTORY AND THEORIES

INTRODUCTION

To develop and embrace our identity as counselors, we probably should have a solid understanding of our history. The counseling profession, overall, has roots in career counseling, which started as early as the late 19th century (Pope, 2000). The career counseling profession (and therefore the counseling profession) has evolved because of early social reform movements, educators seeing a need for a clearer vocational direction, and landmark legislation over the years. The National Career Development Association (NCDA) was one of the initial organizations that created the

American Counseling Association (ACA), although both the ACA and NCDA were named differently at the time.

As the profession has evolved, so have the theories and approaches associated with career counseling and development. Pope (2000) does an excellent job of educating us regarding our history as counseling professionals, and Sampson (2009) explains how we can utilize our past while integrating current thinking and practice in a practical way.

A Brief History of Career Counseling in the United States

MARK POPE

The author presents the 6 stages in the development of career counseling in the United States. In the 1st stage (1890–1919), placement services were offered for an increasingly urban and industrial society. In the 2nd stage (1920–1939), educational guidance through the elementary and secondary schools became the focal point. The 3rd stage (1940–1959) saw the focus shift to colleges and universities and the training of counselors. The 4th stage (1960–1979) was the boom for counseling and the idea of work having meaning in a person's life came to the forefront; organizational career development began during this period. The 5th stage (1980–1989) saw the beginning of the transition from the industrial age to the information age and the growth of both the independent practice of career counseling and outplacement counseling. The 6th stage (1990–present), with its emphasis on technology and changing demographics, has seen an increased sophistication in the uses of technology, the internationalization of career counseling, the beginnings of multicultural career counseling, and the focus on the school-to-job transition.

Mark Pope, "A Brief History of Career Counseling in the United States," *The Career Development Quarterly*, vol. 48, no. 3, pp. 194-211. Copyright © 2000 by National Career Development Association. Reprinted with permission. Provided by ProQuest LLC. All rights reserved.

The birth and subsequent development of career counseling in the United States (U.S) has occurred during times of major societal change (Brewer, 1942). Reviewing such societal changes led Pope (1995) to develop a social transitions stage model to describe the development of the career counseling profession in the U.S. This article expands and clarifies that model. The stages of the social transitions model have been identified from the author's historical research and are an extension of the work of Savickas (1993), Newcombe (1993), Whiteley (1984), Schwebel (1984), Aubrey (1977), Herr (1974), Borow (1964, 1974), Ginzberg (1971), Stephens (1970), Williamson (1965), McDaniels (1964), Super (1955, 1974), Norris (1954a, 1954b), Brewer (1919, 1942), and Bloomfield (1915). In an extension of this model, Zhang and Pope (1997) have applied this model to the development of career counseling in China and Hong Kong.

Some of the above authors have identified stages in the development of career counseling and related such development to the social issues of those times. None, however, have looked at the history of career counseling from an organizational perspective (i.e., the beginnings of organized professional associations), over this particular period of time (i.e., the late 1800s to present), and from an economic-political perspective. Savickas (1993), for example, identified general social stages from the nineteenth to twentieth centuries and related them to changes in a societal work ethic along with specific suggestions for conducting career counseling in the post-modern era. Aubrey (1977) identified social themes in 10-year spans for the guidance and counseling movement, although not specifically for career counseling. Brewer (1919, 1942) described the early history of the profession focusing on the rise of the vocational guidance movement in the U.S. The current article provides important details, extends chronologically the previous publications, and integrates social and organizational history.

It is also important to note that the terms *career counseling, career development,* and *vocational guidance* have distinct meanings that are time and culture specific. *Vocational guidance* was the original term used in the U.S. and was generally used throughout the world at the beginning of the development of a guidance movement. The terms *career counseling* and *career development* came into more common usage in the 1950s through the work of Super (1955) and were institutionalized when the name of the National Vocational Guidance Association (1913–1983) was changed to the National Career Development Association in 1984.

In the first stage of the development of career counseling in the U.S. (1890–1919), placement services were offered for an increasingly urban and industrial society. In the second stage (1920–1939) educational guidance through the elementary and secondary schools became the focal point. The third stage (1940–1959) saw the focus shift to colleges and universities and the training of counselors. The fourth stage (1960–1979) was the boom for counseling, and the idea of work having meaning in a person's life came to the forefront; organizational career development began during this period. The fifth stage (1980–1989) saw the beginning of the transition from the industrial age to the information age and the growth of both the independent practice of career counseling and outplacement counseling. The sixth stage (starting in 1990), with its emphasis on technology and changing demographics, has seen an increasing sophistication in the uses of technology, the internationalization of career counseling, the beginnings of multicultural career counseling, and a focus on the school-to-job transition.

FIRST STAGE: JOB PLACEMENT SERVICES (1890–1919)

Career counseling (then called "vocational guidance") in the U.S. was developed in the latter part of the nineteenth century out of societal upheaval, transition, and change (Brewer, 1942). This new profession was described by historians as a "progressive social reform movement aimed at eradicating poverty and substandard living conditions spawned by the rapid industrialization and consequent migration of people to major urban centers at the turn of the 20th century" (Whiteley, 1984, p. 2). The societal upheaval that gave birth to career counseling was characterized by the loss of jobs in the agricultural sector, increasing demands for workers in heavy industry, the loss of "permanent" jobs on the family farm to new emerging technologies such as tractors, the increasing urbanization of the country, and the concomitant calls for services to meet this internal migration pattern, all to retool for the new industrial economy. Returning veterans from World War I and those displaced by their return also heightened the need for career counseling.

The focus of the first stage was job placement. Parsons (1909) is often called the parent of career counseling and began as a social worker heavily influenced by the work of Jane Addams in Chicago. In Boston, Parsons established a settlement house for young people who were either already employed or currently unemployed, or had been displaced during this period of rapid change. The placement of these young people into new jobs was one of the initial and most important purposes of the new agencies that had arisen during this period.

Parsons's (1909) model of career counseling was largely without theoretical foundations at this stage and was grounded in "simple logic and common sense and relied predominately on observational and data gathering skills" (Aubrey, 1977, p. 290). He stated that "in the choice of a vocation there are three broad factors: (1) a clear understanding of yourself … (2) a knowledge of the requirements and conditions for success … in different lines of work; (3) true reasoning on the relation of these two groups of facts" (Parsons, 1909, p. 5). This largely intuitive and experiential foundation of career counseling formed the basis for Parsons's establishing the Vocation Bureau at Civic Service House in Boston in 1908. This was the first institutionalization of career counseling in the US. (Ginzberg, 1971).

During this first stage, an important factor in the establishment of career counseling was the increasing involvement of psychological testing with career counseling. Psychological tests became an important and necessary part of the first functional stage in career counseling, that is, self-assessment. Testing gave career counseling respectability in American society (Super & Crites, 1862; Whiteley, 1984). Without a scientific procedure to justify this first step of career counseling, it is unlikely that career counseling would have been so popularly accepted. In the late 1800s, Francis Galton, Wilhelm Wundt, James McKean Cattell, and Alfred Binet made important contributions to the newly emerging field of psychological testing and, indirectly, to career counseling. It is important to note that many of the early founders of career counseling were quite hesitant in prescribing psychological tests because many such popularly available tests had not been rigorously studied and researched for specific application to vocations (Bloomfield, 1915; Brewer, 1919).

Another important factor in the establishment of career counseling was the early support for vocational guidance that came from the progressive social reform movement. "The linkage between this movement and vocational guidance was largely built on the issue of the growing exploitation and misuse of human beings" (Aubrey, 1977, p. 290). Child labor laws provided much impetus for such collaboration as this crusade to prohibit the exploitation of children grew. Although some states, beginning with Pennsylvania, had established minimum age laws in the latter half of the nineteenth century, the first decade of the twentieth century continued to see over half a million children from 10 to 13 years of age employed (Bernert, 1958), and effective federal legislation was not enacted until the passage of the 1938 Fair Labor Standards Act. Parsons was a prominent leader in the struggle to eliminate child labor.

Furthermore, laws that were supportive of vocational guidance were beginning to receive significant social support. For example, the landmark Smith-Hughes Act of 1917 established secondary school vocational education training. This legislation was strengthened in succeeding years by the George-Reed Act of 1929, the George-Ellzey Act of 1934, and the George-Deen Act of 1936. Each of these laws supported vocational education as an important part of the public schools. In 1913, the U.S. Department of Labor (DOL) was founded and the Bureau of Labor Statistics (BLS), which had been part of the Department of the Interior, was moved under the auspices of the DOL.

Out of this transition came the founding in 1913 of the National Vocational Guidance Association (NVGA; now the National Career Development Association [NCDA]) in

Grand Rapids, Michigan at the Third National Conference on Vocational Guidance (Brewer, 1942). The first journal of NVGA was the *Vocational Guidance Bulletin,* established in 1915. Volume I, Number 1 was 4 pages, 6" × 8³/₈", and was published for NVGA by the U.S. Office of Education. This publication later became *Occupations: The Vocational Guidance Journal.* The founders of NVGA included Frank Leavitt (first president), Jesse B. Davis (second president), Meyer Bloomfield (third president, Parsons's successor at the Boston Vocation Bureau, and teacher of the first course in vocational guidance in 1911 at Harvard University), and John M. Brewer (fifth president and author of the definitive history of career guidance in the U.S. in 1942). This stage in the development of career counseling in the U.S. was a time for the founders of NVGA of growth and high hopes for vocational guidance.

SECOND STAGE: EDUCATIONAL GUIDANCE IN THE SCHOOLS (1920–1939)

With the end of World War I and the passage of the Smith-Hughes Act, another transition began and, with the economic depression of the 1930s, these social and legislative processes focused U.S. society on educational counseling and solidified the role of vocational guidance in the schools. "The union of education, of social work, and of psychometrics in the vocational guidance of youth and adults was now somewhat more complete" (Super, 1955, p. 4). Elementary and secondary education received an influx of students as a result of increased needs for literacy to cope with increasing demands of industrialization and the increase in numbers of school-age children as a direct result of the boom in pregnancies following the end of World War I (Schwebel, 1984).

Educational counseling emerged from the work of humanitarian, progressive social reformers in the schools. Such reformers included Jesse B. Davis, who served as a "counselor on educational and career problems" at Central High School in Detroit in 1898, and Eli Weaver, who was a principal in the New York City school system in 1906. Promoting career development in the schools, however, was slow work. For example, as late as the 1930s, no vocational guidance programs existed in at least half of the schools in U.S. cities with populations of 10,000 or more (Brewer, 1942).

Organized labor's strength was growing fast in the wake of the economic depression, and President Franklin Roosevelt's New Deal was a response to the growing power of the unions as well as the loss of jobs. The Civilian Conservation Corps (CCC) was established in 1933 to provide training and employment opportunity for unemployed youth, and the educational services of the CCC were supervised by the U.S. Department of Education.

Then, in 1935, the Works Progress Administration was established through federal legislation as an employment source for the millions of people who were out of work at this time. The B'nai B'rith Vocational Service Bureau was opened in 1938 in Washington, D. C., and local Jewish Vocational Services were established in 25 major American cities. Finally, the first edition of the *Dictionary of Occupational Titles* was published in 1939.

In 1921, NVGA published the first version of the "Principles and Practices of Vocational Guidance" (Borow, 1964). This publication contained the Association's statement of principles and has been revised periodically since then, with its most current version published in 1996. Also, the first field secretary of NVGA was hired in 1930. Robert Hoppock served in that role, and his duty was to forge stronger links between the headquarters and regional branches. This office was funded by grants from the J.C. Penney Foundation (in 1929) and later by the Carnegie Corporation (in the 1930s; Norris, 1954a, 1954b).

In addition, the February 1930 issue of *The Vocational Guidance Magazine* (NVGA, 1930) focused on the upcoming annual convention that was held in Atlantic City, New Jersey, at the Hotel Chalfonte February 20–22, 1930. The articles in this special issue focused on educational counseling, and in the tentative program of the annual meeting, the majority of presentations addressed different aspects of vocational guidance in the schools, highlighting again the importance during this period of providing career counseling to students in the schools.

THIRD STAGE: COLLEGES AND UNIVERSITIES AND THE TRAINING OF COUNSELORS (1940–1959)

The third stage in the development of career counseling was characterized by the focus of societal resources on colleges and universities and the training of professional counselors as a direct result of and response to a new social transition engendered by two major events that set the tone for all subsequent world-wide actions: World War II and the USSR's successful launching of rockets that orbited earth and even landed on the moon.

First, World War II focused the energy and attention of all nations of the world on the contest between nationalistic fascism (Germany, Japan, and Italy) and capitalism and communism, which were allied at this time (U.S., USSR, Great Britain, France).

Truman's Fair Deal program was a response to the problems encountered by returning armed services veterans. The lack of jobs and the subsequent displacement of current workers by these returning veterans were important societal problems the Truman program attempted to address.

Second, the USSR successfully launched the first space probe, Sputnik I, in 1957, and followed that with the lunar landing of Lunik II (in 1959). These two events, more than any other, humbled American capitalism for a time. The U.S. had considered itself far superior technologically to any other country on earth; however, when the USSR was so successful in their space program, federal legislators were impelled to begin to address the problems in science and math education across the U.S. The passage of the National Defense Education Act in 1957 was a direct response to the successful launching of Sputnik and the desperation of U.S. government officials over the loss of this supposed U.S. superiority in technology. The Counseling and Guidance Training Institutes were established under the NDEA to provide improved training for counselors who were to identify and encourage science and math majors for college education. This was a boom period for the training of counselors, and almost 14,000 individuals received training in these NDEA institutes (Borow, 1964).

Schwebel (1984) identified two social conditions that characterized the post-World War II period that led to the rise of the professional practice of counseling, especially career counseling: "(1) the personal and career problems of adjustment faced by vast numbers of veterans, including those handicapped during the war; (2) the influx of new types of students to higher education as a result of the G.I. Bill of Rights, an influx comparable to the compositional changes in the secondary school earlier in the century" (p. 285).

As a direct result of the growth of vocational guidance and the realization that there was strength in joining together with other guidance and personnel professional organizations, NVGA became one of the founding divisions of the American Personnel and Guidance Association (APGA; later to become the American Association for Counseling and Development, and then the American Counseling Association) in 1951. Donald Super became the second president of this new association in 1953. NVGA's journal, *Occupations: The Vocational Guidance Journal*, became the *Personnel and Guidance Journal*, the official journal of the new APGA. NVGA then established *The Vocational Guidance Quarterly* as its own journal in 1952.

Another aspect of transition and the organizational response to it was the change in total number of members who chose to join a professional organization. Although the founding of APGA had been a priority of NVGA leadership, NVGA total membership was a victim of this organizational transition. NVGA's membership had risen to more than 6,000 by 1949. It was a healthy and robust organization that had annual conventions across the country; however, with the merger to form APGA, membership in NVGA declined to 2,328 members (NVGA, 1951).

FOURTH STAGE: MEANINGFUL WORK AND ORGANIZATIONAL CAREER DEVELOPMENT (1960–1979)

The 1960s was a time of idealism and hope. John F. Kennedy's election as President of the U.S., Lyndon Johnson's Great Society, the beginning of the great modern day civil rights movements, the Vietnam War, and the economic highs of this stage combined to focus a generation of young people on the potential, myths, and illusions of American society, giving them a new vision of personal, social, and cultural relations (Sale, 1973).

Many young people wanted jobs that were meaningful and that would allow them to change the world for the better. Borow (1974) noted that "the mass of young Americans do not disdain the idea of work as a necessary and at least potentially meaningful and rewarding life activity. Their attack is upon the character of available jobs and the overly conforming and depersonalizing conditions under which most individuals must labor" (p. 25). He captured the tone of the times when he described the mythology regarding the U.S. as "a rich, sophisticated, yet humane nation dedicated to providing all of its citizens with a broad spectrum of services and opportunities for achieving the good life" (Borow, 1974, p. 7).

The type of federal legislation enacted during this period is also illustrative of the expectations of Americans during this fourth stage of career counseling. At the beginning of the 1960s, the unemployment rate was 8.1%, the highest since the 1930s. President John F. Kennedy entered office in 1961 and, as one of his first acts, appointed a panel of consultants on vocational education. They issued a report in 1962, which stated that school counselors need to "have exceptional understanding of the world of work and its complexities. What is obviously needed is a counselor who meets all of the requirements of a professional background in pupil personnel services and who at the same time is a specialist in occupational information, vocational guidance, and counseling" (U.S. Department of Health, Education, and Welfare, 1963, p. 213). Their recommendations became the Vocational Education Act of 1963, which was updated through amendments in 1968 and 1976.

This report was followed by more similarly crafted federal legislation. Not since the founding of the U.S. in 1776 had there been such a plethora of social programs that became laws in such a short time. The Area Redevelopment Act, signed into law in 1961, was to attract new sources of jobs to economically depressed areas. The 1962

Manpower Development and Training Act provided assistance to workers who were "victims of automation." The Economic Opportunity Act of 1964 created several historic social programs including Job Corps, Neighborhood Youth Corps, VISTA, Youth Opportunity Centers, the U.S. Employment Service Human Resource Development Program, and the Head Start Program (Ehrle, 1969; NVGA, 1962).

In addition, in 1965, the Vocational Rehabilitation Administration budget included monies to broaden the scope of vocational rehabilitation agencies to handle impairments to effective vocational life caused by educational, cultural, social, or environmental factors. The 1966 amendments to the Economic Opportunity Act created the New Careers Program to create subprofessional jobs, career ladders, and differentiated staffing. The Social Security Act of 1967 created the Work Incentive Program for welfare clients who wished and were able to become economically self-sufficient. It included funds for training, education, day care for participants' children, and a variety of support services, including counseling. The Elementary and Secondary Education Act as amended in 1969 provided aid for disadvantaged children in schools in impoverished areas, for library resources, and for guidance and counseling services. The Comprehensive Employment and Training Act (CETA) of 1977 extended the life of the CETA programs, which were meant to create jobs and full employment.

Finally, the National Occupational Information Coordinating Committee (NOICC) and the State Occupational Information Coordinating Committees were established by the Vocational Education Act Amendments of 1976. These supra- and intra-governmental coordinating agencies were designated to coordinate the delivery of labor market and other career information among four federal agencies—the Employment and Training Agency, National Center for Education Statistics, Bureau of Labor Statistics, and the Education Commission—and among similar state entities (Lester, 1997). This forced, yet historic, alliance among such federal agencies to make career information available for coordinated public use was to have far-reaching consequences in the next 20 years. Finally, this coordinated effort among federal and state agencies would supply the information needs for both the career counseling and development profession, which require such data for their livelihood, and the general public, which requires such data for career decision making.

Because of the legislation enacted during this fourth stage, career counseling in organizational settings came to the forefront of the career counseling movement. Growth in career counseling in governmental agencies, in nonprofit community agencies, and in business and industry were the hallmarks of this stage. Such governmental agencies as Lawrence Livermore National Laboratories and the Office of Management and Budget had large career development centers and substantial staffs. Companies such as Glaxo Pharmaceuticals, Pacific Bell, and IBM also built career services centers during this time.

This was a time of reconstruction and renewal for the NVGA, which celebrated its 50th anniversary during this period. With 9,000 members, NVGA was the largest and oldest of the vocational guidance and personnel services groups in the U.S. In 1964, Henry Borow was appointed the editor of the book *Man in a World at Work,* which was conceived to celebrate the anniversary and to be a compendium of the "profession's best current thinking on the nature of vocational guidance, the meaning of the human work experience, the relationship of the individual to the labor force, and research and practice in vocational guidance" (Reed, 1964. p. ix). This book was a major project and was funded in part by the Carnegie Corporation and published by Houghton Mifflin Company. The editorial committee consisted of Margaret E. Andrews, Douglas D. Dilenbeck, Barbara A. Kirk, Edward C. Roeber, Joseph Samler, C. Winfield Scott, and Donald E. Super, with C. Gilbert Wrenn as the editorial adviser to the publisher—an illustrious group.

Borow then edited another NVGA book titled *Career Guidance for a New Age,* which was a product of an NVGA committee called Project Reconceptualization, and included papers presented at the NVGA Airlie House Invitational Conference on Implementing Career Development Theory and Research Through the Curriculum.

These two books were followed by a volume in 1974 edited by Edwin Herr, titled *Vocational Guidance and Human Development* and conceptualized as part of a decennial volume series. Also, as testament to the maturing NVGA organization, the Eminent Career Award was established, and Anne Roe was the first recipient in 1966.

FIFTH STAGE: INDEPENDENT PRACTICE CAREER COUNSELING AND OUTPLACEMENT COUNSELING (1980–1989)

The late 1970s was characterized by a declining economic system rather than by the growth and prosperity of the early 1960s. This began the fifth stage of transition for the field—from an industrial age to an information and technology age (Pope, 1995; Toffler, 1990). This new transition spawned another series of problems, such as loss of jobs in the industrial sectors of our economy, increasing demands from employers for technological skills, loss of permanent jobs to contract labor, loss of job security, and marginalization of organized labor, all to retool the economy for the information and technology age.

In 1987, the Hudson Institute commissioned and published a report titled *Workforce 2000,* which laid the foundation for the career development policies of both the Bush (1988–1992) and Clinton (1992–2000) federal administrations. This report was particularly noteworthy in the history of career counseling because of its demographic assumptions about the composition of the new American workforce, that new entrants into that workforce will be predominantly ethnic and racial minorities (Johnson & Packer, 1987).

During this stage, the emergence of the private practice career counselor was the direct result of the beginnings of national acceptance of career counseling as an important service to provide to a citizenry in occupational transition. The practitioner, whose livelihood depended on continuous marketing of short-term career counseling, provided the vitality for the expansion and growth of the professional practice of career counseling during this period as well as for the credentialing of such practitioners.

NVGA had always taken the lead in establishing standards for the profession, such as (a) standards for the practice of vocational guidance, (b) standards for occupational materials, (c) standards for the training of counselors, and (d) standards for vocational counseling agencies (Norris, 1954a, 1954b). As a result of the emergence of the private practice career counselor and under heavy pressure from within the profession, NVGA initiated a specific credential for career counseling professionals. The National Certified Career Counselor credential included substantial academic and experiential requirements along with an examination (National Career Counselor Examination). As a precursor to that credential, NVGA promulgated vocational-career counseling competencies in 1982, which were developed as a "list of competencies necessary for counselors to perform the task of career/vocational guidance and counseling" (NVGA, 1982, p. 1). These competencies were preceded by the American Vocational Association—NVGA Position Paper on Career Development in 1973; the APGA Position Paper on Career Guidance in 1975; the ACES Position Paper on Counselor Preparation for Career Development in 1976; the AIR Report on Competencies Needed for Planning, Supporting, Implementing, Operating, and Evaluating Career Guidance Programs in 1979; and the APGA Career Education Project in 1980.

NVGA then established the National Council for Credentialing Career Counselors in 1983, and using the competencies mentioned, this independent credentialing body developed the National Career Counselor Examination, which was first administered at the 1984 American Association of Counseling and Development (AACD) convention in Houston, Texas. Also in 1984, a letter of intent to affiliate was filed with the new National Board for Certified Counselors (NBCC). The National Certified Career Counselor credential became the first specialty certification area for NBCC.

Concurrent with the emergence of the private practice of career counseling, outplacement counseling had its beginning. *Outplacement* is a term used when a company is having economic difficulties and begins to "downsize" currently employed workers to decrease staffing costs and increase profit margins. Outplacement counselors are then hired to help those workers find new employment-placement outside of their company. Outplacement led to the founding of such firms as Drake, Beam, and Morin; Lee Hecht Harrison; and Right Associates, who competed for these lucrative outplacement contracts side by side with career counselors in independent practice.

The rise in the use of technology in business and industry in the U.S. led to the passage of two very important federal laws during this stage: the Omnibus Trade and Competitiveness Act (1988) and the Carl D. Perkins Vocational Education Act (1984). The Omnibus Trade Act included provisions to assist persons to enter, or advance in, high-technology occupations or to meet the technological needs of other industries or businesses as well as pre-employment skills training, school-to-work transition programs, and school–business partnerships.

The Carl D. Perkins Vocational Education Act was signed into law in October, 1984. The Perkins Act replaced the Vocational Education Act of 1963, which had last been amended in 1976, and extended the federal authorization for vocational education programs through fiscal year 1989. It was notable for strengthening programs for underserved populations, which it listed as "disadvantaged individuals, handicapped individuals, adults requiring training/retraining, Indians, limited English-proficient students, participants in programs to eliminate sex bias in vocational education, native Hawaiians, single parents/homemakers, criminal offenders, and unemployed or workers threatened by unemployment" (Appling & Irwin, 1988, p. 9). The Perkins Act has been amended continuously by the federal government and continues to be the vehicle for career guidance authorization in the schools. Amendments were made by the National Science, Engineering, and Mathematics Authorization Act of 1986 and the Augustus F. Hawkins-Robert T. Stafford Elementary and Secondary School Improvement Amendments of 1988, which also funded the National Center for Research in Vocational Education at the Ohio State University and the University of California-Berkeley.

During the fifth stage, NVGA was in transition as well, and its name change in 1984 to the National Career Development Association (NCDA) completed a process begun by Donald Super in the 1950s (NVGA, 1984). Super's contributions led to a redefinition of vocational guidance. His developmental theory led to what is now termed a career developmental orientation that spans the life of the individual. The acceptance and use of this new concept of career development by practitioners and theoreticians alike was the necessary precursor to the organizational name change.

With the name change and the new NCCC credential came a stronger need for a different identity and increasing autonomy from the more general counseling organization (during this stage called AACD). The hiring of an executive director (Niel Carey) during this period marked the first independent staff since the 1950s, when NVGA founded the APGA. Conducting a national conference separate from the AACD convention began soon after hiring an executive director.

In addition, with the publication of the 1982 edition of *A Counselor's Guide to Vocational Guidance Instruments*, edited by Jerome Kapes and Marjorie Mastie, NVGA began a period of increased publishing for its members on the practice of vocational guidance and career counseling. The Counselor's Guide went into a second edition in 1988, a third edition in 1994, and a fourth edition is planned for 2000. Edwin Whitfield was added as coeditor for the third and fourth editions. Following that publication, in 1985 NCDA published *Adult Career Development: Concepts, Issues and Practices*, edited by Zandy Leibowitz and Daniel Lea. A second edition was published in 1992, and a third is planned for 2000; however, with the death of Zandy Leibowitz in 1997, Carole Minor was added as a coeditor for that edition. Finally, NCDA began collaborating with small publishing companies to develop other materials. The most successful was a series of "how to" books, with the first in the series being a book on how to establish an independent practice in career counseling (Hafer, 1992). Many other books were also published by NCDA during this period, but the Kapes, Mastie, and Whitfield and Liebowitz and Lea books accounted for more than 90% of the publication revenues of NCDA during the period 1982–1996 (Pope, 1996).

SIXTH STAGE: A FOCUS ON THE SCHOOL-TO-JOB TRANSITION, INTERNALIZATION OF CAREER COUNSELING, MULTICULTURAL CAREER COUNSELING, AND INCREASING SOPHISTICATION IN THE USE OF TECHNOLOGY (1990 TO PRESENT)

In the late 1980s and early 1990s, career counseling was extending in various new directions: an upward extension (e.g., outplacement of senior executives); a downward extension (e.g., providing services for poor people, helping homeless people prepare résumés); an outward extension (e.g., providing services to schools and agencies through federal legislation); and an inward development (e.g., developing career specialties).

The upward extension included the populations of senior managers and executives who had rarely used these services before, but through economic imperatives (i.e., they were losing their jobs and had nowhere else to turn), now found themselves looking for work at times in their lives when they should have been planning for a financially successful retirement from the companies that they had spent their entire lives building.

The downward extension included the poor and homeless socioeconomic classes who were being required to go to work because of new governmental policies such as Greater Avenues to Independence (GAIN), the Job Training Partnership Act (JTPA), Welfare to Work WtW), and Workforce Initiative Act of 1998. The WtW Act of 1997 was the harshest of these laws. It set a 5-year limit on any person in the U.S. receiving economic support through a federally administered economic support program called Temporary Assistance for Needy Families, which replaced the federal program called Aid to Families with Dependent Children. The idea was to place individuals who have experienced or have characteristics associated with long-term welfare dependence in lasting unsubsidized jobs—to get them in jobs first (called a "work first" service strategy) and then to train them postemployment.

The role of career counseling and development professionals is to assist in this process in whatever ways they can, which varies from state to state and from local agency to local agency. The focus of federal implementation monies is to help those who are most likely to have the greatest problems, such as individuals with disabilities, individuals who require substance abuse treatment, victims of domestic violence, individuals with limited English proficiency, and custodial parents.

The most recent piece of workforce development legislation has caused concern for both welfare recipient and career development specialists alike. With the focus on "work first" in the current legislation, no provision has been made for assessment and training as a precursor to finding a job, which would then be more likely to be maintained over the individual's lifetime. During the next 10 to 20 years, this program and others like it will be a major employer of career counseling and development professionals.

The outward extension occurred because of renewed interest and support for career development through the policies of the federal government. In fact, not since the 1960s have so many important laws affecting the career development of American citizens been passed by Congress and signed by a president. Beginning with President George Bush and continuing with President Bill Clinton, a resurgence in interest in the lifelong career development of the American populace has occurred. Such federal legislation as the School-to-Work Opportunities Act of 1994 and the One-Stop Career Centers Act of 1994 were important initiatives in this national campaign (Hamilton, 1990; Johnston & Packer, 1987; Marshall & Tucker, 1992; National Center on Education and the Economy, 1990; National Education Goals Panel, 1991; W. T. Grant Foundation, 1988).

The Americans With Disabilities Act of 1990 was the single most important legislation protecting the right to employment of persons who are physically or mentally challenged. Finally, three other bulwarks of career development legislation were also reauthorized during this decade: the Carl D. Perkins Vocational and Applied Technology Education Act Amendments (formerly titled the Carl D. Perkins Vocational Education Act), the Higher Education Act, and the Elementary and Secondary Education Act.

The role of organized career counseling and development professionals and federal agencies working together through the NCDA, the AVA (now called the Association for Career and Technical Education [ACTE]), the NOICC and state OICCs, and American School Counselor Association (ASCA) was pivotal to the final legislation authorizing the School-to-Work Opportunities Act (NCDA, 1993). This legislation is revolutionizing the education process of schooling in the U.S. by refocusing the nation's education resources on the difficult but underattended transition that all students must make from school to jobs (Hoyt & Lester, 1994; Pope, 1997).

Finally, an inward development was that specialities within the field of career counseling began to be developed by private practitioners. Such specialities included multicultural populations (e.g., African Americans, Asian Americans, gay men and lesbians, people with disabilities), attorneys, senior executives, and spousal and international relocation. The increasing specialization within a profession is the result of the maturing of that profession (Pope, 1995).

Quite important as well during this period was the first survey of the attitudes and beliefs of the American workforce regarding career development. With grants from NOICC, NCDA commissioned the Gallup Organization to conduct three national surveys—in 1989, 1992, and 1994—with a fourth survey funded for the year 2000. These survey results were published as books and received much national attention including being cited by federal legislators in their speeches during debate on these issues on the floor of the U.S. Congress. Each national survey covered a topic for which little national data had been published and provided important data on the general population's attitudes toward work and careers, attitudes of ethnic and racial minorities in the U.S. on work and careers, and attitudes of the general population of the U.S. toward how schools were preparing them for work realities and the school-to-job transition in the U.S. (Brown & Minor, 1989, 1992; Hoyt & Lester, 1994). Other books were published by NCDA during this period, including a book on career development and the Internet (Harris-Bowlsbey, Dikel, & Sampson, 1999) and a book providing experiential activities for teaching career development classes in community colleges and to graduate students in counseling, and for facilitating career groups (Pope & Minor, 2000).

The changing demographics of the American workforce also came to the forefront during this period (Johnston & Packer, 1987). Hoyt (1989) addressed the NCDA membership during a luncheon at their annual meeting in Chicago in 1988 and reviewed the progress that women and ethnic and racial minorities in the U.S. have made over the past 20 years. Hoyt, who worked for the U.S. Department of Labor and wrote the definition of "work" for the U.S., was also past president of both ACA and NCDA. These changing demographics have led to a greater emphasis in both counseling, in general, and career counseling, in particular, on multicultural counseling skills (Sue, Arredondo, & McDavis, 1992).

Another aspect of the sixth stage is increasing technological sophistication, which has led to instant communication by telephone, facsimile transmission, and Internet to anywhere in the world. Personal communication devices such as pagers and cellular and digital telephones have made it possible to contact a person wherever they are. Extensions of these changes for the career counselor was the provision of career services using the Internet and the telephone as well as the opening up of career counseling markets in other countries.

NCDA's response to changing technological issues included a conference theme on technology during the presidency of JoAnn Bowlsbey (Daytona Beach, 1997), a book on using the Internet in career counseling (Harris-Bowlsbey et al., 1999), and a statement on the ethics of providing career counseling services on the Internet (NCDA, 1996).

With the dissolution of the former Soviet Union, the opening of economic doors in China, and the steady 7% annual economic growth in Southeast Asia, career counselors from the U.S. have also expanded their practices internationally. This expansion has included substantial energy and economic investment in taking career counseling to other countries. Career counselors from the U.S. now do substantial contract work in various countries, including Singapore, Russia, China, Hong Kong, Malaysia, Australia, Estonia, and Poland (Pope, 1995, 1999). This is only the beginning of this trend, as technological advances drive the worldwide dissemination of information and innovations in the delivery of career counseling services. NCDA responded by designating the theme of its 1999 global conference, led by NCDA President Mark Pope, as "Best Practices in Career Development Across Cultures."

NCDA was in transition as well, returning to its beginnings, as it prepared to meet the challenges of this stage. After much internal debate, NCDA adopted a comprehensive nondiscrimination policy in 1995, which aligned it with its progressive roots and included sexual orientation as a protected category. Furthermore, under NCDA President Ken Hoyt, the NCDA Board of Directors adopted an expansive policy on career development which was to be used in state and federal legislative hearings (Engels, 1994). Also, the composition of the NCDA Board of Directors had been changing from being composed predominantly of counselor educators in academic institutions to being composed predominantly of private practice, business, and agency career counselors and consultants.

During this stage, issues of collaboration with other career-vocational-employment professional associations, both domestically and internationally, also were becoming important, as professional associations similar to NCDA were proliferating and federal legislation dealing with such issues increased. Through the NOICC-funded Career Development Training Institute's Advisory Committee and Workgroup on Workforce and Career Development Competencies, representatives of a variety of professional organizations began to be acquainted with each other's constituencies and issues. NCDA, the National Association of Workforce Development Professionals (NAWDP), the International Association of Personnel in Employment Security (IAPES), and the Interstate Conference of Employment Security Agencies (ICESA) met for the first time in 1998 as a workgroup to discuss workforce and career development competency issues. Out of those meetings came the new Council on Workforce and Career Development Associations—endorsed in 1999 by the NCDA Board of Directors—whose mission is to provide a forum for continued collaboration among the growing number of professional associations whose focus is on career, employment, and vocational issues, broadly termed "workforce and career development associations."

CONCLUSION

There have been several stages in the history of career counseling in the U.S., each presaged by major societal change. Each of these stages has had profound effects on the lives of individuals in this society. In the first stage (1890–1919), placement services were offered for an increasingly urban and industrial society. In the second stage (1920–1939), educational guidance through the elementary and secondary schools became the focal point. During the third stage (1940–1959), the focus shifted to colleges and universities and the training of counselors. The fourth stage (1960–1979) was the boom for counseling, and the idea of work having meaning in a person's life came to the forefront; organizational career development began during this period. The fifth stage (1980–1989) included the beginning of the transition from industrial age to information age and the growth of both private practice career counseling and outplacement counseling. The sixth stage (1990–present), with its emphasis on technology and changing demographics, has seen the increasing sophistication in the uses of technology, the internationalization of career counseling, the beginnings of multicultural career counseling, and the increased focus on the school to job transition.

This article is the beginning of a much larger international study of how economic processes and societal changes have affected the development of career counseling in the U.S. and around the world. If different nations have gone through similar stages in the development of career counseling, then the lessons learned in one nation can be used to assist another in its transition. If, because of increased technological sophistication and increasing internationalization and integration of economic structures, our planet is becoming conceptually smaller with exposure to information as it happens in any part of the world, the stages outlined here may become worldwide phenomena, affecting all nations and their social structures simultaneously, including banking, stock markets, employment, education, and training. The stages that the U.S. has undergone will then become the map for the development of career counseling in other countries and allow career counseling professionals in other countries more time to prepare an even better response to the changes and the transitions based on their knowledge of the past.

The career counseling profession is a product of these changes. With knowledge of the historical processes involved in shaping the profession, career counseling professionals can be ready to provide the social leadership required in times of transition and crisis. As Cicero stated in his oratories in 80 B.C., "Not to know what happened before one was born is always to be a child."

REFERENCES

Appling, R. N, & Irwin, P. M. (1988). *Federal vocational education legislation: Recurring issues during the last quarter century.* Washington, DC: Congressional Research Service, Library of Congress.

Aubrey, R. F. (1977). Historical development of guidance and counseling and implications for the future. *Personnel and Guidance Journal, 55,* 288–295.

Bernert, E. H. (1958). *America's children.* New York: Wiley.

Bloomfield, M. (1915). *Readings in vocational guidance.* Boston: Ginn.

Borow, H. (1964). Notable events in the history of vocational guidance. In H. Borow (Ed.), *Man in a world at work* (pp. 45–64). Washington, DC: Houghton Mifflin.

Borow, H. (1974). Apathy, unrest, and change: The psychology of the 1960s. In E. L. Herr (Ed.), *Vocational guidance and human development* (pp. 3–31). Washington, DC: Houghton Mifflin.

Brewer, J. M. (1919). *The vocational guidance movement.* New York: Macmillan.

Brewer, J. M. (1942). *History of vocational guidance.* New York: Harper.

Brown, D., & Minor, C. W. (Eds.). (1989). *Planning for and working in America: Report of a national survey.* Alexandria, VA: National Career Development Association.

Brown, D., & Minor, C. W. (Eds.). (1992). *Career needs in a diverse workforce: Implications of the NCDA Gallup survey.* Alexandria, VA: National Career Development Association.

Ehrle, R. A. (1969). *Vocational guidance: A look at the state of the art.* Hyattsville, MD: Martin.

Engels, D. W. (Ed.). (1994). *The professional practice of career counseling and consultation: A resource document (2nd ed.).* Alexandria, VA: National Career Development Association.

Ginzberg, E. (1971). *Career guidance.* New York: McGraw-Hill.

Hafer, A. A. (Ed.). (1992) *The nuts and bolts of career counseling: How to set up and succeed in private practice.* Garrett Park, MD: Garrett Park Press.

Hamilton, S. (1990). *Apprenticeship for adulthood. Preparing youth for the future.* New York: Free Press.

Harris-Bowlsbey, J., Dikel, M. R., & Sampson, J.P., Jr. (1999). *The Internet: A tool for career planning.* Columbus, OH: National Career Development Association.

Herr, E. L. (1974). Manpower policies, vocational guidance and career development. In E. L. Herr (Ed.), *Vocational guidance and human development* (pp. 32–62). Washington, DC: Houghton Mifflin.

Hoyt, K. D. (1989). The career status of women and minority persons: A 20-year retrospective. *The Career Development Quarterly, 37,* 202–212.

Hoyt, K. D., & Lester, J. N. (1994). *Learning to work: The NCDA Gallup Survey.* Alexandria, VA: National Career Development Association.

Johnson, W. B., & Packer, A. E. (1987). *Workforce 2000: Work and workers for the twenty-first century.* Indianapolis, IN: Hudson.

Lester, J. N. (1997, July). *The NOJCC/SOICC network: 20 years of change.* Keynote address delivered at the National SOICC Annual Conference, Tacoma, WA.

Marshall, R., & Tucker, M. (1992). *Thinking for a living.* New York: BasicBooks.

McDaniels, C. O. (1964). *The history and development of the American Personnel and Guidance Association 1952–1963.* Unpublished doctoral dissertation, The University of Virginia, Richmond.

National Career Development Association. (1993). *Career development: A policy statement of the 1992–1993 Board of Directors.* Alexandria, VA: Author.

National Career Development Association. (1996). *An ethics statement on the use of the Internet in providing career services.* Columbus, OH: Author.

National Center on Education and the Economy. (1990). *America's choice: High skills or low wages.* Rochester, NY: Author.

National Education Goals Panel. (1991). *Building a nation of learners.* Denver, CO: Author.

National Vocational Guidance Association. (1930, February). *The Vocational Guidance Magazine.* Cambridge, MA: Bureau of Vocational Guidance. Graduate School of Education, Harvard University.

National Vocational Guidance Association. (1951, September). *The National Vocational Guidance Association, Inc. Newsletter.*

National Vocational Guidance Association. (1962, March). *The NVGA Newsletter.* Washington, DC: NVGA.

National Vocational Guidance Association. (1982, June). *The NVGA Newsletter.* Falls Church, VA: NVGA.

National Vocational Guidance Association. (1984, June). *The NVGA Newsletter.* Alexandria, VA: NVGA.

Newcombe, B. H. (1993). *The historical descriptive study of the American Personnel and Guidance Association from April 1963 through July 1983.* Unpublished doctoral dissertation, Virginia Polytechnic Institute and State University, Blacksburg.

Norris, W. (1954a). Highlights in the history of the National Vocational Guidance Association. *Personnel and Guidance Journal, 33,* 205–208.

Norris, W. (1954b). *The history and development of the National Vocational Guidance Association.* Unpublished doctoral dissertation, George Washington University, Washington, DC.

Parsons, F. (1909). *Choosing a vocation.* Boston: Houghton-Mifflin.

Pope, M. (1995). CCDA leadership: Cultivating the vitality of our profession. *CCDA News, 11*(1), 1, 5. [Original publication]

Pope, M. (1996). *Treasurer's report.* Alexandria, VA: National Career Development Association.

Pope, M. (1997, June). *Career counseling comes out: The revolution in schooling in America.* Lecture presented for the Centre for Educational Research, University of Hong Kong, Hong Kong.

Pope, M. (1999). Applications of group career counseling techniques in Asian cultures. *Journal of Multicultural Counseling and Development, 27,* 18–30.

Pope, M., & Minor, C. W. (Eds.). (2000). *Handbook of experiential activities for teaching career development and facilitating career groups.* Columbus, OH: National Career Development Association.

Reed, H. R. (1964). Preface. In H, Borow (Ed.), *Man in a world at work* (p. ix). New York: Houghton-Mifflin.

Sale, K. (1973). *SDS.* New York: Vintage.

Savickas, M. L. (1993). Career counseling in the postmodern era. *Journal of Cognitive Psychotherapy: An International Quarterly, 7,* 205–215.

Schwebel, M. (1984). From past to present: Counseling psychology's socially prescribed role. In J. M. Whiteley, N. Kagan, L. W. Harmon, B. R. Fretz, & F. Tanney (Eds.), *The coming decade in counseling psychology* (pp. 25–49). Schenectady, NY: Character Research.

Stephens, W. R. (1970). *Social reform and the origin of vocational guidance.* Washington, DC: American Personnel and Guidance Association.

Sue, D. W., Arredondo, P., & McDavis, R. J. (1992). Multicultural counseling competencies and standards: A call to the profession. *Journal of Counseling & Development, 70,* 477–486.

Super, D. E. (1955). Transition: From vocational guidance to counseling psychology. *Journal of Counseling Psychology, 2,* 3–9.

Super, D. E. (1974). The broader context of career development and vocational guidance: American trends in world perspective. In E. L. Herr (Ed.), *Vocational guidance and human development* (pp. 63–79). Washington, DC: Houghton-Mifflin.

Super, D. E., & Crites, J. O. (1962). *Appraising vocational fitness.* New York: Harper & Row.

Toffler, A. (1990). *Future shock.* New York: BasicBooks.

U.S. Department of Health, Education, and Welfare. (1963). *Education for a changing world of work* (Panel of Consultants on Vocational Education, pp. 206–214). Washington, DC: U. S. Government Printing Office.

W. T. Grant Foundation Commission on Work, Family, and Citizenship. (Ed.). (1988). *The forgotten half: Pathways to success for America's youth and young families.* Washington, DC: Author.

Whiteley, J. M. (1984). *Counseling psychology: A historical perspective.* Schenectady, NY: Character Research.

Williamson, E. G. (1965). *Vocational counseling.* New York: McGraw-Hill.

Zhang, W. Y., & Pope, M. (1997, June). *The history of career counseling in the USA, China, and Hong Kong.* Symposium presented at the Sixth International Counseling Conference, Beijing, China.

Modern and Postmodern Career Theories
The Unnecessary Divorce

JAMES P. SAMPSON JR.

Postmodern approaches to career counseling are becoming increasingly popular. Part of the impetus for the postmodern view has involved perceived problems in the assumptions and application of the modern approach. Two points of view have emerged: (a) the modern and postmodern approaches are incompatible, and the postmodern approach is superior to the modern approach and (b) the modern and postmodern approaches are compatible, each with specific benefits and limitations, and individual needs and cost-effectiveness should govern the decision of which approach to use. Key issues to examine in this discussion are standardized career assessment, aggregate career information, matching, and cost-effectiveness.

The postmodern approach has made important contributions to the delivery of career resources and services. Theorists, researchers, and practitioners who have advocated a postmodern view have helped those espousing a modern approach to *think* critically about what individuals need and how they can be best served. However, potential problems

James P. Sampson, Jr., "Modern and Postmodern Career Theories: The Unnecessary Divorce," *The Career Development Quarterly*, vol. 58, no. 1, pp. 91-96. Copyright © 2009 by National Career Development Association. Reprinted with permission. Provided by ProQuest LLC. All rights reserved.

can occur when these two conceptual approaches are viewed as mutually exclusive. Problems can result when emphasis is placed on the differences between modernism and postmodernism, the problems as associated with the modern approach, and the benefits associated with the postmodern approach. Creating winners and losers in this discussion is detrimental to the profession and the individuals being served. This article begins with an examination of modernism and postmodernism in terms of career assessment, career information, matching, and cost-effectiveness and concludes with a discussion of the importance of integrating modern and postmodern career theory, research, and practice.

ISSUES RELATED TO USING STANDARDIZED CAREER ASSESSMENTS AND AGGREGATE CAREER INFORMATION

The use of standardized career assessment and aggregate career information from multiple sources is typically identified as part of the modern approach. Two potential problems are usually identified with these resources. The first potential problem is that both individuals and the labor market have changed radically and are now too fluid for assessment and information variables to remain stable over time. Changes have undoubtedly occurred; however, the changes are not at all uniform. Whereas Web designers did not exist 15 years ago, the work of a veterinarian has not changed much with the exception of new technology used to provide medical care. This problem of variability in some of the data can be solved for the most part by investing the funds necessary to keep standardized assessments and aggregate information up to date.

The second potential problem with standardized career assessments and aggregate career information from multiple sources is that a standardized assessment represents someone else's construction of reality, and reality needs to be constructed by each individual on the individual's own terms. Standardized assessments and aggregate career information developed from someone else's experience can be misused by individuals who uncritically accept what they read, especially when they want quick and simple answers to complex problems. Allowing or encouraging individuals to use assessments and information in this way is certainly not good practice. Career assessments and career information should be used as one source of information, among other sources, to help individuals construct their perceptions of themselves and their opportunities in an informed and careful way within their social context.

ISSUES RELATED TO MATCHING

Matching individuals with occupations or educational options has been identified as a component of the modern approach. Matching is sometimes criticized for the historical practice of the matching being done by the practitioner for the individual. Even in countries in which this practice was common in the past, practitioners and policy makers are now realizing that individuals need to learn how to make their own decisions if they are to remain employable because lifetime employment is no longer the norm. Matching has also been criticized for stressing a simplistic, point-in-time approach that ignores intuition, the developmental nature of career choice, and the influence of social context on decision making. In this case, however, matching is not the problem. The problem is using matching as the primary focus of career assistance and failing to incorporate the use of information from multiple sources to generate potential options, as well as failing to deal with other important contextual variables.

Matching is a process, not an event. It is conceptualized as a recursive, evolutionary process in which matches are made, evaluated, and then discarded or kept, as part of a sequence of decisions made over a lifetime. Matching should be viewed as helping individuals use a balance of rational and intuitive processes to create a meaningful understanding of the ongoing choices they make while encouraging an awareness of the positive and negative social forces, including significant others, that influence their decisions (Sampson, 2008; Sampson, Reardon, Peterson, & Lenz, 2004).

Matching still has merit as an aid to career decision making. However, practitioners need to conceptualize matching from a broader perspective: helping individuals understand that matching is best used as a stimulus for exploration as opposed to providing the answer. Doing a better job of helping individuals develop appropriate expectations about the intended outcome of the matching process is imperative for practitioners. The profession must avoid "throwing the baby out with the bathwater" just because some career practitioners conceptualize matching very narrowly or are not effective at helping individuals understand the recursive nature of the matching process.

ISSUES RELATED TO THE COST-EFFECTIVENESS OF CAREER INTERVENTIONS

The cost-effectiveness of career interventions is an increasingly important issue if practitioners are to maintain the funding for services that are necessary to meet individuals' needs. Practitioners must ask themselves vital questions: "Who are we responsible for as career practitioners? Are we responsible only for the clients who come through our doors, or are we responsible for the citizens in our society who need help with career choices?" Blustein, McWhirter, and Perry (2005) reminded the profession of the social justice aspects of its work and its responsibility to address inequity in society. The responsibility of career practitioners is to the citizens who need help and not just to those clients who present themselves at their doorsteps. According to a survey conducted by The Gallup Organization for the National Career Development Association, "Seven in ten adults (69%) report, if they were starting over, they would try to get more information about the job and career options open to them than they got the first time" (The Gallup Organization, 1999, p. 3). The best way of helping citizens to make informed and careful career choices is to maximize the cost-effectiveness of career resources and services (Sampson, 2008).

Using the limited funding for career resources and services wisely is essential. Providing individual counseling to everyone who requests help is simply not possible with the funds available. If one were to divide the number of individuals who need help in making career choices by the number of practitioners available to provide individual counseling, one would realize that, clearly, not enough practitioners exist to fill the need. What is to be done about those individuals who do not have access to the help they need?

Progress has been made in establishing the effectiveness of career interventions in relation to their costs and benefits. Data are available on the outcomes of career interventions (Bowes, Smith, & Morgan, 2005; Brown & Krane, 2000; Folsom & Reardon, 2003; Hughes & Gration, 2006; Kidd & Killeen, 1992; Killeen, 1996; Oliver & Spokane, 1988; Spokane & Oliver, 1983; Whiston, 2002; Whiston, Sexton, & Lasoff, 1998). Examining costs by level of career intervention (Reardon, 1996) is especially important in determining the appropriateness of interventions in relation to the available funding. Data are also available on the economic and social benefits of these interventions (Hughes, Bosley, Bowes, & Bysshe, 2002; Killeen, White, & Watts, 1992; Mayston, 2002). Whiston (2002) noted that "there may be increased interest and support for career counseling interventions if researchers can demonstrate that there are economic benefits to career interventions" (p. 231). Career practitioners need to address this issue or face the consequences of losing funding to other professions that better document the value gained from the financial resources they are given.

Using postmodern assessments, such as card sorts, and postmodern interventions, such as narrative techniques, can be effective. However, practitioners can afford to use such time-consuming (and therefore expensive) resources and services only for those individuals who are not likely to benefit from briefer, less expensive interventions because of their extensive needs.

Practitioners need to determine which interventions, either modern or postmodern, work best with which individuals and in which settings. Differences in decisiveness, personality, culture, verbal ability, learning styles, language skills, disability status, and so forth can make a specific career intervention effective for one individual and ineffective for another. Practitioners need to improve the cost-effectiveness of career interventions by using career resources and services that are most likely to be helpful at the lowest possible cost. This strategy allows practitioners to maximize the number of individuals who can be served in ways that meet their needs.

INTEGRATING MODERN AND POSTMODERN CAREER THEORY, RESEARCH, AND PRACTICE

The test-and-tell career intervention that has sometimes been associated with the modern approach is as bad a practice today as it was 50 years ago. Criticizing the modern approach on the basis of what poorly trained, inadequately supervised, and overworked practitioners do is unfair. Those in the profession should not compare the best practice of the postmodern approach with the worst practice of the modern approach.

Individuals seek assistance with career choices, and those practitioners who seek to help these individuals need to understand and apply an approach that integrates modernism and postmodernism. The stakes are too high for theorists, researchers, and practitioners to assert that one approach is uniformly superior. Both points of view have merit and can be integrated in practice. A well-practiced modern approach is still viable, and a well-practiced postmodern approach has much to offer. Both approaches can also be improved over time. Practitioners need to create cost-effective career services that combine the best of both approaches if they are to serve the large number of citizens who need help in making career choices.

The divorce between theorists, researchers, and practitioners espousing modern and postmodern approaches is unnecessary. Understanding and valuing each approach for its unique contributions is important. Practitioners need to use career interventions that work, irrespective of their philosophical underpinnings. Policy makers who provide the funding for career interventions need to conclude that practitioners are making socially responsible use of the funding they have been given.

It is crucial that the profession understand how the integration of modern and postmodern career theory can help the career practitioner in the Workforce Oklahoma One-Stop Career Center in Shawnee, Oklahoma, on a Friday at 3:30 in the afternoon who has three individuals waiting to be seen. How can the profession integrate these approaches to better prepare this practitioner to help the man who states that he has lost his job and does not know what to do?

REFERENCES

Blustein, D. L., McWhirter, E. H., & Perry, J. C. (2005). An emancipatory communication approach to vocational development theory, research, and practice. *Counseling Psychologist, 33,* 141–179.

Bowes, L., Smith, D., & Morgan, S. (2005). *Reviewing the evidence base for careers work in schools* (iCeGS Occasional Paper). Derby, England: University of Derby, International Centre for Guidance Studies.

Brown, S. D., & Krane, N. E. R. (2000). Four (or five) sessions and a cloud of dust: Old assumptions and new observations about career counseling. In S. D. Brown & R. W. Lent (Eds.), *Handbook of counseling psychology* (3rd ed., pp. 740–766). New York: Wiley.

Folsom, B., & Reardon, R. (2003). College career courses: Design and accountability, *Journal of Career Assessment, 11,* 421–450.

The Gallup Organization. (1999). *National survey of working America, 1999.* Retrieved June 5, 2009, from National Career Development Association Web site: http://associationdatabase.com/aws/NCDA/asset_manager/get_file/3407/ncdareport.pdf

Hughes, D., Bosley, S., Bowes, L., & Bysshe, S. (2002). *The economic benefits of guidance* (iCeGS Research Report Series No. 3). Derby, England: University of Derby, International Centre for Guidance Studies.

Hughes, D., & Gration, G. (2006). *Performance indicators and benchmarks in career guidance in the United Kingdom* (iCeGS Occasional Paper). Derby, England: University of Derby, International Centre for Guidance Studies.

Kidd, J. M., & Killeen, J. (1992). Are the effects of careers guidance worth having? Changes in practice and outcomes. *Journal of Occupational and Organizational Psychology, 65,* 219–234.

Killeen, J. (1996). The learning and economic outcomes of guidance. In A. G. Watts, B. Law, J. Killeen, J. M. Kidd, & R. Hawthorn (Eds.), *Rethinking careers education and guidance: Theory, policy and practice* (pp. 46–58). London: Routledge.

Killeen, J., White, M., & Watts, A. G. (1992). *The economic value of careers guidance.* London: Policy Studies Institute.

Mayston, D. (2002). *Assessing the benefits of careers guidance* (iCeGS Occasional Paper). Derby, England: University of Derby, International Centre for Guidance Studies.

Oliver, L. W., & Spokane, A. R. (1988). Career-intervention outcome: What contributes to client gain? *Journal of Counseling Psychology, 3.5,* 447–462.

Reardon, R. (1996). A program and cost analysis of a self-directed career decision-making program in a university career center. *Journal of Counseling & Development, 74,* 280–285.

Sampson, J.P., Jr. (2008), *Designing and implementing career programs: A handbook for effective practice.* Broken Arrow, OK: National Career Development Association.

Sampson, J. P., Jr., Reardon, R. C., Peterson, G. W., & Lenz, J. G. (2004). *Career counseling and services: A cognitive information processing approach.* Belmont, CA: Thomson/Brooks/Cole.

Spokane, A. R., & Oliver, L. W. (1983). The outcomes of vocational intervention. In W. B. Walsh & S. H. Osipow (Eds.), *Handbook of vocational psychology* (pp. 99–136). Hillsdale, NJ: Erlbaum.

Whiston, S. C. (2002). Application of the principles: Career counseling and interventions. *Counseling. Psychologist, 30,* 218–237.

Whiston, S. C., Sexton, T. L., & Lasoff, D. L. (1998). Career-intervention outcome: A replication and extension of Oliver and Spokane. *Journal of Counseling Psychology, 45,* 150–165.

DISCUSSION QUESTIONS

1   In your opinion, what do you think has been the most important event that has shaped the counseling profession?

2   Do you think the counseling profession's history informs us about the direction that our field will go in the future? Why or why not?

3   In your own history, what has been the worst job you have ever had? What did that job do to you? How did it impact you? How did it change you?

4   In your future career as a counselor, what might happen if you didn't have some knowledge of career counseling (i.e., how to provide career counseling)?

CONCLUSION

Many counseling students over the years, unless specifically focusing on career counseling and development as a specialty area, have begrudgingly studied career counseling as a part of their counselor education. The typical thought is, "Why do I need to study this? I don't plan on being a career counselor." The Council for the Accreditation of Counseling and Related Educational Programs (CACREP) continues to require that all counseling students in a CACREP-accredited program study career development. This isn't a standard that is likely to disappear in the near future.

The knowledge and skills related to career counseling are important. History has shown this as being important within our profession, and the longer you are in the counseling field, the more you will understand and believe it as necessary and highly useful skills for *all* counselors to possess.

INDEX OF KEY TERMS

- American Association for Counseling and Development (AACD)
- American Counseling Association (ACA)
- American Personnel and Guidance Association

- Bureau of Labor Statistics
- career counseling
- career development
- career placement
- Carl D. Perkins Vocational Education Act
- Donald Super
- Frank Parsons, Boston Vocation Bureau
- Jesse B. Davis
- National Career Development Association (NCDA)
- National Vocational Occupational Information Coordinating Committee (NVOICC)
- National Vocational Guidance Association (NVGA)
- postmodern career theory
- Smith-Hughes Act of 1917
- standardized and non-standardized career assessment
- State Occupational Information Coordinating Committee (SOICC)
- U.S. Department of Labor
- Vocational Education Act of 1963
- vocational guidance

REFERENCES

Pope, M. (2000). A brief history of career counseling in the United States. *Career Development Quarterly, 48*(3), 194–211.

Sampson, J. P. (2009). Modern and postmodern career theories: The unnecessary divorce. *Career Development Quarterly, 58*(1), 91–96.

SUGGESTED PUBLICATIONS FOR FURTHER READING

Amundson, N., Harris-Bowlsbey, J., & Niles, S. (2014). Using career theories to help clients. In *Essential Elements of Career Counseling* (3rd ed). New York, NY: Pearson.

Krumboltz, J., Foley, P., & Cotter, E. (2013). Applying the happenstance theory to involuntary career transitions. *Career Development Quarterly, 61*(1), 15–26.

Luke, C., & Redekop, F. (2014). Gottfredson's theory of career circumscription and compromise. In G. T. Eliason, J. Samide, & J. Patrick, (Eds.) *Career counseling across the lifespan: Community, school, and higher education* (pp. 65–84). Charlotte, NC: Information Age.

CHAPTER 3

CAREER ASSESSMENTS AND INTEREST INVENTORIES

INTRODUCTION

For those who are new to the field of career counseling, there is a misconception about career counseling and assessing career exploration. Many people think that career counseling only involves the process of "test them and tell them." This is when a client comes in for services, is given a series of tests (measuring interests, hobbies, and personality), and is then provided a printout with what his or her future career will be for the next 40 years. Professional career counselors know there is so much more to this process. Assessments and interest inventories are valuable tools in career counseling, but they are just one part of the process.

These assessments and interest inventories provide information that both the counselor and client and can use in their career journey. The articles in this chapter will provide an overview of assessments and interest inventories used in career counseling.

Using Theory-Based Career Assessments to Connect Career and Mental Health Issues

V. CASEY DOZIER, JANET G. LENZ, AND VANESSA FREEMAN

INTRODUCTION

As Wood and Hays (2013) noted, "assessment is an integral component of practice for counselors working with clients or students on career related issues" (p. 3). Journal articles, test directories, and conference vendors, provide evidence of the increasing number of assessments available that can be used in the career guidance and counseling process. In addition, the growth of web-based resources has brought a significant increase in the number of career assessments available to consumers and practitioners, with little oversight or quality control associated with these instruments, regardless of whether they are offered for a fee or at no cost (Osborn, Dikel, Sampson, & Harris-Bowlsbey, 2011). Ethical codes in the counseling and career development field stress the importance of considering the reliability, validity, and psychometric properties of any assessments used with clients. The National Career Development Association's code of ethics (2015) states that career professionals must understand the "validation criteria, assessment research, and guidelines for assessment development and use" (p. 13). Another consideration with regard to career assessments is the relationship between theory, research, and practice (Sampson, Hou, Kronholz, Dozier, et al. 2014). The development

V. Casey Dozier, Janet G. Lenz, and Vanessa Freeman, "Using Theory-based Career Assessments to Connect Career and Mental Health Issues," *Career Planning and Adult Development Journal*, vol. 32, no. 1, pp. 100-111. Copyright © 2016 by Career Planning and Adult Development Network. Reprinted with permission. Provided by ProQuest LLC. All rights reserved.

of career theories often leads to the creation of constructs within those theories, e.g., career thoughts, congruence, differentiation, vocational identity, etc. The hallmark of a good theory is that it produces measures to assess constructs derived from the theory, followed by research on those measures and constructs to validate the theory's propositions or assumptions, e.g., negative career thinking is associated with low vocational identity. In reality, many career assessments are created without a clear connection to an associated theory, and/or there is a lack of research on their psychometric properties, and their ability to produce valid results for clients who complete them. Whether via online sites, print materials, or conference presentations, it is not uncommon to see career assessments promoted as being fun, free, quick, and easy to use. However in many instances, these assessments lack any theoretical foundation, research, or supporting materials (e.g., professional manual, intervention tools). Osborn and Zunker (2012) stressed the importance of reviewing an assessment's professional manual prior to use with clients. Promoting the use of career assessments that lack theoretical foundations, supporting research, and guidelines for professional use, seems, at best, at odds with sound practice and, at worst, a violation of ethical codes.

The purpose of this article is to highlight two career assessments, based in theory and research, which can be used in practice to explore the connection between career and mental health issues, which is an increasing area of emphasis in the counseling field (Lenz, Peterson, Reardon, & Saunders, 2010; Zunker, 2008). The first assessment described is the Career Thoughts Inventory (Sampson, Peterson, Lenz, Reardon, & Saunders, 1996a) and the second is the Self-Directed Search (Holland & Messer, 2013). Following the overview of each instrument and its diagnostic components, a case example is provided to illustrate how the results from each assessment can be used in providing a more holistic picture of a client's situation.

CAREER THOUGHTS INVENTORY

The Career Thoughts Inventory (CTI; Sampson, et al. 1996a) is based on cognitive information processing (CIP) theory (Sampson, Reardon, Peterson, & Lenz, 2004) and Beck's (1976) cognitive therapy model. Both of these perspectives describe how negative or dysfunctional thinking can impact feelings and behavior and create difficulties in functioning. CIP theory includes the pyramid of information processing domains: self-knowledge, option knowledge, decision making (CASVE cycle), and thinking about decision making (executive processing). The CTI's 48 items reflect each content domain of the CIP pyramid and CASVE cycle, which includes the following phases: Communication, Analysis, Synthesis, Valuing and Execution.

The CASVE cycle provides a model for career problem solving and decision making (Sampson et al. 2004). An example of a CTI item in the self-knowledge domain is: "I get upset when people ask me what I want to do with my life." A sample CTI item in the Communication phase is: "I get so depressed about choosing a field of study or occupation that I can't get started." A CTI item from Executive Processing is "I get so anxious when I have to make decisions that I can hardly think." The CTI also includes three subscales: Decision Making Confusion (DMC), Commitment Anxiety (CA), and External Conflict (EC).

The CTI Professional Manual (Sampson, et al. 1996b) provides information on the CTI's reliability and validity. Of particular interest in this article is the CTI's convergent validity with selected constructs related to mental health factors. Instruments used in examining the CTI's convergent validity included the My Vocational Situation (MVS), Career Decision Scale (CDS), the Career Decision Profile (CDP), and the Revised NEO Personality Inventory. "Constructs with a negative connotation (e.g., indecision, neuroticism, anxiety, angry hostility, depression, impulsiveness, and vulnerability) were directly correlated with the CTI Total, DMC, CA, and EC" (Sampson, et al. 1996b, p. 59).

The relationship between the CTI and mental health factors was further explored in later research studies. Saunders, Peterson, Sampson, and Reardon (2000) examined the relationship between CTI scores, depression and career indecision in a sample of university students. Dieringer (2012) studied clients seeking career services in a university career center and found that individuals with elevated DMC and CA scores had significantly higher scores on the Beck Depression Inventory and the Beck Hopelessness Scale. Additional studies have been carried out that have examined the relationship of the CTI total scores and the three subscales. Space in this article does not permit a full review of those, but readers are directed to the CIP/CTI bibliography available at the following website: www.career.fsu.edu/content/download/191178/1653555/CurrentCIPBibliography.pdf to learn more about CIP theory and the use of the CTI in research and practice.

The CTI validation studies and subsequent research have provided ample evidence of the CTI's relationship to various mental health factors. **Table 3.1 [see Appendix]** illustrates how CIP content domains relate to CTI items and potential mental health factors. Research suggests that when individuals present with high levels of negative thinking (including elevated CTI total scores and elevated scale scores), career practitioners should be alert to the presence of accompanying mental health concerns. The CTI Manual (Sampson, et al. 1996b), provides guidelines for interpreting the total score, the subscale scores, and individual items, along with suggested interventions, including the CTI Workbook (Sampson, Peterson, Lenz, Reardon, & Saunders, 1996c) which is designed to help individuals identify, challenge, alter their negative thinking, and subsequently take action in their daily lives to engage in more positive thinking.

THE SELF-DIRECTED SEARCH

The Self-Directed Search (SDS), a popular interest inventory utilized by more than 35 million people worldwide, was developed based on Holland's RIASEC theory (Holland, 1997). Holland's theory proposed that personality types and environmental models can be characterized as one of six RIASEC types captured on a hexagonal model: Realistic, Investigative, Artistic, Social, Enterprising, and Conventional. RIASEC theory and its related applications have been referenced in more than 1,600 citations (Foutch, McHugh, Reardon, & Bertoch, 2014).) The Self-Directed Search was revised in 2013 and is now in its 5th edition (Holland & Messer, 2013). The SDS Professional Manual provides detailed information on the reliability and validity of the SDS 5th edition (Holland & Messer, 2013).

While the SDS is commonly used as a tool to relate personal characteristics to occupational alternatives, it also serves as a diagnostic tool (Reardon & Lenz, in press) to help users understand factors that may be impacting their career problem solving and decision making. As Reardon and Lenz noted (in press), the SDS is a career intervention, but its theory-based secondary constructs can also provide insight into client characteristics that may affect clients' readiness to benefit from career interventions. The next section illustrates how selected diagnostic constructs, based on Holland's theory and generated from SDS assessment results, are connected to both career and mental health concerns.

SDS DIAGNOSTIC CONSTRUCTS

In addition to summary scores on Holland's RIASEC types, the SDS provides information on a number of secondary diagnostic constructs that have significant practical implications in understanding a client's career situation. These secondary constructs (e.g., coherence, congruence, differentiation), derived from the SDS and grounded in Holland's theory, not only inform "hypotheses about a person's career path, level of aspiration and achievement, job shifts, educational behavior, social behavior, and environmental responsiveness" (Holland, 1997, p. 40), but they may also have important implications regarding a person's mental health and overall wellbeing. In the section that follows, three of the SDS secondary constructs are discussed, specifically congruence, coherence, and profile elevation, to illustrate how they can provide insight into the intersection of clients' career and mental health concerns.

CONGRUENCE

Congruence is described as the level of agreement between any two Holland codes (Holland & Messer, 2013). When using the SDS, practitioners can determine congruence by comparing the aspirations summary code to the assessed summary code. The SDS Professional Manual (Holland & Messer, 2013) provides a worksheet in Appendix D to use in calculating a congruence score. For example, a client's three-letter summary code from the SDS assessment (e.g., Conventional, Social, and Artistic) can be compared with the aspiration summary code (e.g., Artistic, Investigative, and Realistic) which is calculated based on the RIASEC codes for a person's occupational daydreams. In the example above, the client would have a low congruence level based on the Iachan Agreement Index described in the SDS Professional Manual. A low level of congruence does not automatically indicate that mental health factors are present, but it is a sign that should involve further discussion between the practitioner and the client. The assessed SDS code may simply represent where the client "has been" with regard to his/her occupational history, activities, and competencies, and the daydreams may reflect occupational goals for the future. Of greater concern is when the daydreams seem completely unconnected to clients' self-reported characteristics as reflected in their SDS results, and clients sees no discrepancy between what they aspire to do and their interests and competencies. While practitioners will want to be sensitive to clients' passions about future possibilities, it may be useful to discuss with the client the low congruence, specifically how the occupational dreams might be reached if the client's history and present state suggests a difficult path going forward. From a readiness perspective (Sampson, McClain, Musch, & Reardon, 2013), this situation takes on additional complexity when there are other factors in the person's situation that represent significant barriers to achieve particular occupational goals (e.g., extremely low academic achievement coupled with the desire to become a physician, personality disorders and the desire to be a pilot, etc.). Low congruence may also reflect individuals' intense dissatisfaction with their current job or life activities, and this situation may be connected to other mental health factors associated with a lack of a person-environment match.

COHERENCE

Coherence of aspirations is defined as the "degree to which codes of a person's set of vocational aspirations or occupational daydreams belong in the same RIASEC category" (Holland & Messer, 2013). For example, if the first three daydreams have the same first letter (e.g., Social), then coherence would be high; whereas, if the first letter of the second and third aspirations are different from the first daydream listed, then coherence would be low (e.g., AES, EAS, SIA). Reardon and Lenz (1999) suggested that low coherence may indicate that clients are confused about occupations, their own interests, or how occupations and interests are related. Practitioners may find reasonable explanations for varied daydreams, e.g., the client is multipotential or has diverse interests and skills (Reardon & Lenz, in press). It may be useful to ask clients about themes or patterns associated with their daydreams. Similar to the congruence discussion above, practitioners should take note if the list of unrelated daydreams seem to have no basis in reality and are in no way connected to the client's self-knowledge or personal characteristics. While practitioners will want to be sensitive to clients' self-reported ideas about future occupations and explore any barriers to these goals that could be reduced or eliminated, they also need to discuss with the client any "disconnects" about how these varied occupational dreams might be reached if all the data at hand suggests a difficult path going forward.

PROFILE ELEVATION

Profile elevation is the total sum of the six RIASEC scores on the SDS (Holland, & Messer, 2013). As a positive indicator, high profile elevation has been associated with valuing new experiences. Bullock and Reardon (2008) studied profile elevation in relation to NEO scores and found that high profile elevation was positively related to Openness, Conscientiousness, and Extraversion. In contrast, individuals with "low scores may be less willing to consider new career options and they may display characteristics such as sadness and frustration" (Reardon & Lenz, 2013, p. 23). Holland and Messer (2013) reported significant positive correlations between profile elevation and extraversion, openness, and agreeableness. In situations where clients have a low profile elevation score, which may reflect a number of negative responses and low self-estimate ratings, practitioners should be alert to issues such as depression, lack of engagement with life, low self-esteem, and related concerns. In the section that follows a case study, with both CTI and SDS assessment results will be discussed to highlight the intersection of career and mental health concerns.

CASE OF "MADISON"

Madison is a 34-year-old, married, White female who came into a university-based career center that serves community adults who are seeking career assistance. She has been employed with a government agency for 4 years, but is dissatisfied with her current work environment. She does not enjoy the pressure placed on her to meet various deadlines, and feels like she is not using the skills she possesses. Madison describes her work environment as being one where she "comes into her office space, stares at a computer all day, and has minimal interaction with others." She is often required to work nights and weekends which interferes with her ability to take care of her family. Madison has two small children who are cared for by her husband who works part time. Madison and her husband have discussed the idea of Madison continuing to work while her husband transitions into being a stay-at-home father. At this time, they are unable to complete this transition because they cannot support their family financially without a dual income.

Prior to working in her current position, Madison was employed as a cruise ship performer for several years. She became involved in this work after graduating from college with a political science degree and while looking for a summer job. Madison had been active in theatre and chorus in high school, but had given up these activities while in college. Madison did not have a clear idea of what she wanted to do after college and applied for the position on a whim. She enjoyed this work greatly, including the interaction with others and the creative aspects, but had to quit when she got married and became pregnant with her first child. After the birth of her first child, she became employed in her current job to help pay the bills. She reported feeling overwhelmed, anxious, and saddened by her current situation and described herself as being "at the end of her rope" regarding how to move forward. Madison completed the Career Thoughts Inventory (CTI) to help the practitioner learn more about her current thinking regarding her career situation. At a subsequent appointment, Madison completed the Self-Directed Search (SDS) to further explore what kinds of activities and occupations she might be interested in pursuing. The results of her assessments follow.

Case Data
Career Thoughts Inventory (CTI)
CTI Total Score (T Score): 67 (96th percentile)
Decision-Making Confusion (DMC) (T Score): 61 (86th percentile)
Commitment Anxiety (CA) (T Score): 66 (95th percentile)
External Conflict (EC) (T Score): 60 (84th percentile)

CASE ANALYSIS

Madison's CTI results suggest that she is having many negative career thoughts. Her elevated Decision-Making Confusion (DMC) score points to difficulties she is having in making a career decision, and is reinforced by her past experiences in making career decisions. She lacked clarity about her career goals following graduation and randomly chose to become a cruise ship performer without considering her interests, skills, and values. Additionally, she seems to have chosen her current job in the same manner. This lack of understanding of how to make career decisions may have also contributed to her elevated Commitment Anxiety (CA) score. This scale assesses an individual's feelings about making career choices and the level of anxiety that accompanies this process. The CTI results highlight Madison's confusion and anxiety associated with making a career decision at the present time. At age 34, and in light of the family's financial situation, Madison feels pressure about choosing the "right" job which in turn makes it difficult for her to proceed in the job search process. She feels caught between the need to keep her job and the associated benefits, but feels extremely discouraged about finding a satisfying alternative. Lastly, her scores on the External Conflict (EC) scale suggest that her family, and the role she plays in it, interferes with her ability to navigate the career development process. Her expressed feelings of anxiety and discouragement are supported by her CTI results.

The diagnostic signs from Madison's SDS results contain both positive indicators and some areas for further discussion. On the positive side, the congruence level between her assessed summary code, ESR and her Daydreams summary code, EAS, was high. However, her daydreams had low coherence. As noted previously, these options may simply reflect her diverse skills and interests, but the career practitioner will want to explore the extent to which these alternatives contribute to her uncertainty and anxiety associated with considering future career choices. In addition, while the first two letters of her SDS summary code, ES, are high in consistency, the challenge of this code combination is that it relates to a wide variety of occupational alternatives and this could be contributing to her commitment anxiety as reflected in the CTI results. Madison's profile elevation is average, but her differentiation is low. Differentiation relates to the "distinctness in an SDS profile" (Reardon & Lenz, 2013, p. 23). Low differentiation may reflect many high or low SDS scores, which results in a flat profile. Reardon and Lenz (2013) suggested that users with low differentiation may present more "interpretation challenges for practitioners" (p. 23). Madison's anxiety and confusion, as reflected in her CTI scores, may be connected to her low differentiation. She may be overwhelmed with options or she may feel confused by the variety of options across the different Holland areas.

While some career counseling models encourage embracing a diverse array of options, not all clients feel comfortable with the ambiguity associated with this type of approach to career choice. The practitioner working with Madison used a CIP-based approach to career decision making called the CASVE cycle. The visual figure of this approach that the practitioner shared with Madison, along with the accompanying "Guide to Good Decision-Making Exercise" (Sampson, Peterson, Lenz, & Reardon, 1998) helped her see a process for moving forward in her career problem solving. The practitioner highlighted CTI items related to various aspects of the CASVE cycle and CIP pyramid. This helped Madison see why she was feeling confused and anxious, but also helped her see specific areas that could be addressed by various career interventions. To address the career and mental health concerns reflected in Madison's elevated CTI scores, the practitioner used the CTI Workbook (Sampson, Peterson, Lenz, Reardon, & Saunders, (1996c) as part of the counseling process to help Madison challenge and reframe her negative career thoughts.

The practitioner also talked with Madison about ways to explore and prioritize options that better fit with her self-knowledge. Madison's SDS summary code (ESR) helped her and the practitioner understand her unhappiness with her current job. Her lack of interest in Conventional occupations, as reflected in her SDS results, lends further support to this conclusion. She has a strong interest in working with people (S) as a leader or motivator to achieve a common goal (E) which she is unable to do in her current work. Madison also appears to enjoy activities and occupations that allow her to use her hands and body in a more flexible work environment (R). These interests are supported by the fact that she enjoyed her job as a cruise ship performer where she was able to use these interests in her work every day. The practitioner helped her brainstorm ways to learn about options and make a plan for next steps.

CONCLUSION

This article and the accompanying case highlight how theory-based career assessments can provide a window into the intersection of career and mental health concerns. Clients who present for career assistance may be experiencing a range of emotions, including anxiety, confusion, frustration, etc., accompanied by negative thinking. Saunders (2014) noted that adult clients, in particular, who are dealing with greater life complexity, may need assistance in confronting negative thinking early in the career counseling process, in order to move forward with other career tasks. Theory-based assessments like the Career Thoughts Inventory and the Self-Directed

Search can point to not only career areas that need attention, such as self- and options knowledge, and decision-making difficulties, but also other areas that cross over into mental health factors such as stress, anxiety, confusion, and family conflict. Use of theory and research-based instruments that provide a more complete picture of a client's situation offer practitioners a more efficient and holistic way to assist clients in navigating their life career journey.

REFERENCES

Beck, A. T. (1976). *Cognitive therapy and the emotional disorders.* New York: International Universities Press.

Bullock, E. E., & Reardon, R. C. (2008). Interest profile elevation, big five personality traits, and secondary constructs on the Self-Directed Search. *Journal of Career Assessment* 16, 326–338.

Dieringer, D. D. (2012). Dysfunctional career thinking as a predictor of depression and hopelessness in students seeking career services (Doctoral dissertation). Available from ProQuest Dissertations and Theses database. (UMI No. 3519307)

Foutch, H., McHugh, E. R., Bertoch, S. C., & Reardon, R. C. (2014). Creating and using a database on Holland's theory and practical tools. *Journal of Career Assessment* 22, 188–202. DOI: 10.1177/1069072713492947

Holland, J. L. & Messer, M. A. (2013). *Self-Directed Search Form R.* 5th ed. professional manual. Odessa, FL: Psychological Assessment Resources.

Holland, J. L. (1997). *Making vocational choices* (3rd ed.). Odessa, FL: Psychological Assessment Resources.

Lenz, J. G., Peterson, G. W., Reardon, R. C., & Saunders, D. (2010, July). Connecting career and mental health counseling: Integrating theory and practice. *VISTAS 2010.* Retrieved from: http://counseling-outfitters.com/vistas/vistas10/Article_01.pdf.

National Career Development Association. (2015). *NCDA Code of ethics.* Broken Arrow, OK: Author. Retrieved from http://ncda.org/aws/NCDA/asset_manager/get_file/3395.

Osborn, D. S., Dikel, M. R., Sampson, J. P., Jr., & Harris-Bowlsbey, J. (2011). *The internet: A tool for career planning* (3rd ed.). Broken Arrow, OK: National Career Development Association.

Osborn, D. S., & Zunker, V. G. (2012). *Using assessment results for career development* (5th ed.). Belmont, CA: Brooks/Cole.

Reardon, R. C., & Lenz, J. G. (in press). *The handbook for using the Self-Directed Search: Integrating RIASEC and CIP theories in practice.* (2nd ed.). Odessa, FL: Psychological Assessment Resources.

Reardon, R. C., & Lenz, J. G. (2013). Use and interpretive guide. In J. L. Holland & M. A. Messer (Eds.). *Self-Directed Search professional manual* (5th ed., pp. 15–29). Odessa, FL: Psychological Assessment Resources.

Reardon, R. C., & Lenz, J. G. (1999). Holland's theory and career assessment. *Journal of Vocational Behavior* 55, 102–113. http://dx.doi.org/10.1006/jvbe.1999.1700

Sampson, J. P., Hou, P. C., Kronholz, J., Dozier, C., McClain, M. C., Buzzetta, M., Pawley, E., Finklea, T., Peterson, G. P., Lenz, J. G., Reardon, R. C., Osborn, D. S., Hayden, S. C. W., Kennelly, E. L., & Colvin, G. P. (2014). Annual review: A content analysis of career development theory, research, and practice—2013. *The Career Development Quarterly* 62, 290–326.

Sampson, J. P., Jr., McClain, M-C., Musch, E., & Reardon, R. C. (2013). Factors affecting readiness to benefit from career interventions. *The Career Development Quarterly* 61, 98–109. doi: 10.1002/j.2161–0045.2013.00040.x

Sampson, J. P., Jr., Peterson, G. W., Lenz, J. G., & Reardon, R. C. (1998). A guide to good decision making exercise. Unpublished manuscript, Florida State University, Center for the Study of Technology in Counseling and Career Development, Tallahassee, FL.

Sampson, J. P., Jr., Peterson, G. W., Lenz, J. G., Reardon, R. C., & Saunders, D. E. (1996a). *Career Thoughts Inventory.* Odessa, FL: Psychological Assessment Resources, Inc.

Sampson, J. P., Jr., Peterson, G. W., Lenz, J. G., Reardon, R. C., & Saunders, D. E. (1996b). *Career Thoughts Inventory: Professional manual.* Odessa, FL: Psychological Assessment Resources, Inc.

Sampson, J. P., Jr., Peterson, G. W., Lenz, J. G., Reardon, R. C., & Saunders, D. E. (1996c). *Improving your career thoughts: A workbook for the Career Thoughts Inventory.* Odessa, FL: Psychological Assessment Resources, Inc.

Sampson, J. P., Jr., Reardon, R. C., Peterson, G. W., & Lenz, J. G. (2004). *Career counseling and services: A cognitive information processing approach.* Pacific Grove, CA: Brooks/Cole.

Saunders, D. E. (2014). Using the Career Thoughts Inventory in practice: Helping clients shift from self-doubt to certainty. *Career Planning and Adult Development Journal* 30 (4), 101–114.

Saunders, D. E., Peterson, G. W., Sampson, J. P., Jr., & Reardon, R. C. (2000). The relation of depression and dysfunctional career thinking to career indecision. *Journal of Vocational Behavior* 56, 288–298. doi:10.1006/jvbe.1999.1715

Wood, C., & Hayes, D. G. (2013). *A counselor's guide to career assessment instruments* (6th ed.). Broken Arrow, OK: National Career Development Association.

Zunker, V. (2008). *Career, work, and mental health: Integrating career and personal counseling.* Thousand Oaks, CA: SAGE.

Table 3.1 CIP contest domains for CTI items & potential mental health factors

CTI Domain Based On CIP Theory	Dysfunctional Thoughts	Potential Mental Health Factors
Self-knowledge	Unstable or weak self-knowledge schemata that compromise one's identity	Low vocational identity, e.g., "I'm unsure of myself in many areas of my life"
Occupational knowledge	Difficulty in developing a conceptual framework or schema of the occupational world	Disturbed thinking relative to the world of work; potential options
Communication	Presence of disabling emotions or cognitions that block progress through the CASVE cycle	Anxiety, depression, frustration, unwillingness to acknowledge nature of the problems which include a combination of career and mental health issues
Analysis	Lack of motivation to expend the effort related to solving a career problem, intimidated by the task	Feeling "stuck"; unable to examine information need to solve a career problem; fear of moving forward with next steps
Synthesis	Inability to use information about self and options to identify plausible alternatives and create a manageable list of options	Cognitive distortions; inability to process information; overwhelmed by information; inability to focus on & use resources

CTI Domain Based On CIP Theory	Dysfunctional Thoughts	Potential Mental Health Factors
Valuing	Inability or unwillingness to balance input from significant others and self interests; unable to rank options; not wanting to take responsibility for choices	Anxiety; fear of making a wrong choice; fear of disappointing important people
Execution	Unable to develop a plan of action to pursue choice; lack of persistence in reaching a goal	Procrastination; fear of failure; lacking in skills needed to execute next steps (e.g., social anxiety)
Executive Processing	Lack of confidence as a career problem solver or decision maker; lack of persistence or self control	Depression or anxiety over resolving a career problem, finding a satisfactory solution; Perfectionism related to career outcomes

Reproduced by special permission of the Publisher, Psychological Assessment Resources, Inc., 16204 North Florida Avenue, Lutz, FL 33549, from the Career Thoughts Inventory by Sampson, Peterson, Lenz, Reardon, and Saunders, Copyright 1994, 1996 by PAR, Inc. Further reproduction is prohibited without permission from PAR, Inc.

Table 3.2 Self-Directed Search Summary Scores

SDS SECTION	R	I	A	S	E	C	CODE
Activities	8	3	8	5	10	1	ERA
Competencies	6	1	5	8	5	10	CSR
Occupations	1	1	2	2	5	1	EAS
Self-Estimates I	4	2	5	7	4	6	SCA
Self-Estimates II	5	2	3	6	5	3	SRE
Summary scores	24	9	23	28	29	21	ESR
Percentiles	77	20	59	41	64	23	

Reproduced by special permission of the Publisher, Psychological Assessment Resources, Inc., 16204 N. Florida Avenue, Lutz, FL 33549, from the Self-Directed Search Professional Report, by Robert C. Reardon, PhD, Melissa A. Messer, MHS, and PAR Staff, Copyright© 1985, 1987, 1989, 1994, 1996, 1997, 2001, 2010, 2013, 2015 by PAR, Inc. All rights reserved. May not be reproduced in whole or in part in any form or by any means without written permission of PAR, Inc. O*NET is a trademark of the U.S. Department of Labor Employment and Training Administration.

ABOUT THE AUTHORS

V. Casey Dozier is the Program Director of Career Advising and Counseling at the Florida State University Career Center. She earned the PhD in the Combined Counseling Psychology and School Psychology program at Florida State University. Her professional qualifications include: Licensed Psychologist (State of Florida); and National Certified Counselor (NBCC). Her publications include refereed journal articles, book chapters, and national presentations. She has provided clinical interventions in a variety of settings, with an emphasis on personal and career counseling to assist college students of all ages. Her professional passions have been related to supervision and training, underserved populations, work-life balance, and integrating theory, research, and evidence-based practice.

Janet G. Lenz, PhD, is the Program Director for Instruction, Research, & Evaluation in the Florida State University Career Center, and an Associate-In faculty member in FSU's Department of Educational Psychology and Learning Systems (EPLS). She earned the BS in Sociology at Virginia Commonwealth University, the MS in Student Personnel Administration and PhD in Counseling and Human Systems at Florida State University. She is a National Certified Counselor (NCC), Master Career Counselor (MCC), and a Career Development Facilitator Instructor. She is past-president of the National Career Development Association (NCDA) and an NCDA Fellow.

She has authored or co-authored more than 70 publications in the career area. Her research interests include the application of cognitive information processing and Holland's RIASEC theory to career counseling and services, the relationship of client characteristics to career constructs, and the connections between career and mental health issues.

Vanessa Frierson Freeman, MA, is a career advisor and career planning class instructor at the Florida State University Career Center. She is currently an advanced doctoral student in the Combined Counseling and School Psychology program at Florida State University. Vanessa earned the master's degree in Counseling in Higher Education at the University of Delaware. Prior to returning to school, Vanessa was an academic advisor at the University of Maryland working with students who were undecided about their majors. Her areas of interest include first generation college student's transition to college and their career development, as well as students who are undecided about their majors.

The History of Interest Inventories and Career Assessments in Career Counseling

THOMAS HARRINGTON AND JENNIFER LONG

Interest inventories and career assessments continue to be used to support practitioners as they work to uncover client interests, abilities, skills, motivations, values, and other personal factors that help individuals self-define and construct their career. The skilled use of career inventories and assessments remains a minimum competency of career service providers' ability to successfully partner with their clients. A history of the evolution of assessment from 1914 through 1974 and considerations for the future of assessment are highlighted to provide historical perspective to inform practitioners as they serve the diverse needs of complex client populations.

Although interest inventories have been a dominant career practitioner methodology for service delivery to clients, few have studied or recognized the changes that have occurred within these instruments over the years. As a significant component in the field of career counseling, career assessment can be seen as a "bridge from career development theory to practice, a method of operationalizing theoretical constructs by incorporating them into career interventions and, in particular, into tests and other

Thomas Harrington and Jennifer Long, "The History of Interest Inventories and Career Assessments in Career Counseling," *The Career Development Quarterly*, vol. 61, no. 1, pp. 83-92. Copyright © 2013 by National Career Development Association. Reprinted with permission. Provided by ProQuest LLC. All rights reserved.

measurements" (Whitfield, Feller, & Wood, 2009, p. 14). A history of the development of assessments, tools, and interventions allows us to understand motivations, trends, and environmental/social/political factors that have affected how we historically and currently serve clients. Practitioner knowledge of the evolution of assessment in the field of career counseling is critical to inform how career counselors move forward to ensure that clients remain the top priority as career counselors continue to innovate and develop career services.

With an ever-changing U.S. workplace and economic environment, clients face a future where 63% of all jobs will require a postsecondary education, more than one third of all job openings will not require a college degree, one third of the jobs will require 1 month or less of on-the-job experience to fully qualify, and only 76% of public high school students will earn a diploma within 4 years of entering the ninth grade (otherwise stated, 1 million students will fail to earn a high school diploma each year; Rumberger, 2011). In reaction to these factors, career counselors may search for additional applications of inventories to cope with and support their clients, which increasingly include returning veterans, laid-off workers, and students leaving school with skills deficits and heavy debt.

To serve the complex needs of diverse client populations, career practitioners will benefit from a history of the evolution of assessment from 1914 through 1974, past uses of available resources, and key takeaways that inform the future of assessment on a global level. The majority of inventories in this history are out of print. Inventories that continue to be in use or were developed in the second half of the history (beyond 1974) are referenced for the reader to obtain more information in the National Career Development Association's (NCDA) *A Counselor's Guide to Career Assessment Instruments* (hereinafter referred to as *A Counselor's Guide;* Whitfield et al., 2009).

EARLY PIONEERS OF INTEREST INVENTORIES

This history begins with Jesse Davis (1914) publishing the Student Vocational Self Analysis for all public school 10th graders. Davis systemized an analysis of self-awareness to occupations process. Although Davis was an educator, a principal in the Detroit and Grand Rapids public schools, the majority of the authors to follow were psychologists serving primarily adult and college student clients. In 1917, the first of these psychologists, James Miner, studied whether students' preferences were their own or due to teachers' influence and he then went on to develop interest questions with weighted scores. Brewer's (1942) *History of Vocational Guidance* described Miner's work extensively and cited his questionnaire on interests as "the forerunner of Strong's later researches" (p. 203).

THE CARNEGIE INSTITUTE OF TECHNOLOGY ERA

The Carnegie Interest Inventory (1920) was the first standardized interest inventory published by the Carnegie Institute of Technology's Bureau of Personnel Research in Pittsburgh, Pennsylvania. It had no authors and used the same directions, questions, and interpretations for all forms of the inventory. Prior to this (a logical sequence to Miner's work), in 1919, Clarence Yoakum ran a seminar on how to measure interests where students developed 1,000 survey questions, many of which can be found throughout today's inventories. In 1921, Bruce Moore expanded interest inventories even further by using the Carnegie Interest Inventory to differentiate such interests/occupations as sales engineers from design engineers. Max Freyd quickly followed, in 1923, by recognizing gender differences and developing separate instruments for men, with 80 occupations listed, and women, with 67 occupations listed. Then, in 1924, Karl Crowdery became the first to separate occupational groups by their interests with the use of different question formats and seven classifications of items: 84 occupational titles, 25 school subjects, 34 hobbies and amusements, 23 miscellaneous activities, 78 types of people, six kinds of pets, and 13 kinds of reading. In fact, Crowdery developed 182 items (questions) and their formats, which were used in Strong's 1927 inventory. During this intensified developmental period, E. K. Strong worked at the Carnegie Institute of Technology, and, in 1923, he was recruited to Stanford University. Two resources that further explore the Carnegie era are Fryer's (1931) *The Measurement of Interests* and Fryer and Henry's (1950) *Handbook of Applied Psychology*. Across the decades to come, the publication and utilization of Strong's work accelerated and became a dominant influence within the field.

AN EARLY STABILIZATION PERIOD AND THE INFLUENCE OF THE STRONG INTEREST INVENTORY

E. K. Strong developed The Strong Vocational Interest Blank (SVIB), which was published in 1927 by Stanford University Press, in Stanford, California, and The Vocational Interest Blank for Women in 1933. Strong used the same eight types of items for both genders: occupational titles, school subjects, hobbies and amusements, occupational activities, kinds of people, forced choice of preferences and activities, and self-identification with various personal characteristics. The first page of the SVIB asserts that "it is possible with a fair degree of accuracy to determine by this test whether one would like certain occupations or not" (Strong, 1927, p. 1).

Strong's adherence to empirical methodology for occupational scale development primarily sets it apart from most other interest inventories, "though the techniques have varied slightly in the various forms, the method remains essentially the same" (Strong & Campbell, 1966, p. 26). Each occupational scale has been developed by contrasting the SVIB responses of men for a specified occupation (the criterion sample) with a group of men in general, representing a sample of men from many diverse occupations. Each scale contains items that discriminate between interests of these two groups; thus, a person's score provides an index of similarity between his interests and the characteristic interests of men in the designated occupation. The women's occupational scales were developed the same way.

Key differences in editions have been the number of occupational similarity/dissimilarity indices reported; for example, in 1938, 34 were reported, in 1945, 49 were reported, and in 1966, 54 were reported. In 1974, the Strong-Campbell Interest Inventory (SCII) moved away from separate gender-specific booklets as a means of eliminating sex bias and promoting more equal gender treatment. The items for the SVIB–SCII were, with two exceptions, taken from the earlier Strong booklets, either from the men's form, published in 1966, or the women's form, published in 1968 (Campbell, 1974, p. 5). At this time, John Holland's theory was integrated within the instrument's framework. A complete overview of this instrument can be found in NCDA's *A Counselor's Guide* (Whitfield et al., 2009, p. 309).

EXPANSIONARY EXPLORATION PERIOD

Simultaneously, through Strong's influence in the previously outlined period, the foundation of career assessment continued to expand through the development and utilization of various tools to support occupational guidance and career counseling. In 1931, the University of Michigan School of Business Administration at Ann Arbor published Grace Manson's *Occupational Interests and Personality Requirements of Woman in Business.* This instrument was a revision of the Carnegie Interest Inventory, consisting of two parts: 160 occupational titles commonly open to women and 30 personality traits of items from job analysis and job requirements of specific occupations. Interpretation of this instrument shows the extent that a person's scores are above or below an average score for 10 occupational groups: private secretary, office manager, bookkeeper, stenographer, office clerk, high school teacher, grade school teacher, nurse, sales proprietor, and retail sales women. Manson's contribution highlighted the role of personality in career counseling, extensive research on the development of scoring keys, and validation work.

Later, in 1937, Bruce Le Suer developed the Occupations Interest Blank, which was published by The Psychological Corporation in New York, New York. The instrument was developed for high school boys and included 100 occupations printed on one page on which a student checked if he *liked, had no decided feelings,* or *disliked the job.* The assessment took 10 minutes to score, and interpretation was a comparison to a specific job or to the highest total score on 10 areas: professional, technical, clerical, sales, artistic/creative, skilled trades, semiskilled work, adventuresome work, personal service, and agricultural occupations.

In 1947, the University of Chicago's Psychometric Laboratory published L. L. Thurstone's An Interest Schedule. This was the first time an assessment was theory based, and statistical factors played a dominant role in test development. Thurstone combined Eduard Spranger's six types of men theory (Spranger, 1928) with the results of his factor-analytic research showing that physical and biological sciences were distinct. The instrument generated 10 career fields: physical science, biological sciences, computation, business, executive, persuasive, linguistic, humanitarian, artistic, and manual. The instrument was self-scoring, used raw scores, de-emphasized norms, and introduced an ipsative scoring methodology.

In contrast to Thurstone's ipsative method, Bertram Forer (1948) developed the Diagnostic Interest Blank based on a projective methodology with 80 incomplete sentences scored on the following: reactions to authorities, coworkers, criticism, challenge, taking orders, responsibility, causes of aggression, anxiety, failure, job turnover, and vocational goals. Introduction of this information was certainly additive, leading to more holistic and more personal interpretations. As career assessments and inventories continued to develop within graduate school programs and their use with younger people was encouraged, the field shifted to emphasize a commercially focused approach to the publication of these resources.

BEGINNING OF THE COMMERCIAL PUBLICATION PERIOD

Science Research Associates, a subsidiary of IBM in Chicago, Illinois published Frederic Kuder's *Kuder Preference Record* in 1940 and *The Kuder Occupational Survey, Form DD* in 1956. There were several forms of the Preference Record. They included seven scales to which mechanical and clerical occupations were later added. In 1948, the Kuder Preference Record, Vocational, Form C, proved to have the greatest use. It had 10 scales: Science, Computational, Art, Music, Literary, Social, Persuasive, Clerical, Mechanical, and Outdoors. Research-based interest inventories could be faked, so a verification scale was included in the instrument to identify people who were intentionally trying to make a good impression and manipulate results. The item format of a triad with three choices, where the respondent selected the *most liked option* and the *least liked option,* was a unique contribution. A separate interpretive booklet displayed a listing of appropriate related occupations for each of the two highest interest scales.

Form DD incorporated a new approach that produced a machine-scored report and the publisher claimed that "it can now *be* said with considerable confidence that a person's pattern of interest is, for example, more like that typical of chemists than of pediatricians, or more like that of electricians" (Kuder & Diamond, 1966, p. 1). The report also showed the degree of relationship between interest patterns with college majors, with different profiles being used for men and women. A predictive research study over a 12- to 19-year interval found that slightly more than 50% of 882 participants were in occupations that would have been suggested by their Form DD report results (Kuder & Diamond, 1966). In addition, a complete overview of this instrument can be found in NCDA's *A Counselor's Guide* (Whitfield et al., 2009, p. 163).

In 1943, McKnight and McKnight published Glenn Cleeton's The Cleeton Vocational Interest Inventory in Bloomington, Indiana, which included separate forms for men and women. The inventory introduced several noteworthy features, including a 700-item inventory that represented a good collection of items used in inventories at this time period, expressed stated choice of job types, and interviewed people for their preferences toward people and things. Interpretation suggested advice or recommendations in four areas that included vocational, educational, health, and personal adjustment. Interpretive material displayed clear connections between jobs, school subjects, and personal characteristics to provide a more holistic interpretation.

A PROLIFIC PERIOD

NINE NEW INSTRUMENTS FROM 1956 TO 1974

The context that surrounds the advent of nine new instruments in this prolific period was the following: professionals and the public recognized the need for and accepted interest inventories, universities invested in students to construct instruments and encouraged their students to use them, and companies accepted interest inventories as products worthy for investment.

Lee and Thorpe developed The Occupational Interest Inventory published by the California Test Bureau in Los Angeles, California, in 1956. An Intermediate and an Advanced Form were available, and each instrument had 120 descriptions of work and 30 activities in a triadic format. Its uniqueness was the introduction of the level of interest and groups of occupations that were differentiated by the amount of proficiency required in verbal, mechanical manipulation, and computation. Job level was based on degrees of responsibility, capacity, and skill needed, and scores were reported in gender-based percentiles.

The U.S. Department of Labor in Washington, DC, published its Interest Checklist in 1957 and revised it in 1967 and 1979 when the U.S. Department of Labor structures for delivering occupational information changed. Thus, when the third edition of the *Dictionary of Occupational Titles (DOT;* U.S. Department of Labor, 1965) was published, this necessitated the need for the 1967 revision of the Interest Checklist. The Interest Checklist is self-administered with no scales and takes approximately 20 minutes to complete, with the options of selecting *like, don't like,* or *not certain* for each item. In 1961, Leonard Gordon designed the Gordon Occupational Checklist (published by Harcourt, Brace, and World, Inc., in New York, New York) to assess those who were not college bound. Based on Anne Roe's (1956) Two-Way Classification of

Occupations, the Gordon Occupational Checklist used five groups: business, outdoors, arts, technology, and science, and the levels of degree of autonomy and the level of skill and training required by an occupation. The assessment was easy to use: Individuals simply underlined the activity that they wanted to perform in a job, and each of the 240 activities was then related to a specific job.

The Educational Test Service in Princeton, New Jersey, published the Interest Index in 1961; it was unique because it was an interest measure integrated within an aptitude test for students entering 2-year community colleges, with items focused on academic-related activities. The 1971 edition included 176 items and 11 scales: Health, Business, Mathematics, Physical Sciences, Engineering Technology, Biology, Home Economics, Secretarial, Social Sciences, The Arts, and Music. Scores for this index were reported as raw scores.

The Guilford-Zimmerman Interest Inventory was developed by Wayne Zimmerman and Joan Guilford, published by Sheridan Supply Company in Beverly Hills, California, in 1963 to identify areas that bring the most satisfaction. A vocational and personal satisfaction areas are measured through items with high reading levels and are reported on 10 scales: Mechanical, Natural, Aesthetic, Services, Clerical, Mercantile, Leadership, Literary, Scientific, and Creative. Items are rated on a 5-point Likert scale, ranging from *definitely dislike* to *definitely like*.

The Minnesota Vocational Interest Inventory, by Kenneth Clark, was published in 1965 by The Psychological Corporation of New York, New York, for vocational students, noncollege attendees, apprenticeship candidates, and students who drop out. It included 158 items for individuals to select the most and least liked activities in triadic form. The inventory was scored like the Strong Interest Inventory, with specific occupations that empirically differentiated a group from a Tradesman-in-General group. Illustrative scales are Baker, Printer, Carpenter, Plumber, Machinist, and Electrician.

Additionally, in 1965, Consulting Psychologists Press in Palo Alto, California, published John L. Holland's Vocational Preference Inventory (VPI). Although the instrument's primary purpose was to assess personality, it has also been used as an interest inventory. The VPI is composed entirely of occupational titles. This is significant because of its long history in career guidance and its being a part of the Self-Directed Search. A similar version of the VPI was copyrighted in 1961 in the National Merit Student Survey, and, in 1968, Holland incorporated it in the ACT Guidance Profile. Holland (1965) highlighted that "selected VPI scales are predictive of academic and extracurricular achievements for one- to three-year intervals. Generally, these predictions are inefficient although they are statistically significant" (p. 13). For more information, a complete overview of this instrument can be found in NCDA's *A Counselor's Guide* (Whitfield et al., 2009, p. 296).

The Ohio Vocational Interest Survey, created by D'Costa, Winefordner, Odgers, and Koons, was published by The Psychological Corporation located in New York, New York, in 1968. These authors plotted the Data-People-Things values of jobs in the U.S. Department of Labor *DOT* and categorized them into homogenous clusters. From these clusters, they developed 24 scales: Manual Work; Machine Work; Personal Work; Caring for People or Animals; Clerical Work; Inspecting and Testing; Crafts and Precise Operations; Customer Services; Nursing and Related Technical Services; Skilled Personal Services; Training; Literary; Numerical; Appraisal; Agriculture; Applied Technology; Promotion and Communication; Management and Supervision; Artistic; Sales Representative; Music; Entertainment and Performing Arts; Teaching, Counseling, and Social Work; and Medical. The second edition, in 1980, updated the occupational information components based on changes in the U.S. Department of Labor's 1977 *DOT* and the 1979 *Guide for Occupational Exploration.*

Robert Knapp and Lila Knapp's California Occupational Preference System (COPS) was published by Educational and Industrial Testing Service in San Diego, California, in 1974, and was originally published as an interest inventory along with Career Briefs, which were integrated into the COPS interpretation. The COPS continues to be developed, with later editions published up to 2004. The NCDA most recently listed the system as COP System Career Guidance Program in *A Counselor's Guide* (Whitfield et al., 2009). The COPS's three instruments are designed to provide individuals with coordinated measures of interests, abilities, and work values within eight major career clusters. COPS has 168 activity items and takes 20 to 30 minutes to complete. Scores are reported in percentiles compared with norms for 14 career clusters (scale names): Science Professional, Science Skilled, Technology Professional, Technology Skilled, Consumer Economics, Outdoor, Business Professional, Business Skilled, Clerical, Communication, Arts Professional, Arts Skilled, Service Professional, and Service Skilled. The 14 clusters resulted from factor analysis. Different forms are available for college students and adults, those with a fourth-grade reading level and special education populations, as well as middle school students and above. A complete overview of this instrument can be found in NCDA's *A Counselor's Guide* (Whitfield et al., 2009, p. 119).

REFLECTION ON HISTORICAL TAKEAWAYS THAT INFORM THE FUTURE OF CAREER ASSESSMENT

In the first author's experience, the most effective components of career/employment counseling are the people who provide it. Positive orientation, flexibility, competence, good mental health, and competency to work creatively with customers/clients are not only helpful, but critical assets for all practitioners within the field. The basis of this belief is the overwhelming ratio of those in need of services in comparison to the number of service providers available. The first author reflected on the use of interest inventories to deliver minimum competencies in order to effectively provide career services to all contractual clients so as to allow for time to serve those in greater need. Competent career counseling is challenging and complex, with additional factors presenting themselves as part of the counseling service desired. Changing and diversified client needs may be moving practices away from where some practitioners feel most comfortable, such as primarily providing information, and are challenging professionals to expand their competencies and tackle new developmental issues. With an ever-changing and challenging marketplace, counselors are not just working with a person who is unemployed but are also forced to attend to the anger the person projects and his or her feelings about concerns such as insufficient funds to support a desired living or lifestyle. Although counselors are accustomed to working with those with inadequate skills for employment and poorly defined goals, evidence now indicates that a client's significant difficulty maintaining relationships will negatively affect a counselor's effectiveness in job placement if this issue is not addressed.

Integration of abilities along with the use of interests will increase more so in the future. Behaviorally, what a person can do well translates to skills that one possesses and will be important to communicate to others. Abilities are also critical components of self-concepts.

This more holistic perspective fits with a more comprehensive/multidimensional portrayal that computers and technology can deliver. Current instruments that highlight the importance of abilities are the Harrington–O'Shea Career Decision-Making System-Revised by O'Shea and Feller; the COPSystem Career Guidance Program developed by Knapp, Knapp, and Knapp-Lee; the O*NET (Occupational Information Network) Ability Profiler created by the U.S. Department of Labor, Employment and Training Administration; and the Ability Explorer by Harrington, Harrington, and Wall (Whitfield et al., 2009).

The third edition of the Ability Explorer–developed by Harrington, Harrington, and Wall in 2012 with JIST Publishing, Inc., in Indianapolis, Indiana—assesses individuals' 16 career-related abilities. The underlying theory asserts that people can improve their abilities somewhat through additional activities/experiences, both inside and outside of school. Interpretive materials display the two or three empirically determined abilities needed for performance of a specific occupation. Users observe the match between their current ability levels and the skills identified as needing improvement for a desired occupation. This approach is described for those practitioners who do not want the computer to do all of the client's work in clarifying self-concepts and uncovering any lack of information needed to identify occupations, serving as an alternative for teaching people how to manage their career development.

SUMMARY

Twenty inventories were presented with many different forms tailored for specific audiences, with the intent to show the creative thinking of past practitioners that may relate to the diverse populations that career counselors are now being asked to serve. Enlightened career practitioners and inventory administrators are critical for effective service delivery to provide staff with copies of and training in alternative instruments, because the one-size-only approach does not fit all.

The following highlights an important challenge of interest-focused inventories and assessments in career development:

> Similarly, although a man's performance on the job depends on his abilities and motivation, whether or not he stays on the job will largely reflect whether he likes or dislikes it. For this reason, interest ratings are better indices of job persistence than of job success. In most selection techniques, too much attention is given to efficiency and too little to satisfaction and enjoyment—what does it avail us if our trainee becomes an immediate success but then leaves the job? (Campbell,1969, p. 1)

The second half of this history is found in NCDA's *A Counselor's Guide*, the most recent being the fifth edition (Whitfield et al., 2009). This book is a living up-to-date reference, including updates and advances to current additions, as well as validation information, which serves as the most critical information needed to assess an instrument. The combination of insights into the first half of the history within this article and the extensive summary of reviews of assessment in *A Counselor's Guide* fill a regrettable gap of testing and career assessment textbooks, which provide coverage of only several interest inventories and neglect the expansive richness of this major service delivery tool within the field (Whitfield et al., 2009).

A significant foundation of career assessment exists to inform practitioners by providing additional insights, information, and resources to support client growth and awareness. As the profession moves forward faced with an increasingly global world and evolving workplace, the question relative to career assessment is: do our current instruments measure personal flexibility, commitment to continuous learning, comfort with cultural diversity, ability to work in teams, willingness to engage in multitasking, self-initiative, the ability to be creative, and the motivation to be responsible for one's own career development? (Whitfield et al., 2009, p. 17)

REFERENCES

Brewer, J M. (1942). *History of vocational guidance: Origins and early development.* New York, NY: Harper & Brothers Publishers.

Campbell, D. P. (1969). *Strong Vocational Interest Blanks manual supplement.* Stanford, CA: Stanford University Press.

Campbell, D. P. (1974). *Manual for the Strong-Campbell Interest Inventory.* Stanford, CA: Stanford University Press.

Carnegie Institute of Technology: Bureau of Personnel Research. (1920). *Carnegie Interest Inventory.* Pittsburgh, PA: Author.

Clark, K. (1965). *Minnesota Vocational Interest Inventory.* New York, NY: The Psychological Corporation.

Davis, J. B. (1914). *Vocational and moral guidance.* Boston, MA: Ginn and Company.

D'Costa, A.G., Winefordner, D. W., Odgers, J. G., & Koons, P. B. (1968). *Ohio Vocational Interest Survey.* New York, NY: The Psychological Corporation.

Educational Test Service.(1961). *Interest Index.* Princeton, NJ: Author.

Educational Test Service. (1971). *Interest Index.* Princeton, NJ: Author.

Forer, B. R. (1948). A diagnostic interest blank. *Journal of Projective Techniques, 12,* 119–129.

Fryer, D. H. (1931). *The measurement of interests.* New York, NY: Henry Holt and Company.

Fryer, D. H., & Henry, E. R. (1950). *Handbook of applied psychology.* New York, NY: Rinehart and Company.

Gordon, L. (1961). *Gordon Occupational Checklist.* New York, NY: Harcourt, Brace, and World.

Harrington, J.C., Harrington, T. F., & Wall, J. E. (2012). *Ability Explorer* (3rd ed.). Indianapolis, IN: JIST Publishing.

Holland, J. L. (1965). *Holland Vocational Preference Inventory: Manual.* Palo Alto, CA: Consulting Psychologists Press.

Knapp, R., & Knapp, L. (1974). *California Occupational Preference System.* San Diego, CA: Educational and Industrial Testing Service.

Kuder, F., & Diamond, E. (1966).*Kuder DD Occupational Interest Survey general manual* (2nd ed.). Chicago, IL: Science Research Associates.

Le Suer, B . (1937). *Occupations Interest Blank.* New York, NY: The Psychological Corporation.

Manson, G. (1931). *Occupational Interests and Personality Requirements of Woman in Business.* Ann Arbor: University of Michigan School of Business Administration.

Roe, A. (1956). *The psychology of occupations.* New York, NY: Wiley.

Rumberger, R. W. (2011). *Dropping out: Why students drop out of high school and what can be done about it*. Cambridge, MA: Harvard University Press.

Spranger, E. (1928). *Types of men*. Halle, Germany: M. Niememeyer.

Strong, E. K. (1927). *The Vocational Interest Blank*. Stanford, CA: Stanford University Press.

Strong, E. K. (1933). *The Vocational Interest Blank for Women*. Stanford, CA: Stanford University Press.

Strong, E. K., & Campbell, D. P. (1966). *Strong Vocational Interest Blanks manual*. Stanford, CA: Stanford University Press.

Thurstone, L. L. (1947). *An Interest Schedule*. Chicago, IL: University of Chicago's Psychometric Laboratory.

U.S. Department of Labor. (1965). *Dictionary of occupational titles* (3rd ed.). Washington, DC: Government Printing Office.

Whitfield, E. A., Feller, R.W., & Wood, C. (2009). *A counselor's guide to career assessment instruments* (5th ed.). Broken Arrow, OK: National Career Development Association.

Zimmerman, W., & Guilford, J. (1963). *Guilford–Zimmerman Interest Inventory*. Beverly Hills, CA: Sheridan Supply Company.

DISCUSSION QUESTIONS

1 Describe how you could use career assessments and inventories in your work with clients.

2 What can you learn about a client by using some of the most current career assessment tools?

3 What are some pros and cons with using career assessments and inventories?

CONCLUSION

Career assessments and inventories are part of the career counselor's toolkit. These are not stand-alone techniques, but are used in combination with counseling to assist the client in his or her career journey. Career assessments continue to expand and work toward increased reliability and validity. Meeting the needs of diverse client populations will be one of the top areas of focus for career assessments in the future.

INDEX OF KEY TERMS

- career assessments
- career counseling
- career exploration
- interest inventories
- self-directed search

SUGGESTED PUBLICATIONS FOR FURTHER READING

Burns, S. (2014). Validity of person matching in vocational interest inventories. *The Career Development Quarterly, 62*(2), 114–127. doi:10.1002/j.2161–0045.2014.00074.x

Etheridge, R. L., & Peterson, G. W. (2009). The measurement and development of competence in the use of career assessments. *Career Planning and Adult Development Journal, 25,* 14–28.

ETHICS IN CAREER COUNSELING

INTRODUCTION

As a counseling professional (or aspiring counseling professional), you are expected to adhere to an ethical code. Hopefully, at this point in your training, you have already been exposed to various codes of ethics (the American Counseling Association's code of ethics being the primary one; ACA, 2014). Ethical codes are intended to provide guidance, direction, and information about a professional's expected conduct and practice. What we would like to emphasize, and make sure that you are aware of, is that the National Career Development Association (NCDA) also has its own code of ethics (NCDA, 2015). However, the two sets of codes do not work against one another. The NCDA Ethics Committee "endeavored to follow the structure of ACA's Ethics Code so that the two codes would be compatible with each other, while developing, adding, and enhancing profession-specific guidelines" (NCDA, 2015, p. 2). The same professional values that are present within ACA's code of ethics are present within NCDA's code of ethics (e.g., autonomy, non-maleficence, beneficence, justice/objectivity, fidelity/accountability, and veracity).

The two articles presented in this chapter are published by the National Career Development Association, and each does a good job of providing specific and practical information related to standards, competencies, and ethics. We recommend that you review these articles in addition to consulting the ethical codes directly.

Professional Standards, Competencies and Ethics

CAROLYN D. JONES

C areer counselors carry out a wide range of assistance at the various stages of career services. The provision of these services is guided by the professional standards and NCDA Code of Ethics that have built a framework to use in delineating best practices. Administrators, managers and practitioners must understand and incorporate professional Codes of Ethics when providing career services for their students/clients to sustain the ethical guidelines of the profession. For many, the knowledge and application of these standards and codes have been acquired over time through academia, training and work experience. A current dilemma of the field of career counseling in particular, is the credentialing processes and management of adequate service provision across such a diverse group of settings. This article will offer a centralized discussion of the areas within the NCDA Code of Ethics that inform the required level of knowledge, training and experience needed to offer specific types of assistance.

Carolyn D. Jones, "Professional Standards, Competencies and Ethics," *Career Developments*, vol. 33, no. 4, pp. 6-9. Copyright © 2017 by National Career Development Association. Reprinted with permission.

OVERVIEW OF TERMS

Career counseling is defined in the NCDA Career Counseling Competencies Statement "as the process of assessing individuals in the development of a life-career focus on the definition of the worker role and how that role interacts with other life roles". The NCDA Code of Ethics includes statements, ethical standards and the professional competencies of career counselors.

Ethical Standards as defined by NCDA's Code of Ethics are "Standards of practice (also known as Ethical Guidelines) include general, counseling relationship, measurement and evaluation, research, publication, consulting, private practice, and procedures for processing ethical complaints. NCDA's Code of Ethics was revised in 2015". The following excerpts from the Code are relevant for this discussion:

A.1.B. DIFFERENTIATION BETWEEN TYPES OF SERVICES PROVIDED

"Career planning" services are differentiated from "career counseling" services. Career planning services include an active provision of information designed to help a client with a specific need, such as review of a resume; assistance in networking strategies; identification of occupations based on values, interests, skills, prior work experience, and/or other characteristics; support in the job-seeking process; and assessment by means of paper-based and/or online inventories of interest, abilities, personality, work-related values, and/or other characteristics. In addition to providing these informational services, "career counseling" provides the opportunity for a deeper level of involvement with the client, based on the establishment of a professional counseling relationship and the potential for assisting clients with career and personal development concerns beyond those included in career planning. All career professionals, whether engaging in "career planning" or "career counseling", provide only the services that are within the scope of their professional competence and qualifications.

C.2.A. BOUNDARIES OF COMPETENCE

Career professionals practice only within the boundaries of their competence, based on their education, training, supervised experience, state and national professional credentials, and appropriate professional experience. Whereas multicultural counseling competency is required across all counseling specialties, career professionals gain knowledge, personal awareness, sensitivity, dispositions, and skills pertinent to being a culturally competent career professional.

PROFESSIONAL VALUES AND REQUIRED COMPETENCIES

The NCDA statement on Professional Values and Principles further states that "In order to work as a professional engaged in Career Counseling, the individual must demonstrate minimum competencies in eleven designated areas. These eleven areas are: Career Development Theory, Individual and Group Counseling Skills, Individual/Group Assessment, Information/Resources, Program Management and Implementation, Consultation, Diverse Populations, Supervision, Ethical/Legal Issues, Research/Evaluation, and Technology".

The success and satisfaction of the students and/or clients are assured when the professional standards and ethics codes are followed and the services are being provided based on required competencies of those in the profession. Competent practitioners must be able to assist students/clients in all areas of the career development process. And, in like manner the efficacy of the work also requires administrators and managers to have appropriate career development training and experiences so that they can ensure the best practices of their staff.

It is well understood that professional standards and Codes of Ethics are in place for academic advisors, counselors and a multitude of other professions, as well. Hiring practices and the creation of appropriate job requirements must be based on the training and experiences of those persons being hired. Having a deeper understanding of the differing roles of counseling, career development, academic advising, and other partnerships that serve the student/client could maximize the benefits of each individual. This differentiation allows for each service provider to optimize their assistance as they will be able to focus solely on the part of the person's profile for which they are responsible.

However, the reality in actual practice is oftentimes the sharing of job responsibilities, such as budget cuts, may have staff members wearing several "hats", e.g., providing career services and academic advising services. In such cases, collaboration is highly recommended to enhance services such that the duties and responsibilities are consistent with professional standards, competencies and ethics required to do the job. There is a need for career counselors and professionals their work environment to work together for a solution that best fits the needs of students and/or clients.

According to Jack Zibert, et al., (1995), "ethical standards are not static, legalistic, or explicitly definitive documents designed to preempt professionals' decisions. Rather, they are designed to guide an active educational process through which counselors enhance, inform, expand, and improve their ability to serve as effectively as possible those clients seeking their help".

The implementation of this approach may be complicated by the fact that professionals coming into the field are from different educational backgrounds. References to professional standards and Codes of Ethics does, to some extent, establish the criteria for the creation of job descriptions that include appropriate qualifications for the position. In as much as having appropriate credentials is very important, hiring individuals who have a passion for career exploration and providing services is critical. And, as previously stated, it is the responsibility of the institution to provide quality programs and services and recognize the value of career development for its students/clients. The consideration of work and job characteristics and requirements is also extremely important.

Particularly in line with sometimes limited budgets, the hiring of competent career professionals is sometimes influenced by the availability of funds. And, oftentimes are influenced by minimum job requirements based on state guidelines or the governing or policy making entity. According to Spencer G. Niles, Dennis Engels and Janet Lenz (2009), career services practitioners are the best advocates for change in the public policy arena in terms of the types of services being provided and are best qualified to conduct a needs analysis of potential clients. Justification for career services to be provided by competent professionals must be be made available to support accountability and value within the scope of services for students/clients.

The ongoing review and assessment of services and data collection are critical to the survival of these centers and agencies. This is necessary to demonstrate the significance of the work provided by professional career counselors at the institution.

However, the challenge that arises in such efforts is that student satisfaction and career success are oftentimes difficult to measure. It is very necessary for the survival of the profession if the value is to be understood by the decision and policy makers at institutions, community, local, state and federal governing bodies. Another challenge lies in the personalized application and accountability to use the research findings to inform change. In some instances, the transfer of the responsibility to those who lack training and experience only serve to marginalize the significance and value of the support made available to students/clients.

Niles (2003) further suggests that career counselors and professionals need to communicate the expertise that they bring to their work by engaging in research demonstrating accountability and the effectiveness of services being provided to their students/clients. Sharing best practices as often as possible and in various venues will enhance credibility. He also stated that it's critical to share their contributions with various stakeholders (e.g. school boards, university administrators, legislators) that are part of groups that are making funding decisions about providing resources for career counseling services.

> *It is also well understood that organizations uphold ethical principles in the community when they ensure that all members know the principals that govern their actions. And, all members of the community know and appreciate that their interests are being accounted for and awareness by society that benefits and burdens are being distributed. Members of the community will then want to support the organization because one is then aware of the optimization of the mutual advantages of living in a community.*

Zibert, Engels, Kern, Durodoye, (1998).

ACTION STEPS

may include:

Share data as a result of student satisfaction surveys of the services and programs in which they have participated.

Sharing the results of the data from employers and the impact the services provided had on preparing students for the job market and securing employment.

Share data that identifies the impact on student employment that contributed to the local economy and tax base.

The data must demonstrate the improvements students have experienced in choosing a major after being in contact with professional career counselors.

Include the results in reporting outcomes about employment or continuing education in public documents and the social media of the institution.

Interview with
DR. CONSTANCE PRITCHARD
NCDA Credentialing Commission Chair

Recently Dr. Pritchard, Chair of the NCDA Credentialing Commission, was interviewed regarding the responsibility of career counselors and professionals to serve as advocates of the profession.

Dr. Constance J. Pritchard is well known for her work in leadership, business consulting, and career development. As President of *The Pritchard Group*, a training and consulting firm she founded in 1993, Dr. Pritchard presents seminars and workshops around the country on career, life management, and organization development topics. She has delivered career training and consulting training nationally and internationally. Dr. Pritchard is an NCDA Master Trainer and NCDA Fellow. She is also the Chair of NCDA's Credentialing Commission.

Q: Should NCDA or representatives in the field advocate for career development professionals in work places whose positons are being redefined or transferred to other departments and/or staff members who do not have appropriate career counselor training as quoted in our Code of Ethics? If so, how would you encourage them to do so and what would justify them not doing so?

A: Without a doubt, any employer would like to have the most qualified individual in a position. My impression is that the career services field is changing rapidly, perhaps at a faster rate than we have previously seen. Professionals in our business are being asked to show quantifiable evidence concerning their work with clients. This trend has long existed in the delivery of career services in the workforce sector, but is now becoming more prominent in education, business, and private sectors. It seems to me that as NCDA representatives we must continue to educate others about what it means to be a career professional, what services we can provide, and how we are held accountable. And NCDA has a responsibility to continue to understand the delivery of career services in all the sectors and industries where we work. Dialogues among the diverse membership of NCDA, including our colleagues working internationally, are key to the organization's leadership in our field.

Although research on staffing ratios in college career centers are limited there are some studies that suggest increased data management systems. An increased use of data to demonstrate career counseling effectiveness in counseling and supervision and frequency by which services are utilized, and collaboration with multiple departments to foster increased awareness of these services are mentioned (Van Brunt, 2008; Varlotta, 2012). When shared with administrators in decision-making power roles, numbers may often speak for themselves.

Q: What do you consider to be the significance of educating the membership on the importance of data collection demonstrating the value of the work and the improvements in decidedness or professionalism and career outcomes?

A: I think it is very important for us as practitioners and NCDA to gather data to demonstrate the value of our work and outcomes. We are probably not very good at gathering or citing data from· the practitioner side. Since our workforce colleagues have been forced to gather data for a long time, certainly we can learn from their experience. What information matters? To which stakeholder? What is the ROI? Some of the questions that are being asked now might make us a bit uncomfortable, but we need to learn how to response in ways that satisfy and educate stakeholders and decision makers. And, oh yes, we probably need to make that response no longer than a tweet or two! NCDA is the leader in our field, and we need to grow in how we talk about our work. I think NCDA can help us gathering and communicating data about what we do".

SUMMARY

In summary, institutional commitment is critical if professional standards, competencies and ethics are to receive the attention necessary to provide effective career services for students/clients. Employee performance and job satisfaction overall impact the success of the organization. Employees are more likely to excel in the workplace if they feel that they are not being professionally compromised or marginalized.

Career counselors and specialist play an important role in the world providing services that help others deal with unemployment, work stress, and work strain in these uncertain economic times and related job market shifts. Career counseling services impacts how our students/clients deal with daily life issues. The work day encompasses most of our time on any given day. Dealing with these shifts affects our mental health and sense of well-being. Career counselors help students/clients to better understand life's issues and gain skills to adapt and continue to function and create a meaningful existence, (Erford and Crockett, 2011). As practitioners, this will serve as motivation to uphold the purpose of the profession and thereby successfully upholding the expectations set forth by a longstanding field of dedicated professionals.

Carolyn D. Jones, M.ED (ethics@ ncda.org) is the chair of the NCDA Ethics Committee, a member of the NCDA Awards Committee, President of the Florida Career Development Association and President/CEO of CDJ Consulting, LLC. Her private practice provides expert services in professional development coaching, team building strategies, human capital management, talent acquisition, and leadership and resource development. She also has an extensive professional background in higher education administration as a manager.

What Does the NCDA Code of Ethics Call For?

EDWARD MAINZER AND ABIOLA DIPEOLU

W riting about higher education in the 21st century, Zakaria and Warren (2016) state "in the journey of becoming a professional, a person learns skills important for the specific profession. Counseling ethics education is one of the most important areas of knowledge acquisition in the counseling profession" (p. 83). Codes of ethics must evolve to meet changing times, such as developments in information and communication technology (compare Sampson and Makela, 2014) and serving different populations, such as those with special needs (compare Mainzer and Dipeolu, 2015), but as Welfel (2016) wrote, "the [ethical] codes and guidelines are not dry, intellectual documents, but rather, they represent the passion and commitment of the profession to serve the public well" (xvii).

What does it mean to be a professional? Do you know what the NCDA Code of Ethics calls for in any given situation? Do you know when to consult the Code or seek assistance? The NCDA revised its Code of Ethics in 2015, and while every NCDA member should consult the entire code on an ongoing basis, this article provides a brief overview.

The first section covers Professional Relationships. Differentiating between career planning and counseling, it notes career professionals' obligation to only provide services within the scope of their professional qualifications and to keep appropriate records. The Code also reminds

Edward Mainzer and Abiola Dipeolu, "What Does the NCDA Code of Ethics Call For?," *Career Convergence Web Magazine.* Copyright © 2016 by National Career Development Association. Reprinted with permission.

us of the importance of developmental and cultural sensitivity, and of the need to assure that clients understand confidentiality and its limitations, including involving in the decision making process individuals who may be unable to give consent because of their age (which is particularly common in K–12 school settings) or other factors.

Other ethical obligations include requesting consent to share information when assisting clients also served by others and being aware of our own values. Sexual or romantic relationships with clients or their families are prohibited, as are such relationships with former clients for at least five years, at which time they still require careful consideration, as do nonprofessional relationships, even though non-sexual or romantic, with clients families at any time. The Code requires us to obtain client consent prior to engaging in advocacy. Career professionals are ethically bound not to abandon or neglect clients, and should avoid entering into a relationship with a client who they will be unable to assist. If it is necessary to terminate, pre-termination services and recommendations for other practitioners should be provided when feasible and necessary.

CONFIDENTIALITY AS A MATTER OF ETHICS

Regarding confidentiality, we are called on to recognize different cultural views toward information disclosure and to engage in ongoing discussions with clients regarding information sharing. Career professionals are also reminded to solicit private information only when it is beneficial to the working relationship. There are confidentiality exceptions in accord with state laws, such as suspected child or elder abuse or when a client has a communicable life threatening condition and may infect an identifiable third party. If faced with court-ordered disclosure we should take steps to limit it as narrowly as possible and whenever possible inform clients before disclosing.

Career professionals are also responsible to make every effort to assure that client confidentiality is maintained by others in their workplaces, and to strive to work only in settings which reasonably ensure client privacy. In the absence of such a setting, career professionals have an ethical obligation to discuss the limitations with clients and seek their consent to proceed. We're also obligated to take precautions to assure confidentiality of information transmitted through any medium. Special obligations around explaining the parameters of confidentiality arise when providing services to groups and/or families. Practitioners should clearly identify "the client" and discuss expectations and limitations of confidentiality. When serving minors or adults who lack the capacity to voluntarily consent, providers discuss their role with parents or other legal guardians and are as always sensitive to issues of culture as well as client welfare.

WORKING WITHIN OUR COMPETENCIES

Career professionals must provide reasonable access to records, limiting access only when there is compelling evidence that it would cause harm and in accord with relevant statues, which must be accordingly documented. When providing access we additionally provide assistance in interpreting records. Following service termination, records should be stored in a manner that allows reasonable access, but providers are also encouraged to purge and dispose of files in time frames called for by governmental and/or institutional regulations. The Code also has sections regarding research and consultation, including obtaining consent and assuring privacy.

There is an ethical obligation to only practice within the boundaries of our competence and only accept positions for which we qualify. Ethical providers must continually monitor their effectiveness, consult and engage in continuing education. We must take care if advertising and take reasonable measures to assure the accuracy of other's statements about us; we are prohibited from using our places of employment or institutional affiliations to recruit clients without permission. We are also mandated to disclose if using our own products or training events and must accurately represent such matters as credentials, educational degrees and professional memberships.

The Code of Ethics specifically prohibits sexual harassment. It calls on career professionals to use techniques/procedures/modalities that are grounded in theory and considered to be established professional practices. Nonetheless, we are also called upon to be respectful of different approaches to career services. Additional obligations include alerting employers to inappropriate policies and practices and attempting to change them; however, when it is not possible to do so, providers are called upon to take additional steps, including if necessary voluntary termination of employment.

ASSESSMENT, EVALUATION, AND RESOLVING ETHICAL CONFLICTS

Further, the Code covers evaluation, assessment and interpretation, calling upon professionals to only use assessments for which they have training and which are in the best interests of clients who have given informed consent and for whom providers have considered the personal/developmental, cultural/diversity and socioeconomic implications of each assessment. A more recent addition to the Code looks at online service provision and technology and the implications of social media for career service providers. It requires consideration of technical, ethical and legal dimensions, including assuring that clients are free to choose whether to engage in online services and that confidentiality and security are provided. Supervision, Training and Teaching are covered in their own section as are Research and Publication.

The Code of Ethics concludes with a section on Resolving Ethical Issues, explicating the need to incorporate ethical practice into daily work through understanding of the NCDA Code and those of other applicable professional or regulatory organizations. These ethical obligations include the duty to consult when ethical questions arise and to take appropriate action when there are doubts as to the ethical practices of another career professional. The NCDA Code of Ethics also makes particular note that those professionals who affiliate with other organizations, such as school counselors who are members of the American School Counselor Association (ASCA), should consult their codes of ethics as well. The ASCA Ethical Standards for School Counselors were last issued in 2010 and are currently under revision. As Makela (2009) wrote in her casebook study on the previous revision of the NCDA Code of Ethics, "Codes of ethics have considerable educational and advocacy value. Yet, harnessing that value requires an active reflection and integration of the code within practice" (p. 10).

REFERENCES

American Counseling Association. (2014). *2014 ACA Code of Ethics*. Alexandria, VA: Author. Retrieved from https://www.counseling.org/resources/aca-code-of-ethics.pdf

Mainzer, E. A., & Dipeolu, A. (2015). Doing right by those we serve: Law, ethics and career services for individuals with disabilities. *Career Planning and Adult Development Journal, 31*(4), 131–141.

Makela, J. P. (2009). *A case study approach to ethics in career development: Exploring shades of gray.* Broken Arrow, OK: National Career Development Association.

National Career Development Association. (2015). *2015 NCDA Code of Ethics.* Retrieved from http://www.ncda.org/aws/NCDA/asset_manager/get_file/3395?ver=366559

Sampson, J. P. & Makela, J. P. (2014). Ethical issues associated with information and communication technology in counseling and guidance. *Florida State University Libraries Faculty Publications*. Retrieved from http://diginole.lib.fsu.edu/islandora/object/fsu:210480/datastream/PDF/view

Welfel, E. R. (2016). *Ethics in counseling and psychotherapy, standards, research, and emerging issues* (6th ed.). Boston: Cengage Learning.

Zakaria, N. S. & Warren, J. (2016). Counseling ethics foundation: Teaching and learning development reformation. In I. H. Amzat and B. Yusuf (Eds.), *Fast forwarding higher education institutions for global challenges, perspectives and approaches* (Chapter 8). Singapore: Springer.

DISCUSSION QUESTIONS

1   What is meant by the phrase "practice only within the boundaries of your competence"? What does this mean for you specifically related to career counseling?

2   What do you think are some of the challenges related to confidentiality in career counseling?

3   What will be your plan for resolving ethical dilemmas when they occur?

CONCLUSION

What we have learned in our own careers is that ethical dilemmas are a reality of our profession. It isn't a question of *whether* they will occur, because they will. What is most important to consider is *how* you will work to resolve the ethical dilemma when it happens. Both ACA and NCDA expect you, as a professional counselor, to carefully consider the dilemma, engage in an ethical decision-making process, and consult resources (which includes other professionals) as needed.

INDEX OF KEY TERMS

- autonomy
- beneficence
- boundary of competence
- career planning vs. career counseling
- confidentiality
- ethical obligation
- fidelity
- justice
- nonmaleficence
- resolving ethical conflicts
- veracity

REFERENCES

American Counseling Association. (2014). *2014 ACA code of ethics*. Alexandria, VA: Author.
National Career Development Association. (2015). *2015 NCDA code of ethics*. Broken Arrow, OK: Author.

SUGGESTED PUBLICATIONS FOR FURTHER READING

American Counseling Association. (2014). *2014 ACA code of ethics*. Alexandria, VA: Author.
Anderson, S. K., Peila-Shuster, J. J., & Aragon, A. (2012). Cross cultural career counseling: Ethical issues to consider. *Career Planning and Adult Development Journal, 28*(1), 127–138.
Habbal, Y., & Habbal, H. B. (2016). Identifying aspects concerning ethics in career counseling: Review on the ACA code of ethics. *International Journal of Business and Public Administration, 13*(2), 115–125.
Makela, J. P. (2009). *A case study approach to ethics in career development: Exploring shades of gray*. Broken Arrow, OK: NCDA.
National Career Development Association. (2015). *2015 NCDA code of ethics*. Broken Arrow, OK: Author.

ADDRESSING DIVERSITY IN CAREER COUNSELING

INTRODUCTION

As the population in the United States and other countries becomes more diverse, there is an increased need for career counselors who can address the needs of diverse clients. Career exploration will need to include issues related to diversity and culture, and career counselors will need to have an understanding of how diversity will play a role in career exploration and career development. Areas of focus will be centered around developing a conceptual framework for working with diverse clients, multicultural competency, and using appropriate strategies and techniques. The selected readings in this chapter will discuss issues related to addressing diversity in career counseling settings.

A Conceptual Framework for Culturally Competent Career Counseling Practice

COURTLAND C. LEE

ABSTRACT

Among the contemporary issues facing career counseling professional addressing the career development and choice issues of the growing number of clients from culturally diverse backgrounds is, perhaps, the most challenging. Contemporary career counseling theory and practice has been greatly impacted by changing demographics and social dynamics that characterize the 21st century. For example, projections of the United States population indicate that by the year 2050, the non-Hispanic White population will decrease to 46 per cent of the total population, while 30 per cent of the population will be Hispanic; 13 per cent Black; 1 per cent American Indian, Eskimo, and Aleut; and eight per cent Asian and Pacific Islander (U.S. Bureau of the Census, 2008).

Cultural diversity, therefore, has become widely recognized as a major factor deserving increased understanding on the part of career counseling professionals. Within this context, career counselors must provide services that help people to make career decisions in the midst of sweeping demographic and sociological change. The past two decades have seen a growing realization that career counseling services often do not have broad applicability across the range of cultural backgrounds represented

Courtland C. Lee, "A Conceptual Framework for Culturally Competent Career Counseling Practice," *Career Planning and Adult Development Journal*, vol. 28, no. 1, pp. 7-14. Copyright © 2012 by Career Planning and Adult Development Network. Reprinted with permission. Provided by ProQuest LLC. All rights reserved.

by clients (Bowman, 1993; Fouad & Bingham, 1995; Fouad & Byars-Winston, 2005; Leong, 1995; Pope, 2003; Walsh, Bingham, Brown & Ward, 2001). With this awareness has come frustration that in attempting to promote career development, the values inherent in career counseling and those of culturally diverse clients often come into conflict in the career exploration and choice process (Fouad & Bingham, Leong). In order to resolve this conflict and the frustration which often accompanies it, cultural differences must be effectively addressed in the provision of career counseling services. It is evident that career counselors need a conceptual framework from which to operate if they are going to insure that clients from culturally diverse backgrounds have access to competent career services.

This article provides such a conceptual framework. It explores the acquisition of multicultural career counseling competence from a developmental perspective. The conceptual framework examines the foundational aspects as well as the aspects of culture that must form the basis of multicultural career counseling competency. It is based on the knowledge and skills considered essential in relating to diverse populations that impact the career counseling and development process that are outlined in the National Career Development Association's Career Counseling Competencies (1997).

THE CONCEPTUAL FRAMEWORK

The conceptual framework focuses on the development of culturally competent career counselors who apply their practice in a diverse society. The framework is comprised of eight themes organized into three areas: foundational dimensions, multicultural dimensions, and multicultural competency.

Foundational Dimension. The foundational dimension consists of four themes. While these themes are the foundation of multicultural career counseling competency they can also be considered the essence of competent counseling in general.

SELF-AWARENESS

The basis for culturally competent career counseling practice is counselor self-awareness. It is important that counselors fully experience themselves as cultural beings. An individual who expects to work cross-culturally must first be anchored in his or her own cultural realities. This process should start with explorations of how one's own cultural background has influenced his or her career development. It is of critical importance that a person considers the role that cultural heritage and customs play in shaping his or her personality characteristics. It is also crucial that a person assess his or her own process of cultural identity development. The significant questions that one must ask in this regard are "How do I experience myself as a member of Cultural Group X?" "How do I experience others members of Cultural Group X?" and "How do I experience people of other cultural backgrounds?"

As part of this self-exploration process, it is also important that a counselor evaluate the influences that have shaped the development of his or her attitudes and beliefs about people from different cultural backgrounds. It is important to evaluate the explicit, as well as the often subtle messages one has received throughout his or her life about people who are culturally "different." A career counselor must evaluate how his or her personal attitudes and beliefs about people from different cultural groups may facilitate or hamper counseling effectiveness.

Multicultural competency begins with an exploration of personal issues and questions, no matter how uncomfortable, in an attempt to discern how one's own cultural heritage, values and biases might impact upon the career counseling process. Self-exploration leads to self-awareness, which is crucial in developing a set of personal attitudes and beliefs to guide culturally competent career counseling practice. Culturally competent career counselors are sensitive to cultural group differences because they are aware of their own identity as cultural beings.

GLOBAL LITERACY

Global literacy refers to the knowledge base that every culturally competent individual should possess in the contemporary interconnected world. It is a reflection of one's exposure to and knowledge of the contemporary world. Global literacy is the breadth of information that extends over the major domains of human diversity. In modern society a globally literate person, for example, would be one who has a knowledge of ethnic variations in history, has travel experience, and is knowledgeable about current world events (Lee, In Press).

FOUNDATIONAL KNOWLEDGE OF TRADITIONAL CAREER DEVELOPMENT/COUNSELING THEORY

The concept of multicultural career counseling competency must also rest on an understanding of traditional counseling theory. Although there have been criticisms of the Eurocentric nature of traditional career counseling theories (Fouad & Bingham, 1995; Leong, 1995), each has important aspects that contribute to best practice in career counseling. Therefore, it is important that the foundation of career counseling practice laid down by pioneering thinkers such as Anne Roe, Donald Super and John Holland are incorporated into culturally diverse concepts and approaches to career counseling.

ETHICAL KNOWLEDGE AND ASPIRATIONS

Another crucial foundational aspect of multicultural career counseling competency is knowledge of ethical standards. Indeed, the integrity of the entire counseling profession rests on ethical practice. Importantly, the ethical standards of the American Counseling Association call on counselors to actively attempt to understand the diverse cultural backgrounds of the clients they serve (ACA, 2005). Best practice in career counseling, therefore, is putting ethics in the forefront of all professional activity. It is safe to assume then that career counselors who are culturally competent aspire to high ethical standards.

Multicultural Dimension. The multicultural dimension of the conceptual framework consists of three themes. These themes reflect the theory and practice multicultural counseling.

MULTICULTURAL COUNSELING THEORETICAL KNOWLEDGE

In addition to knowledge of traditional career counseling theory, it is imperative that counselors have a knowledge base which includes culturally diverse ideas on the nature of career development from which to plan, implement and evaluate services in a cross-cultural context. Significantly, Sue, Ivey, and Petersen (1996), proposed a theory of multicultural counseling that forms the basis for understanding career development and counseling from culturally diverse perspectives. The basic assumption of this theory is that it is a metatheory of counseling that recognizes that both counselor and client identities are embedded in multiple levels of experience and context. It posits that cultural identity development is a major determinant of both counselor and client attitudes, which are also influenced by the dominant and subordinate relationships among groups. Cultural identity refers to an individual's sense of belonging to a cultural group and the part of one's personality that is attributable to cultural group membership. Multicultural theoretical knowledge must also include an understanding that career counseling is most likely enhanced when modalities and goals are consistent with the life experiences and cultural values of the client.

Another crucial aspect of multicultural knowledge is an understanding of how social systems operate with respect to their treatment of culturally diverse groups of people (Lee, 2007; Ratts, Toporek, & Lewis, 2010). Culturally competent career counselors must have an understanding of the impact that systemic forces such as racism and classism can have on career development and career choice.

CROSS CULTURAL ENCOUNTERS

Multicultural career counseling competency must be predicated on one's ability to acquire working knowledge and information about specific groups of people. This should include information about the histories, experiences, customs, and values of culturally diverse groups. However, the acquisition of such knowledge must not be limited to books, classes, and workshops. A crucial way to acquire such knowledge is through ongoing professional, and perhaps more importantly, personal encounters with people from diverse cultural backgrounds. Such encounters may entail getting outside of the familiarity of one's own cultural realities and experiencing diversity first hand. An important component of any cross cultural encounter is the ability to get beyond stereotypes and ensure that one sees people as individuals within a cultural context.

CROSS CULTURAL CAREER COUNSELING SKILL DEVELOPMENT

It is imperative that career counselors enter a cross cultural helping relationship with a repertoire of skills. They should develop career counseling strategies and techniques that are consistent with the life experiences and cultural values of their clients. Such skill development should be based on the following premises. First, cultural diversity is real and should not be ignored in career counseling interactions. Second, cultural differences are just that—differences. They are not necessarily deficiencies or pathological deviations. This suggests having the ability to meet clients where they are, despite obvious cultural gaps between helper and helpee. Third, when working with clients from culturally diverse groups, it is important to avoid stereotypes and a monolithic perspective. It is crucial that career counselors consider clients as individuals within a cultural context.

In developing culturally competent career counseling skills, a number of theoretical approaches should be included in a helping repertoire. It is important that one's counseling approach be eclectic enough that he or she can use a variety of helping interventions. Any counseling approach should incorporate diverse worldviews and practices.

Upon actually encountering a client from a different cultural context, a career counselor's skill set must proceed from important answers to the following questions, "What 'buttons,' if any, does this client push in me as a result of the obvious cultural difference between us?" "What are some cultural blind spots I may have with respect to this client?" "As a result of my cultural realities, what strengths do I bring to this counseling relationship?" "As a result of my cultural realities, what limitations do I bring to this counseling relationship?"

MULTICULTURAL CAREER COUNSELING COMPETENCY

The apex of this conceptual framework is multicultural career counseling competency. This is based on a construct that has received significant attention in the cross cultural literature—multicultural counseling competency (Arredondo, Toporek, Brown, Jones, Locke, Sanchez, & Stadler, 1996; Roysircar, Arredondo, Fuertes, Ponterotto, & Toporek, 2003; Sue, Arredondo & McDavis, 1992). Multicultural counseling competency defines a set of attitudes and behaviors indicative of the ability to establish, maintain, and successfully conclude a counseling relationship with clients from diverse cultural backgrounds. Given this therefore, multicultural career counseling competency can be conceptualized as a set of attitudes and behaviors indicative of the ability to establish, maintain and successfully conclude a career counseling relationship with clients from diverse cultural backgrounds in a global marketplace. In essence, career counselors who are culturally competent have heightened awareness, an expanded knowledge base, and use helping skills in a culturally responsive manner.

In the developmental process that has been described in this conceptual framework, three important questions summarize the evolution of multicultural career counseling competency. First, those counselors who demonstrate multicultural career counseling competency possess selfawareness that is grounded in an exploration of the question, "Who am I as a cultural being?" Second, in addition to knowledge of traditional career counseling theory and ethical principles, multiculturally competent career counselors consider the question, "What do I know about cultural dynamics?" Third, the counseling practice of career counselors who exhibit multicultural competency is predicated on the question, "How do I promote career development and facilitate the career choice process in a culturally competent manner?"

CONCLUSION

American society in the 21st century is characterized by ever-increasing cultural pluralism. This phenomenon has had a profound effect on career counseling. No longer can career counseling theory or practice be considered exclusively within the confines of one cultural perspective. Instead, important aspects of cultural diversity, such as race/ethnicity must be factored into effective career counseling practice. Therefore, if career counselors are to have an impact on the career development of increasingly diverse client groups, then their practice must be grounded in multicultural competency. The development of such competency must be an integral part of the personal and professional growth process of all career counselors. This process involves acquiring not only the awareness and knowledge, but also the skills for effective multicultural career intervention.

REFERENCES

American Counseling Association. (2005). *Code of ethics*. Alexandria, VA: Author.

Arredondo, P., Toporek, M. S., Brown, S., Jones, J., Locke, D. C., Sanchez, J. and Stadler, H. (1996) *Operationalization of the Multicultural Counseling Competencies*. AMCD: Alexandria, VA

Bowman, S.L. (1993). Career intervention strategies for ethnic minorities. *The Career Development Quarterly*, 42, 14–25.

Fouad, N. A., & Bingham, R. P. (1995). Career counseling with racial and ethnic minorities. In W. B. Walsh & S. H. Osipow (Eds.), *Handbook of vocational psychology: Theory, research, and practice* (pp. 331–365). Mahwah, NJ: Erlbaum.

Fouad, N. & Byars-Winston, A. (2005). Cultural context of career choice: Meta-analysis of race/ethnicity differences. *The Career Development Quarterly*, 53, 223–23.

Lee, C.C. (Ed.). (2007). *Counseling for Social Justice*. Alexandria, VA: American Counseling Association.

Lee, C.C. (In Press). Global literacy: The foundation of culturally competent counseling. In C.C. Lee (Ed). *Multicultural issues in counseling: New approaches to diversity* (4th Edition). Alexandria, VA: American Counseling Association.

Leong, F.T. (Ed.). (1995). *Career development and vocational behavior of racial and ethnic minorities*. Mahwah, NJ: Erlbaum.

National Career Development Association (1997). *Career counseling competencies*. Alexandria, VA: Author.

Pope, M. (2003). Career counseling in the twenty-first century: Beyond cultural encapsulation. *The Career Development Quarterly*, 52, 54–63.

Ratts, M.J., Toporek, R.L. & Lewis, J .A. (Eds.) (2010). *ACA advocacy competencies: A social justice framework for counselors*, (pp. 3–10). Alexandria, VA: American Counseling Association.

Roysircar, G ., Arredondo, P., Fuertes, J. N ., Ponterotto, J. G. & Toporek, R. L. (2003). *Multicultural counseling competencies 2003: Association for Multicultural Counseling and Development*. Alexandria, VA: Association for Multicultural Counseling and Development.

Sue, D.W., Arredondo, P. & McDavis, R.J. (1992). Multicultural counseling competencies and standards: A call to the profession. *Journal of Counseling & Development*, 70, 477–486.

Sue, D.W., Ivey, A.E., and Pedersen, P.B. (Eds.) (1996). *A theory of multicultural counseling and therapy.* Pacific Grove, CA: Brooks/Cole.

U.S. Bureau of the Census (2008). *Projected population by single year of age, sex, race, and Hispanic origin for the United States: July 1, 2000 to July 1, 2050.* Washington, D.C: Author.

Walsh, W.B., Bignham, R.P., Brown, M.T. & Ward, C.M. (Eds.). (2001). *Career counseling for African Americans.* Mahwah, N.J.: Erlbaum.

ABOUT THE AUTHOR

Courtland C. Lee is Professor of Counselor Education at the University of Maryland, College Park. He earned the PhD at Michigan State University. He is the author, editor, or co-editor of five books on multicultural counseling and two books on counseling and social justice. He is also the author of three books on counseling African American males.

In addition, he has published numerous book chapters and articles on counseling across cultures. He is the former editor of the *Journal of Multicultural Counseling and Development* and the *Journal of African American Men.* He has also served on the editorial board of the *International Journal for the Advancement of Counselling* and was a Senior Associate Editor of the *Journal of Counseling and Development.* He is the President of the *International Association for Counselling.* He is also a *Fellow* and Past President of the American Counseling Association and a past President of the *Association for Multicultural Counseling and Development.* He is also a *Fellow of the British Association for Counselling and Psychotherapy,* the first and only American to receive this honor.

Multicultural Career Counseling Strategies

An Update for 21st Century Career Professionals

LEE COVINGTON RUSH

Strategies and techniques in the development of multicultural career counseling skills and competencies are discussed. The focus is on instructional applications which may enhance student learning.

> "Career development involves one's whole life, not just occupations. As such, it concerns the whole person, needs, and wants, capacities and potentials, excitements and anxieties, insights and blind spots, warts and all. More than that, it concerns him/her in the ever-changing contexts of his/her life. The environmental pressures and constraints, the bonds that tie him/her to significant others, responsibilities to children and aging parents, the total structure of one's circumstances are also factors that must be understood and reckoned with. In these terms, career development and personal development converge. Self and circumstances—evolving, changing, unfolding in mutual interaction—constitute the focus and the drama of career development" (Wolfe & Kolb as cited in Gysbers 2004).

Lee Covington Rush, "Multicultural Career Counseling Strategies: An Update for 21st Century Career Professionals," *Career Planning and Adult Development Journal*, vol. 25, no. 1, pp. 82-96. Copyright © 2009 by Career Planning and Adult Development Network. Reprinted with permission.

This expansive and inclusive definition of career development contemporaneously informs the way in which the construct is now articulated. The process of career development includes the individual's entire life span, incorporating the varying life roles, contexts, environmental opportunities and barriers, cultural reference points, racial/ethnic implications, gender variables, sexual orientation status, and disability status. This view provides us a richly textured framework within to discuss multicultural career counseling strategies. Teaching career counseling from a multicultural perspective can indeed be a great joy, whether you are a career professional or career practitioner. This joy and excitement emerge when you observe your students having moments when a light goes on in their heads as the connections between career and multicultural counseling skills occur. This pleasure and excitement also manifests itself when your students begin to examine themselves in the context of their burgeoning career and multicultural competencies, and also as they immerse themselves in beginning to development their counselor identity. This article is thus framed to provide the counselor educator or practitioner trainer with instructional strategies and techniques which will hopefully aid you in providing your students a foundation within which they can begin to build their multicultural career counseling skills and competencies. The incorporation of career and multicultural counseling constructs requires hard work, creativity, and dedication. The rewards can be exceptionally self-affirming from an instructional perspective.

WORLD MULTICULTURAL CAREER COUNSELOR EDUCATOR/ PRACTITIONER/STUDENT

"Counselor: Know Thyself" (Hulnick, 1977, p. 69). Hulnick's now classic dictum holds true today as it did some three decades ago. The initial task for us, in our roles as multicultural career counselors, practitioners, and students, is that of first and foremost examining ourselves. That is, undertaking an introspective evaluation of our values, beliefs, biases, prejudices, world views and overall personal perspectives as cultural beings. This journey requires considered thought and reflection in combination with a "realization [that] the universe itself is infinite and any beliefs we hold concerning its reality are subject to question ... [and that] the second quality ... for self knowledge [is] openness to experience" (Hulnick, 1977, pp. 70–71). This self-knowledge is of importance for any counselor, yet it takes on additional implications for students engaged in multicultural career counseling given the diversity of the 21st Century. Locke and

Parker (1991) have provided a cross-cultural awareness continuum which provides a useful model for such exploration. Thus it is proposed that if we as multicultural career counselors/practitioners/students undertake this intrapersonal exploration in combination with our training, we will be reasonably prepared to work towards becoming multiculturally competent in general counseling as well as career counseling. This self exploration is clearly in keeping with the multicultural competencies as articulated by Sue, Arredondo, and McDavis (1992). They proposed that multicultural competencies are framed upon three broad areas; (a) the counselor's awareness of his/her own cultural values and biases; (b) counselor's awareness of the client's culture and values; and (c) the counselor's use of culturally appropriate intervention strategies (p. 481). Each of these broad headings are further explicated in terms of the specific attitudes/beliefs, knowledge and skills required within each category. The significance of this multicultural counseling knowledge, awareness (including self-awareness), beliefs, attitudes, and skills are such that the American Counseling Association (ACA) specifically addresses various competencies in its ACA Code of Ethics (2005). For example Section A, Introduction states that *"Counselors also explore their own cultural identities and how these affect their values and beliefs about the counseling process"* (p. 8). Further, Section C. 2.a. indicates that "counselors gain knowledge, personal awareness, sensitivity and skills pertinent to working with a diverse client population (p. 9). Additionally the National Career Development Association's Board (2009) recently approved a statement on the *Minimum Competencies for Multicultural Career Counseling and Development,* which incorporates the professionals' self-awareness components. Extrapolating from Gay (1985), this self exploration has the potential for transforming and liberating the individual. Thus the implications of this transformative process include enhanced self-awareness and self understanding, along with a heightened appreciation of and sensitivity to others who are different, which are the initial steps towards multicultural career counseling efficacy.

MULTICULTURAL CAREER COUNSELING STRATEGIES

For the multicultural career counselor or practitioner, one of the key challenges in career instruction is that of finding various strategies for fully incorporating multicultural components into the course curriculum. Among career researchers and theorists there seems to be some consensus with regard to specific variables of import in addressing the career related behaviors/needs of non-majority clients, (e.g. Byars-Winston

& Fouad, 2006; Leong and Hartung, 1997). Among the often cited variables are the clients' world view, the clients' racial-identity status, and attendance to culturally appropriate assessment and cultural contexts.

In an effort to explicate strategies that may be used in exploring these variables for multicultural career counseling instructional purposes, the following recommendations are proposed:

WORLD VIEW

According to Ibrahim, Ohnishi, and Wilson (1994) an individual's world view relates to the prism or lenses through which the person interprets his or her world. "It represents our beliefs, assumptions, and attitudes about people, relationships, institutions, nature, time and activity in our world"(p. 280). Accordingly in career counseling, as in most counseling dyads, it is the counselor's ability to understand and respond to the cultural reference point or world view of the client. Leong and Hartung (1997) maintained that *"understanding and intervening with clients in terms of how culture influences their world view emerges as a vitally important part of the career assessment process"* (p. 190).

ACTIVITIES FOR CONSIDERATION:

1   One method to aid students in beginning to conceptualize the differences between their world views and a culturally different person's world view could incorporate the use of films. For example, the film *The Color of Fear* (1995) explores the attitudes, cultural values and indeed cultural fears and barriers of a group of culturally different men. Each of the eight participants explores what it means to be Asian-American, Africa-American, Hispanic-American and European-American in America and the implications of racism. While this film is not about career counseling per se, it provides its viewers affective moments wherein understanding the cultural context of another emerges. Another film which speaks to the world view of Chinese-Americans is the Joy *Luck Club* (1993). This film explores the relationship between a Chinese born immigrant and her American born daughter. The world view of the immigrant parent is contrasted with the daughter's, and the strained relationships between these differing cultural contexts are explored. Again, this film could serve as a vehicle by which the implications of cultural context is framed for the career counseling student and as importantly the construct of world view is visually demonstrated.

2   Another activity by which students can examine their own world views is by focusing on who they are, using *value orientations/emphasis* exercise by Kluckhohn as cited in Ibrahim et al. 1994. In highly diverse classes, this exercise can be done in culturally different dyads so that students can discuss their differing world views and cultural assumptions.

a.   How [is] human nature perceived by [me]? Is it essentially good … bad or a combination?

b.   How are social relationships perceived and organized in [my] world? Are they organized hierarchically, with power at the top … do people within this system see group goals as superordinate to individual goals?

c.   Do the familial or societal ends (good or bad) justify the means? Are social relations defined in a collateral-mutual manner [or from an individualistic perspective]?

d.   How do [I] perceive nature? … Is nature perceived [by me] as something that can be controlled?

e.   How do [I] conceptualize time? Do [I] emphasize the past, the present, or the future?

f.   How [do I] define human activity? Is the focus on being spontaneous … Is the emphasis on inner development (spiritual) and material attainment as result of work/living? Is the emphasis of life and work on outward success or material gain only? (pp. 280–281)

3   Another means by which students can begin to understand cultural context or world view of another is through reading a novel that involves characters from a cultural/ethnic group other than their own. In this instance the instructor can assign a list of appropriate novels. Some examples are:

African-American world view exploration:
Makes Me Wanna Holler: A Young Black Man In America, Nathan McCall (1994).
When and Where I Enter: The Impact of Black Women On Race and Sex In America, Gloria Naylor (1986)

Asian-Americans:
The Kitchen God's Wife, Amy Tan (1991).
China Men, Maxine Kingston (1980).

Hispanic-Americans:
The Infinite Plan, Isabel Allende (1993).
Hunger of Memory: The Education of Richard Rodriguez, Richard Rodriguez (1983).

Upon completion of the novel the students should write a paper addressing the following type questions:

1   Identity the ways in which you identify with and are different from the protagonists(s).

2   How did this novel help you in understanding the world views of those who are culturally different than yourself?

3   Identify a character(s) in the novel for whom you could do a career intervention/career counseling.

4   What are the cultural implications that may be of particular significance, and how would you address them with the client?

5   How is the client's career-decision making, and career maturity impacted by his/her world view?

The aforementioned activities are designed to assist students in conceptualizing the significance of the client's world view on the multicultural career counseling process. The client in his or her cultural context is the frame within which career counseling has to occur. These activities could be used in combination with chapters on career theories, with skills and techniques chapters, and with chapters related to career counseling with diverse populations.

RACIAL IDENTITY DEVELOPMENT

Helms (1994) proposed that Racial Identity Models [Statuses] could be of use in explaining and assessing the career behaviors of non-majority clients. Specifically, as noted by Trusty (2002):

"One quality of racial-ethnic identity development models that renders them useful in career development counseling is that they address experience, cognition, affect, and overt behavior in terms of people's selves, their own and other racial-ethnic group cultures, and the mainstream or dominant culture ... [therefore] racial identity ego-statuses should influence how people experience and perceive discrimination; and these perceptions, in turn, influence career-related variables such as perceived opportunity, choices, and job satisfaction" (pp. 199–200).

Currently many career texts incorporate discussions surrounding the implications of clients' Racial Identity Status (RID) in relationship to the multicultural career counseling processes (e.g., Niles & Harris-Bowlsbey, 2009; Capuzzi & Stauffer; 2006). It therefore seems of importance that career counseling students both understand RID models as well as how they might influence the career development of racial/ethnic clients. Prior to discussing specific activities that may enhance student understanding of RID, a brief review of the constructs such as conformity, dissonance, immersion/emersion, internalization, and integrative awareness, based upon the work of Helms (1994), is recommended.

ACTIVITIES FOR CONSIDERATION:

Among the most context rich instructional activities can be that of using a case study approach. Krieshok & Pelsma (2002) proposed that the use of case studies for career counseling instruction are especially useful because *"work stories are life stories ... each case teaches students a small amount of content ... [and] true stories are never boring"* (pp. 837–838). Thus for exploration of RID constructs the use of case studies may serve as an invaluable tool for students. One source of career related case studies is the *Career Counseling Casebook: A Resource for Practitioners, Students, and Counselor Educators (2002)* by Niles, Goodman and Pope. Other sources are some case studies that were published in the 1980's and 1990's in *The Career Development Quarterly*, under the heading *Getting Down to Cases*. The following case study provides an example for activities:

Mr. Ebo is a genteel, 40-year-old Black man who came in for career counseling because he is currently unemployed and experiencing significant financial stressors (i.e., outstanding student loans and a delinquent home mortgage). He reports having had a series of self-employment ventures that all culminated in failure. These ventures included attempts to establish an international import and export consulting business, being a general building contractor, owning a restaurant, and operating a carwash. As he relates these past business experiences, Mr. Ebo offers numerous reasons/excuses for the demise of all his businesses. He has a BS degree in Business Administration, but feels that the *"world is simply against a Black man trying to get ahead."* Mr. Ebo's wife, Louise, left him several years ago because she could not put up with his anger at the world, and his continued business failures and excuses. Study extrapolated from Cultural Changes and Career Changes: The Case of Ebo, *The Career Development Quarterly* (1991), by Spencer Niles. Some possible questions for discussion include:

1   What career development theory would you use as a guide in working with this client and why?

2   Where (what stage) would you assess the client's RID status to be based upon this vignette? What are the career implications for this particular status?

3   How might the client's RID status impact his career development and behaviors? His career maturity? His vocational exploration?

4   What barriers do you see in his career growth and development?

5   How can you aid this client in overcoming these barriers?

A second activity would be Career Genograms, emerging from the family counseling literature (Bowen, 1978), can provide another tool for exploring RID status along with myriad other cultural markers. Heppner, Obrien, Hinkelman and Humphrey (1994) articulated that the use of the career genogram is a creative method by which the counselor and client can identify:

1   Occupations represented in the family for several generations.

2   How family members rank these occupations in terms of value and status.

3   What patterns of career choice emerge within the family and how they change.

4   Evidence of family values or ethics as they relate to the world of work. (pp. 80–81)

In using the career genogram the counselor, in encouraging the client to explore his/her family story, has the ability to aid the client in reflecting upon *"meaning, values, expectation, roles, secrets, traditions, memories, myths, and misperceptions intersecting with career patterns,"* (Andersen & Vandehey, 2006, p. 192). Within the parameters of the client narrative, the RID Status may become apparent. The technical/pictorial of a family genogram can be located in many family therapy/counseling texts. For instructional purposes, it is of value to have students construct their own career genograms, which provides them a fuller understanding of its use for career exploration.

From the multicultural counseling perspective, McGoldrick, Giordano & Garcia-Preto (2005) provided a series of *cultural genogram questions* which can be easily adapted for the career counseling framework. Some of their questions include:

1   What ethnic groups, religious traditions, nations, racial groups, trades, professions, communities, and other groups do you consider yourself to be part of?

2   When and why did you or your family come to the United States? To this community?

3   How old were family members at the time?

4   Do they and do you feel secure about your status in the United States?

5   What language do they (do you) speak at home? In the community? In your family of origin?

6   What burdening wounds has your racial or ethnic group experienced?

7   What burden does your ethnic or racial group carry for injuries to other groups?

8   How have you been affected by the wounds your group has committed, or that have been committed against your group?

9   What experiences have been most stressful for family members in the United States?

10 To whom do family members in your culture turn when in need of help?

11 What are your culture's values regarding male and female roles? Education? Work and success? Family connectedness? Family caretaking? Religious practices?

12 Have these values changed in you family over time?

13 What do you feel about your culture(s) of origin?

14 Do you feel you belong to the dominant U.S. culture? (p. 762)

McGoldrick et al. (2005) suggested that these genogram questions assist clients in looking at their histories, present cultural context and their futures. For career counseling purposes, embedded in reframed career questions, the counselor and client are afforded opportunities to explore important cultural variables related to the client's career/vocational RID statuses, gender statuses, disability statuses, and GLTB statuses. The implications of these cultural contexts are then examined in relationship to career attitudes, barriers, career exploration or the lack therof, and the career decision-making processes or difficulties of the client.

A third activity that has the potential to increase career counseling students' overall multicultural awareness, especially in terms of the world views of others, differing cultural values, and RID is provided from the book, *Experiential Activities for Teaching Career Counseling Classes and for Facilitating Career Groups*, Vol. One, Mark Pope and Carole W. Minor (Eds.) (2000). This activity is authored by F. Leong & H. Kim.

CAREER-RELATED INTERCULTURAL SENSITIZERS

Learning Objectives: As a result of this critical incident activity, students will increase their cultural knowledge and enhance their multicultural career counseling skills.

Incident: Mr. Chin, a Chinese student with a 3.9 GPA, has come in for career counseling because he is very interested in a career in social work. He is however, highly distressed, because his family is expecting him to pursue a career as a surgeon. Given this client's GPA, the counselor encourages Mr. Chin *follow his interests and his dreams.* Though the session went well, Mr. Chin does not return for further sessions, and the counselor is perplexed as to why the client does not respond to phone calls.

Question for students: Why did Mr. Chin not continue his career counseling sessions? Provide students with several possible reasons why this client discontinued his counseling. After discussing several possible reasons, provide students with the following explanation:

Highly developed feelings of obligation and filial piety govern much of the traditional life of people from Asian cultures … Thus, regardless of Mr. Chin's personal wishes, no decision can possibly be made without acknowledging and respecting the wishes of his family which the counselor in this case completely disregarded. (p. 207).

CULTURALLY APPROPRIATE ASSESSMENT

According to Niles & Harris-Bowlsbey (2009) assessment is defined as: "the use of any formal or informal technique or instrument to collect data about a client ... its most important use is to assist individuals at a given point in time to identify their current interests and skills in order to identify the next educational or vocational choice in the sequence that makes up career development" (p. 160).

In terms of career assessment with culturally diverse or historically disenfranchised clients, it is of utmost importance that career counselors be culturally competent and have an understanding the cultural characteristic and cultural context of the client (Capuzzi & Stauffer, 2006). Several models for multicultural career counseling and assessment have been proposed (e.g. Flores, Spanierman, & Obasi, 2003); Leong & Hartung, 1997). Assessment techniques can include formal and informal instruments, in combination with a particular counseling modality. Assessment efforts for culturally diverse clients should however take into account the possibility of barriers to their career development. These barriers might include disability status; racial discrimination; gender variables; sexual orientation and discrimination; parental influence; the client's level of acculturation; collectivistic values; limited vocational knowledge and exploration; limited role models; economic constraints; environmental constraints; RID status; and client's level of career maturity and decision-making.

For instructional purposes, one model that multicultural career counseling students might examine for application is the **Culturally Appropriate Career Counseling Model—CACCM,** as developed by Fouad & Binghman (as cited in Byars-Winston & Fouad 2006). It is proposed by the authors that this model "incorporates culture as a critical factor in every aspect of the counseling process" (Byars-Winston et al., 2006, p. 193). CACCM **Step (1)** Counselor's establishment of a culturally appropriate relationship with the client; **Step (2)** The identification of the career issues; **Step (3)** Assessment of the impact of cultural factors on identified career issues; **Step (4)** Appropriate goal setting; **Step (5)** Determination and implementation of culturally appropriate intervention; **Step (6)** Culturally appropriate decision making (concentrate on the counselor and client developing specific career counseling strategies to address client's career concerns); **Step (7)** Focus on the implementation of the client's plan and follow-up (pp. 193).

Byars-Winston et al. (2006) further expanded the original model incorporating metacognitive components, which are: **Step 1. Plan:** what is my plan for working with this client? What are any gaps in my knowledge about the client's context? What are my strengths and areas of challenge? What are my initial goals and intentions in working with this client?; **Step 2. Monitor:** What is the client's cultural context and what are my reactions to that? How might the client's information be conflicting? Are there some career issues that I am willing to address more than others? Are there some issues that I am avoiding? **Step 3. Monitor:** What are my own thoughts and reactions about the possible impact of cultural variables on career issues? Are there some cultural variables that I am emphasizing more than the client? **Step 4. Monitor:** How are my goals appropriate for the client's cultural context? Are there some gaps in my knowledge about what might be appropriate goals? How will I respond if the client's goals differ from my own? **Step 5. Evaluate:** How helpful are my interventions? On what basis am I determining how helpful my interventions are? **Step 6. Evaluate:** What are the consequences of my behavior or intervention strategy? How culturally congruent are the counseling outcomes with the client's desired goals? Reclarify issues. (p. 195).

This is but one model that may be useful in multicultural career counseling and assessment for students to explore. As is evident in the expanded version, this model includes the cultural contexts of the client, but further calls upon the counselor to examine his/her cultural knowledge and skills in tandem with his/her values and cultural awareness. Ponterotto, Rivera & Sueyoshi (2000) developed *The Career-in-Culture Interview CiCI,* an assessment protocol that can be used during the intake process. As noted by Niles et al. (2009) this tool *"focuses on the client from five spheres of career development influence: culture; family and religion; community and larger society; self-view and self-efficacy; barriers and oppression; and narrative and relationship"* (p. 146). This semi-structured instrument and its questions may provide students additional understanding of the importance of cultural context in the assessment processes. Selected questions from Ponterotto et al. (2000) include:

1. Introduce yourself and inquire: Is there anything you would like to know about me and my role as a career counselor? (If at any point during your session you have any other questions you would like to ask me, please feel free to do so.)

2. Tell me about yourself and include any information that you believe is important for me to better understand you.

3. Tell me a little about your career concerns and goals.

4. What are some things that are important/not as important to you in a career?

5. What type of occupations were you aware of growing up?

6. Do you believe/feel that you can accomplish whatever goals you set for yourself? Why or why not?

7   Tell me about your cultural and ethnic background (consider asking the client about language preference, immigration/migration history, and level and place of education).

8   Tell me about your religious background.

9   How has your family, both immediate and extended, influenced your career goals? How do your career goals match or conflict with your family's expectations?

10   I would like you to draw a family genogram and then tell me about the lives and career/work experiences of the family members identified.

11   Who are some of the people in your community and/or the larger society (teachers, neighbors, religious leaders, grandparents, etc.) who have influenced your career goals, and why?

12   How has your life style/life choices influenced what you see as possible career options?

13   As a (race/ethnicity, female/male, older/younger, heterosexual/homosexual/bisexual, abled/disabled) person, what do you see as your greatest challenge/barrier to pursuing your career goals, and in what ways do you confront these challenges?

14   We have covered a lot of information today; how are you feeling about what we have discussed?

15   Is there anything you would like to add? Perhaps we missed some information that you would like to share (pp. 95–96).

Any discussion regarding multicultural career counseling and assessment has of necessity to address instruments that may be used. Of particular importance in working with culturally diverse clients, assessment tools should be appropriate for the client in his/her cultural context and it should be understood that assessment instruments are but one small portion of the process. Following are some guidelines that students should consider in deciding to use assessment instruments in the multicultural career counseling process. These guidelines were proposed by Evans (2008).

1   Review the purpose of test collaboratively with clients to ensure that the test utilized will meet client needs.

2   If the test seems to meet client needs, investigate the test by reading all available information about its cultural inclusiveness, including information on language and reading levels.

3   Pay special attention to the standardization sample.

4   Ensure that diversity percentages are close to population numbers of diverse groups.

5   If the test utilizes ethnic minorities or other special populations in the normative sample, pay close attention to how close the ethnic population compares to that of the U.S. general population.

6   If there is data concerning testing differences between culturally different groups, note the data and make a decision as to whether or not to proceed with testing.

7   Always explain to clients any caveats before administering a test and again when you interpret the test for clients.

8   Provide the best interpretation of the test results you can, taking into consideration the client's race, culture, and environment. (pp. 132–133).

FURTHER REFLECTIONS

This discussion has been offered to articulate and identify strategies and techniques which may be useful in guiding students toward the development of their multicultural career counseling competencies. In concluding this article, there are two additional recommendations that this author would wish to provide. Instructors may find the paperbound book, *Gaining Cultural Competence in Career Counseling* by Kathy Evans (2008) an invaluable tool in providing students multicultural career counseling knowledge, awareness, and skills. This book can be used in combination with a standard career theory text or independently. Secondly, the American Psychological Association's Video series offers Professor Nadya Fouad (often cited in this article) working in a *Culturally Oriented Career Counseling* session. This video could also serve to enhance student learning vis-à-vis multicultural career counseling. The engagement with and skill development in multicultural career counseling competency has the potential to be an extraordinary learning adventure. It can be a source of great professional and personal growth for career educators, practitioners, and students. Effort and commitment are required, but the journey is well worth it.

REFERENCES

American Counseling Association (2005). *ACA code of ethics.* Alexandria VA: Author.

Andersen, P. & Vandehey, M. (2006). *Career counseling and development in a global economy.* Boston MA: Lahaska Press.

Bowen,. M. (1978). *Family therapy in clinical practice.* New York: Aronson.

Byars-Winston, A. & Fouad, N. (2006). Metacognition and multicultural competence: Expanding the culturally appropriate career counseling model. *The Career Development Quarterly* 54, 187–201.

Capuzzi, D. & Stauffer, M. (2006). *Career counseling: Foundations, perspectives, and applications.* Boston, MA: Pearson Education, Inc.

Evans, K. (2008). *Gaining cultural competence in career counseling.* Boston-New York: Lahask Press.

Flores, L., Spanierman, L., & Obasi, E. (2003). Ethical and professional issues in career assessment with diverse racial and ethnic groups. *Journal of Career Assessment* 11, 76–95.

Gay, G. (1985). Implications of selected models of ethnic identity development for educators. *The Journal of Negro Education* 54, 1, 43–55.

Gysbers, N. (2004). *Life career development: A needed perspective for all counseling.* VISTA 2004 (pp 79–87). Alexandria VA: American Counseling Association.

Helms, J. (1994). Racial identity and career assessment. *Journal of Career Assessment* 2, 199–209.

Heppner, M., O'Brien, K., Hinkelman, J., & Humphrey, C. (1994). Shifting the paradigm: The use of creativity in career counseling. *Journal of Career Development* 21, 77–86.

Hulnick, H. R. (1977). Counselor: Know thyself. *Counselor Education & Supervision* 17, 69–72.

Ibrahim, F., Ohnishi, H., & Wilson, R. (1994). Career assessment in a culturally diverse society. *Journal of Career Assessment* 2, 276–288.

Krieshok, T. & Pelsma, D. (2002). The soul of work: Using case studies in the teaching of vocational psychology. *The Counseling Psychologist* 30, 833–845.

Leong, F. & Hartung, P. (1997). Career assessment with culturally different clients: Proposing an integrative-sequential conceptual framework for cross-cultural career counseling research and practice. *Journal of Career Assessment* 5, 183–202.

Leong, F. & Kim, H. (2000). Career-related intercultural sensitizers. In M. Pope & C. Minor (Eds.).Vol. I, *Experiential activities for teaching career counseling classes and for facilitating career groups* (pp. 203–207). Tulsa, Oklahoma: National Career Development Association.

Locke, D. & Parker, L. (1991). A multicultural focus on career education. Information Series No. 348. *ERIC Clearinghouse on Adult, Career, and Vocational Education.* Columbus, Ohio: ERIC Clearinghouse Products.

McGoldrick, M., Giordano, J., & Garcia-Preto, N. (Eds.) (2005). *Ethnicity & family therapy,* 3rd Ed. New York: The Guilford Press.

National Career Development Association (2009). *Minimum competencies for multicultural career counseling and development.* Broken Arrow, OK: Author.

Niles, S., & Gibbs, A. L., Jr. (1991). Cultural changes and career changes: The case of Ebo. *The Career Development Quarterly* 40, 20–23.

Niles, S. & Harris-Bowlsbey, J. (2009). *Career development interventions in the 21st century, 3rd Ed.* Upper Saddle River, NJ: Pearson Publishing.

Ponterotto, J., Rivera, L., & Sueyoshi, L. (2000). The career-in-culture interview: A semi-structured protocol for the cross-cultural intake interview. *The Career Development Quarterly* 49, 85–96.

Sue, D. W., Arredondo, P., & McDavis, R. (1992). Multicultural counseling competencies and standards: A call to the professions. *Journal of Counseling & Development* 70, 477–486.

Trusty, J. (2002) Counseling for career development with persons of color. In S. Niles (Ed.). *Adult career development: Concepts, issues and practices* 3rd ed. (pp. 191–214). Tulsa, Oklahoma: National Career Development Association.

ABOUT THE AUTHOR

Lee Covington Rush, PhD, NCC, is an Assistant Professor in the Department of Counseling, Adult and Higher Education, at Northern Illinois University. He is the supervisor and coordinator of the Career Exploration Program, assisting undergraduate students in their career development, and is the coordinator for Career Counseling Certificate Program. He was previously on the Counseling faculties at North Dakota State University and Wilmington University. He earned the PhD in Counselor Education and Supervision in 2002 at The Ohio State University. His cognate was Life-Span Career Development with an additional specialization in Multicultural Counseling and Diversity. He was employed for twenty years with the New York State Department of Labor as a Job Placement Counselor, and as a Workforce Development and Training Specialist. He participated in the Emerging Leader Training of the American Counseling Association in 2003. In 2003–2004 he received an Outstanding Teacher Award in the College of Human Development and Education at North Dakota State University. He participated in the National Career Development Association's Leadership Academy, Class of 2008–2009. He is a life time member of Chi Sigma Iota: Counseling Academic and Professional Honor Society International. His research interests include career and multicultural counseling interventions. He has presented on both subjects. He has authored one and coauthored another book chapter and has coauthored several journal articles. He served as co-chair 2007–2008, for the Association for Multicultural Counseling and Development's Graduate Student Committee, and he was a National Committee Member in 2003, for Counselors for Social Justice, both American Counseling Association affiliates.

DISCUSSION QUESTIONS

1   What specific skills will counselors need to possess to effectively provide career counseling to diverse populations?

2   Discuss ways in which you feel prepared and not prepared to provide career counseling services to diverse clients.

3   What are some current barriers to providing career counseling to diverse clients?

4   What are some obstacles in your current life that may hinder your work with diverse clients?

CONCLUSION

Providing career counseling to clients from diverse backgrounds will require counselors to expand their worldview and to respect clients and their worldviews. Understanding how culture will play a role in career exploration will need to be a top priority for counselors. The selected readings in this chapter provided an overview of topics related to providing culturally competent career counseling to diverse clients.

INDEX OF KEY TERMS

- culture
- culturally appropriate assessment
- culturally competent counseling
- diversity
- diversity in career counseling
- worldview

SUGGESTED PUBLICATIONS FOR FURTHER READING

Bledsoe, D., & Owens, E. (2014). Multi-cultural issues in career development: Advocacy and social justice. In G. T. Eliason, J. L. Samide, & J. Patrick (Eds.), *Career development across the lifespan: Counseling for community, schools, higher education, and beyond* (pp. 789–811). Charlotte, NC: Information Age.

Pope, M. (2011). The career counseling with underserved populations model. *Journal of Employment Counseling, 48*(4), 153–155.

CHAPTER 6

TECHNOLOGY IN CAREER COUNSELING

INTRODUCTION

Here are some interesting things to consider:

- The World Wide Web has only been available since 1993. Now, nearly four billion people across the world use the Internet—over half of the world's population (Internet World Stats, 2018). Eighty-eight percent of the population of North America are Internet users.
- Wifi (Wireless local area networking) has been available since 1997.
- Amazon.com was founded in 1994.
- eBay launched in 1995.

- Netflix started with DVD sales and rentals in 1997.
- Google was created in 1998.
- Facebook launched in 2004. At the end of 2017, there were 2.2 billion monthly active Facebook users (Statista, 2018).
- LinkedIn was founded in 2002, YouTube started in 2005, Twitter launched in 2006, Instagram was developed in 2010, and Snapchat was created in 2011.

Some of the largest corporations and most important businesses and entertainment industries in our worldwide economy have only been around a short amount of time. The Internet has dramatically changed the career counseling field.

The career counseling field has always focused heavily on information: Career information, occupational information, educational information, labor market information, just to name a few. Prior to the end of the 20th century, career counselors relied on paper copies of information, paper-and-pencil assessments, and printed (book) resources. The *Dictionary of Occupation Titles* (or *DOT*, published by the United States Department of Labor), physically a thick printed resource with multiple volumes, was released periodically and could routinely be found on a career counselor's bookshelf. Once the World Wide Web was available, the *DOT* was rendered obsolete and replaced by an online database referred to as the O*NET (Occupational Information Network). On that same counselor's bookshelf, at the end of the 20th century, you might also find a printed copy of the *Occupational Outlook Handbook (or OOH)*. Although the *OOH* is still released every other year, it can also be found online.

These days, career counselors have much more space on their bookshelves and lots of technology at their fingertips. We've included some articles here to help illustrate how career counselors use technology to provide information, help with decision making, assess career interests or personality, provide educational information and school information, search for jobs, explore careers, network, and the provision of actual counseling services.

Career Development and the Role of Technology as an Agent of Change

JEFF L. SAMIDE, KELSEY BRACKEN, AND JAKE MCELLIGOTT

TECHNOLOGY AND CAREER DEVELOPMENT

Technology means many different things to different people. But over the course of history, it has always been a harbinger of change. The institutions charged with educating the masses are no different in this respect than is business and industry.

When one considers the role of technology in our culture, thoughts move towards devices: smartphones, HDTV, the newest laptops and tablets, high speed Internet access and countless other consumer goods. If we were to ask autoworkers about technology, they might have a similar initial reaction to the word, but they would also likely include concepts such as robotics, less overtime, job layoffs and a shrinking workforce. Like most parts of modern American life, the integration of technology into everyday life has downsides as well as upsides. However, no one can rationally deny the fact that "the times are a changing" and technology is one of the major forces that shapes our everyday lives.

The role of the professional counselor in the twenty-first century continues to grow. The future of our profession can be viewed with great

Jeff L. Samide, Kelsey Bracken, and Jake McElligott, "Career Development and the Role of Technology as an Agent of Change," *Career Counseling Across the Lifespan: Community, School, and Higher Education*, ed. Grafton T. Eliason, Jeff L. Samide, John Patrick, and Trisha Eliason, pp. 295-311. Copyright © 2014 by Information Age Publishing. Reprinted with permission.

optimism and enthusiasm. Counselors are meeting with greater acceptance amongst other professionals and governmental agencies, private businesses, industries and healthcare organizations. Our role in the schools and in our communities at large is perhaps greater than it has ever been in at any time in the past.

Like other professionals, counselor too struggle with the role that technology will play in their professional lives. As Dollarhide and Saginak (2008) stated,

> we can't deny technology's effect on the world, including counselors. Like the autoworker, we appreciate the increased productivity that good technology brings … but many of us fear losing the primary elements that make our profession unique. We struggle to integrate computers and software programs, the Internet and video conferencing into our work—but equally, we seek to maintain the one-on-one intimacy, trust and humanity in all of the interactions with our students.

CAREER DEVELOPMENT IN COUNSELING

The practice of career development in counseling has long been an important part of our profession (Brown, 2007). From its beginnings, career development has been dependent on information. Not only information about careers but also information about the individual's aspirations and aptitudes was critical.

Psychometric testing in the form of career inventories and intelligence tests has long been a staple of the career/vocational counselor (Brown, 2007). Through its use, counselors have been able to determine the interests and aptitudes of their students. And once identified, the student's "search" for a vocation could be narrowed to fit a set of manageable choices.

The interest inventories also served another purpose. They significantly reduced the amount of information a counselor had to present to a student. Since most career awareness information was presented in the form of books, pamphlets and in some cases, filmstrips, films and fieldtrips, it was important that information be managed in a manner that "funneled" clients from a broad variety of choices into more reasonable sets of options as efficiently as possible.

Technology has altered that process in two very crucial ways. First, the advent of computers, robotics, high speed communications, healthcare technology, and many other advances has moved our society to one whose career choices are profoundly variant and complex. Second, technology has altered the very relationship between the counselor and the client. Where counselors once "funneled" clients from numerous career clusters to a specific job within that career, counselors can now utilize technology to "shape" career preferences already formed (through the technology of the Internet and television), through a process that is still well represented by a funnel … but now the funnel is pointed the other way! Instead of hearing the words, "these are your options," today's and tomorrow's career counselor will more likely say, "look at all of the possibilities."

Nonetheless, some counselors might claim that the promise of the twenty-first century has somewhat of a hollow ring. Of course, we use databases to follow our students' progress. We use the Internet in a variety of ways to gather and distribute information. However, overall these authors posit, career counselors tend to perform their duties in a manner that is more similar with the means of the past than the hopes of the future.

However, technology is a tool mankind created to meet a specific need. One might believe that the effectiveness of a given tool determines if its use continues or if it is discarded. However, tools, like people, interact with their environment and evolve. Sometimes the evolution, in effect, completely leaves its initial purpose behind. The profoundly creative process of a human being interacting with a tool within his or her environment over time determines the ultimate effect a tool has on its environment and its overall worth to the user. Such a process occurs today in career counseling, as counselors seek to integrate technology into their work—to the benefit of all.

Computers, the internet, and high-speed telecommunications are still relatively young. In fact, the personal computer has been a staple in schools and homes for little longer than about twenty years. The evolutionary process between these technologies of progress and career counseling is even younger. In due time, the technology will do for career counseling what it has done for many other professions: it will greatly enhance our effectiveness while providing an almost limitless capacity for exploration and growth.

The purpose of this chapter is to describe the evolutionary processes that are in play today in career counseling and to illustrate the role that technology has in shaping career awareness and career choice in students both at home and in the schools. In doing so, one comes to understand that career awareness and choice are shaped by technology early on and throughout our students' educational experience. Historically, television, career-assisted career guidance systems (CACGS), Web-based software such as DISCOVER and Choices, the Internet on its own merit, and many other resources all played and continue to play an important role in the evolution of technology in career development. Together, they continue to broaden options and choices in a very efficient manner that preserves and individualizes a student's decision-making process in ways hardly imagined twenty years ago.

TECHNOLOGY AND CHOICE AWARENESS IN SMALL CHILDREN

It is no more evident that technology has played a large role in developing career awareness than it is in young children. Marland (1974) described career awareness as being in evidence when a child has recognition of the broad spectrum of careers open to an individual. Children are in many ways a blank slate awaiting such awareness.

When we ask young children, "what they want to be when they grow up," they invariably respond in a manner that is reflective of their environment and their experiences. A child who has had opportunities to see doctors and nurses perform their duties (and has had a positive experience) might well suggest that they would like to become a physician or a nurse. Children whose parent is a soldier or a law enforcement officer might tend to gravitate towards favoring those types of jobs. It is safe to state that the child's perspective of his or her world is a significant determinant of the type of "job fantasies" he or she will gravitate towards early on. As a child's world expands with his or her years, job choices expand as well.

The technology of television has greatly expanded and broadened the world of young children. Turn on a television to children's programming today, and we are likely to see naturalists interacting with playful chimpanzees, swimming with dolphins, gently handling exotic poisonous snakes or following the icy tracks of polar bears in the arctic. Equally, children can view astronauts performing intricate and exciting spacewalks high above the earth or learn how radio telescopes study stars thousands of light years away. It is no wonder that many children in kindergarten today want to become veterinarians, marine biologists, astronauts, astronomers, and zookeepers. Unlike earlier generations of the 70s and 80s, the youngster of the twenty-first century lives in a world that encompasses everything from the micro-biologic to the black holes of deep space ... much to the credit of television. Public television in particular has played an important role in expanding the world of young children.

While it can be argued that such activities are outside of the officially sanctioned curriculum of the schools, their effects on children and on the counselors who work with them cannot be ignored. The curiosity and enhanced awareness of the world that results from television and the mass media significantly contribute to children's readiness to effectively and energetically immerse themselves into the activities of career counseling.

The dividends derived from a greater awareness of the world of work also pushes the career counselor to expand their repertoire of techniques and activities to meet and exceed that which the students of today can access themselves via television or the almost ubiquitous home computer. Without such continued development, career counselors would run the very real risk of becoming redundant—or even worse—irrelevant to the leisure-time activities of watching television or "surfing" the World Wide Web.

PUBLIC TELEVISION

One of the most powerful forces for the enhancement of early childhood and primary school age learning, (including career awareness), had its beginnings through an act of the United States Congress in the 1960s. That year marked the passing and the federal funding of The Public Broadcasting Act of 1967. The act declared that, "it is in the public interest to encourage the growth and development of public radio and television broadcasting, including the use of such media for instructional, educational, and cultural purposes." It also specifically stated, "it is in the public interest to encourage the development of programming that involves creative risks and that addresses the needs of unserved and underserved audiences, particularly children and minorities."(Public Broadcasting Act of 1967, 1967)

The act created the non-profit Corporation for Public Broadcasting. It sponsored two major arms, National Public Radio and The Public Broadcasting System (PBS). PBS is owned by its affiliates who pay licensing fees to air PBS programming. These educational licensees numbered 169 in 2005. (PBS 2005 Financial Report, 2007) Together they operate 354 PBS member stations, nationwide. Typically, licensees are non-profit organizations themselves, frequently owned by institutions of higher education, community organizations and municipalities. (About PBS.org.)

CHILDREN'S PROGRAMMING AND CAREER DEVELOPMENT

Today, PBS is a major source of young children's programming. Career education activities on PBS, while many are not so named, vary from introducing children to the world of work to developing good work habits. Overall, PBS sponsored children's programming and other commercial programming, routinely highlight the essential role that work plays in a healthy, adaptive, and productive community.

For instance, the long running PBS television show, *Mister Roger's Neighborhood*, features a segment entitled, *Appreciating the World*. In a quiet and slow-paced manner that characterizes the entire show, Mister Roger's Neighborhood has introduced younger children to activities as diverse as making crayons to creating music. Such video tours of workplaces and factories "help children value work and know that things are made through a process with a beginning, middle, and end. With the focus on people, children gain an understanding of work and an appreciation for the work that people do." (Mister Roger's Neighborhood, Appreciating the world, 2007)

Over the course of 45 years and hundreds of episodes, Mister Roger's Neighborhood has focused on weekly themes that assist young children in a variety of career-related areas, covering a wide range of topics such as:

- Helping children to develop self-discipline
- Developing creativity
- Accepting and expecting mistakes
- Parents who work
- Feelings about work, money and choices
- When things get broken (Mister Roger's Neighborhood, Weekly Themes, 2001)

Through such programming, television is able to take young children into actual workplaces and show work processes in an engaging manner that can be geared to a young child's interests and intellectual capabilities.

Another popular children's show of more recent origin, challenges children aged five through eleven to "turn off the TV and do it!" (Zoom, 2005) *Zoom* has a strong focus on science and engineering. The show features bright and energetic children-hosts performing a wide variety of fun yet educational activities and experiments. Good work habits such as talking through construction problems, cooperating with and valuing the ideas of others, and making choices based on reason—instead of impulse—are in abundant evidence.

Zoom regularly features the emails and letters from its audience. The content of these letters are generally comments on favorite parts of the show, suggestions for other activities and descriptions of the audience member's experiences. All of this interaction, either via "snail mail" or cyber, tends to involve the youthful audience more and assist them in feeling as though they too play an important role in the show.

Many adults grew up with the admonishment from their parents that "cartoons will rot your brain." Animation has come a long way from being only entertainment. The animated series, *Magic School Bus,* (Magic School Bus, 2012) features a group of school-aged children and their teacher, Ms. Frizzle. This fast-paced show mixes solid scientific facts with adventure and fantasy. Together with a school bus that flies, swims, shrinks and seemingly thinks, the students and their teacher explore the worlds of physics, biology, earth science, engineering and more (Magic School Bus, Theme index, 2012).

As an example, one episode features the transformation of the bus into a "Weathermobile." The episode discusses the science of meteorology and gives one of the cartoon characters the opportunity to become the "meteorological hero of his dreams" (Magic School Bus, Kicks up a storm, 2012). The science of meteorology is presented in an easy to understand manner along with rudimentary concepts of how weather is created.

In addition to these examples of shows that have been around for years, there have been recent developments in career exploration for children on television programming. For example, SciGirls and Design Squad focus on adolescents that are facing the new challenges that come when entering high school. Descriptions from the PBS Kids website include

SCIGIRLS

The bold goal of SciGirls is to change how millions of girls think about science, technology, engineering, and math—a.k.a. STEM. Research shows that, for a variety of reasons, some girls begin to lose interest (and confidence in their abilities) in math and science in middle school. SciGirls engages girls between 8 and 13 years old, helping them through these challenging tween years to arrive in high school with a positive attitude toward STEM and STEM careers (PBS Kids, 2013).

DESIGN SQUAD

Design Squad is a reality competition series where eight teenagers learn to think smart, build fast, and contend with a wild array of engineering challenges. With Design Squad Nation, engineer co-hosts Judy and Adam travel across the country, working side by side with kids and using engineering to turn kids' dreams into reality (PBS Kids, 2013).

REAL LIFE 101

This 30 minute program is geared to the middle school and high school student. It features in-depth looks at a wide range of careers that sometimes are overlooked by other career resources. A viewer might encounter episodes that feature nurse anesthetists, career counselors, attorneys, occupational therapists and much more. (The Television Syndication Company, 2013)

COMPLEMENTARY WEBSITES

Much of children's television programming is further enhanced by complementary websites. These sites offer opportunities for children to explore topics more deeply, to link to other similar subjects or interests, or to conveniently communicate via email with the programming staff and/or hosts. The marriage of television to webpages on the Internet allows a child to examine a career option, its educational requirements, salary expectations, job tasks, related fields, and other issues immediately and in-depth. Moreover, with the growing computer proficiency and accessibility among children at home and at school, the door to deeper understanding is almost always open.

A second important feature of these complementary websites is that they all provide links to information for both parents and teachers. In them, teachers can find written resources, ready-made lesson plans, alternative activities, and other materials that could bring children's television programming alive in their classroom, equally, parents can find games, books, video resources, homework help, and more. Through these sites, parents can take an active role in educating their children about the world of work and the role it plays in the lives of their family and their community … well beyond acting only as a role model for the type of work that they perform.

As television evolved into a potent force that educated as well as entertained, the use of computers in the schools was initiating its evolutionary process in the 80s. From its beginnings as disconnected PC's running pricy career development software, to the wide-open Internet as it is today, the computer stands as an essential tool for career counselors with a potential not yet near its zenith.

1980S & 1990S

Technology first impacted school counseling, as it did most school functions, in the 1980s. It was not, however, altogether paradigm-shifting. In a way, it was just a replacement for the paper-and-pencil processes and the booklets/binders of a counseling office. As Herr, Cramer and Niles (2004) point out, in the 1960s and 1970s it was anticipated that computer technology would revolutionize career and vocational counseling, a revolution that has yet to take place or, at best, is only now in its infancy decades later. While a notion of computers and technology impacting career development had been prevalent for decades, only in the 1980s did career-assisted career guidance systems

(CACGS) emerge as a broadly adopted tool in career and vocational counseling (Katz & Shatkin, 1983).

A comprehensiveness in career development services that had been difficult, if not impossible, before CACGS software such as DISCOVER and the System of Interactive Guidance and Information (SIGI) now allowed for integrated career development functionality. Whether the software was geared toward information gathering and sorting or was geared toward career development processes, the goal was the same: harnessing technology to provide deeper, more wide-ranging, and consistent career development services in the schools. Throughout the 1980s and 1990s the number of CACGS increased in number and sophistication to the point where, even today, there are a range of choices for school counselors looking for a CACGS (Brown, 2003). Indeed, the substantive use of computer technology in school counseling, aside from merely administrative use, was spearheaded by career development software (Hardesty & Utesch, 1994).

Adoption was slow at first, which was as much a function of school district resources as it was school counselor attitudes toward the new technology (Gerler, 1995; Harris-Bowlsbey, 1990). Casey (1995) modified Rogers' (1983) model to describe the adoption of innovative strategies and applied it to the adoption of technology by school counselors, finding that a few school counselors were true innovators or early adopters. Indeed, the Rogers' model posits that the intermediate stage (mass acceptance) requires adoption by 80% or more of users. While data on the adoption, particularly, of technology geared specifically to career development is not available, one can posit that it was well into the 1980s and perhaps even the mid-1990s before CACGS software had reached the level of mass adoption. For example, in Moore's study (1992), only 30% of his sample reported using computers in their school counseling duties. Even by the end of the 1990s, Trilling and Hood (1999) found a particular resistance by school counselors to fully embrace technology and its uses.

This slow diffusion and acceptance of technology in school counseling, even with software as accessible and comprehensive as CACGS, is reinforced by the sense that technology was many times viewed only as something to assist with administrative tasks (communication, collaboration, presentation) rather than any substantive application (Bowers, 2002; Coy & Minor, 1997; Van Horn & Myrick, 2001). In Williams' and Buboltz's (1999) content analysis of the *Journal of Counseling & Development* over the period 1988–1996, a period at the heart of the adoption and maturation of technology like CACGS in school settings, full-length articles with abstracts addressing the topic of Technology & Media represented only 0.81% of the total topics identified (8 topic identifications out of a total of 991). Perhaps it is unfair to view technology retrospectively in this way. In a sense, events were unfolding rapidly and dramatically, and it may be viewed as unfair to use words such as "slow" and "resistance." Yet those events unfolded over roughly two decades, a time span that would allow even laggard adopters (in Rogers' terminology) to embrace technology.

Regardless, the rate of adoption of software such as CACGS, among software geared to other areas of substantive school counseling, over these decades did not fundamentally alter the provision of career development services out of the school counseling office. *How* a school counselor provided career and vocational guidance had changed, but the *'what'* remained the same. In short, CACGS and technology were a better way to do the same old thing. In doing this, it served its purpose. It was the necessary pivot toward an entirely new technological advance: the internet. It is the internet era of school counseling, an era just maturing, that may fundamentally alter substantive career development approaches in school counseling (D'Andrea, 1995; Elias, Hoover, & Poedubicky 1997; Glover, 1995; Shulman, 1995).

CAREER COUNSELING AND THE INTERNET

A proliferation of Web-based career tools has closely followed the dramatic increase of computer-competent teens. As teens became increasingly sophisticated in their understanding and more comfortable in its use, the "web" opened doors to a world that paradoxically became larger and smaller at the same time. Among the leaders in Web-based career exploration programming is DISCOVER and Choices.

DISCOVER

DISCOVER is a web-based application that is used in middle schools, high schools and university settings throughout the nation (Act, 2007). Like many websites, it is password protected, requiring the sponsorship of a subscribing organization or school. Once admitted, it offers the student a plethora of information. It focuses on three interrelated tasks. They are: know yourself, explore options & choose direction, and make plans & take action. The initial screen is fresh and welcoming with colorful graphics and smiling faces. Along the top of the screen are the following options:

- Home
- Inventories
- Occupations

- Majors
- Schools
- Job search
- My portfolio (ACT, homepage, 2007)

DISCOVER seeks to broadly engage a student in exploring their values, attitudes, likes, dislikes and strengths, rather than simply provide a listing and descriptions of potential occupations. The pacing through the program is logical and reinforces a process that is thorough.

The following is a brief description of the content as viewed by a student exploring the site:

INVENTORIES (ACT, INVENTORIES, 2007)

Interests, abilities and values are each assessed through interactive inventories that are engaging, of relatively short duration, and many times accompanied with colorful content-supporting graphics. The immediacy of the results, (the click of a button), is a motivator to continue with the inventory process. The final step of the inventory process labeled *inventories summary* pulls together all of the parts of the evaluative process and provides relatively succinct yet valuable insight into the likes and dislikes of the student's interests, abilities, and values.

OCCUPATIONS AND MAJORS (ACT, OCCUPATIONS, 2007)

These menu items represent much more than a listing of occupations. They use a variety of sort techniques to stimulate curiosity. For instance, a student can search through an alphabetical listing of colleges and majors by keywords, through college majors, according to a world of work map, by a listing of "hot" occupations, by military specialties, and more. The site "tags" the student's career choices that coincide with interests earlier identified in the inventory section of the site.

SCHOOLS (ACT, SCHOOLS, 2007)

This menu item contains a comprehensive listing of schools throughout the nations. Students can explore the many institutions by sorting according to regions, degrees offered, keywords, college majors, scholarships or aid offered, and more. An even more fascinating aspect of this menu item is contained in the *search by characteristics* area. In it, a student is able to choose an assortment of school characteristics such as costs, special programs, or services for students with disabilities.

After a student chooses their preferred characteristics, a sub-menu then offers a check list of relevant subtopics. For instance, a student seeking a school that had a strong sports program would choose their preferred sports. After choosing their favorites, the site would take these preferences and match them up with all of the other vital characteristics chosen and present the student with schools that matched the chosen criteria as closely as the student's choices permitted.

JOB SEARCH (ACT, JOB SEARCH, 2007)

This feature assists the student in writing resumes and cover letters, preparing for job interviews, and finding resources that identify job openings. Additionally, it assists students in identifying jobs that accept apprenticeships and internships. As in the other menu selections, it highlights favorites from other areas of the website so that students can readily focus on jobs that match their strengths, likes, and values.

MY PORTFOLIO (ACT, MY PORTFOLIO, 2007)

This is a storage site where students can work on creating resumes, review career inventory results, identify preferences in potential majors, and more. An interesting aspect of this tab is the *Chosen Path* sub-menu. It provides structure to individuals who might not have used the site in a systematic fashion and therefore missed important activities. It describes the steps to take to successfully accomplish career choice tasks and also importantly lists the many questions that might be answered if the student accomplishes each task.

CHOICES

Choices, by Bridges Transitions Inc., is organized similarly. It consists of an extensive database that is organized around three concepts … exploring careers, planning your future, and college & post secondary (Bridges, Student homepage, 2007).

Under the *Exploring Careers* menu (Bridges, Exploring, 2007) students will find numerous choices. There is a *Career Finder* that matches important job characteristics such as education level, earnings, jobs outlook, work conditions and more to the student's preferences. As the student selects more job characteristics, the webpage selects careers and specific types of jobs that match their preferences. As with anyone who has used an online search engine, a student who uses Career Finder will discover that very specific career needs will result in less choices regarding career opportunities.

The *Interest Profiler* and the *Career Quiz* are inventories that break down students' top interests and categorize their personal characteristics into easy to understand descriptors that include categories such as: Realistic, Investigative, Artistic, Conventional, Enterprising and Social. After the student chooses their preferred categories, a data base of occupations is presented, followed by detailed descriptions of each potential career.

Do What You Are matches personality traits to the individual in order to assist the student in matching their unique qualities and strengths to specific occupations and occupational categories. Also included in the webpage is a wide variety of links to short, engaging articles of interest to students involved in career activities. Examples of such linked topics include: Do You Need A Degree to See the Money? Internships: Are They Worth It? Gain Job Skills By Volunteering, and much more. The webpage also deals with important "how to" topics such as starting a business and describing the process of arranging a shadowing experience.

Under the menu tab Planning your Future (Bridges, Planning, 2007) students can find help with choosing schools through the identification of preferred school characteristics. Other links provide concrete information on planning high school coursework so that it better meets the student's future career paths. A large number of informational links categorized under the topics of Career Planning, Educational Planning, and Career and Training Alternatives provides easy to understand information that is essential to making good educational and career choices. An activity entitled "What I Have To Offer" assists students in identifying the skills, credentials, and social and business connections needed to gain employment in chosen careers.

Finally, under the College and Post Secondary menu, (Bridges, College and post secondary, 2007) there is assistance in choosing a college program that matches the student's needs, a financial aid overview, and an introduction to scholarships and tips on the college application process. Informational links categorized under the headings, College Planning, Preparing and Applying for College, and Paying for College also provides timely and important information. Information on budgeting, planning for unexpected expenses and other information "brings home" the realities of paying for a college and post secondary education.

Unlike DISCOVER and Choices, Education Planner provides information to students, parents, and counselors at no cost. The state of Pennsylvania provides the website 'Education Planner' for students of Pennsylvania at no cost. Students are encouraged to access this website when looking to clarify what major they would like to pursue, what school they would like to attend, and also to gather information about scholarships and FAFSA.

Information for Students—Under the *Students* tab (Pennsylvania Higher Education Assistance Agency, 2011), there are five subsections. Each subsection helps the student realistically look at their future. Information about career planning, preparing and paying for school, and self-assessments are provided for the student to analyze what kind of future they are looking for, as well as what they can achieve. In addition, there is a section that allows students to "Ask a Counselor" if there is a topic of interest that has not been answered in any of the other sections.

INFORMATION FOR PARENTS

The *Parents* tab (Pennsylvania Higher Education Assistance Agency, 2011) of the website has more information regarding the cost of college. There is also a section that describes the SATs and ACTs and what they mean for students who are applying to college. Under this tab, there are also pointers and goals for searching for scholarships, as well as information about filling out the FAFSA.

INFORMATION FOR COUNSELORS

The *Counselors'* tab (Pennsylvania Higher Education Assistance Agency, 2011) may be the most use in a school setting. Education Planner provides counselors information about how to use the website with students during school hours. There is a computer lab activity, information on how to set up a Job Shadowing event, as well as setting up a career fair in the school. All of this information is neatly organized for everyone to view. It is easy to access and very informative for everyone involved in the career and college process.

The above listed websites are just a few examples and it is not our intention to exclude any other valuable programs. Due to limits on space, we chose these general examples in the field of technology.

SUMMARY

If the past is an indication of the evolutionary potential of technology as it applies to career development, the future is bright. As it is currently being utilized, Web-based career tools provide a highly interactive, informative, entertaining, and most important, enriching experience to students. There is little doubt that "tech savvy" students naturally look to the World Wide Web for much of the information they use to gain a perspective on the world. The melding of the web with the natural inquisitiveness of youthfulness creates an environment where Websites are a vehicle that first broadens, focuses, and directs students into career choices that are thoughtful, meaningful, and ultimately fulfilling.

While the evolution of technology certainly can change the interactions of counselors and students, these authors believe that the change is good and beneficial to both parties. The counselor has the means to provide extensive information, support, and encouragement with a minimum of "busy work" to a student who is better prepared and more knowledgeable about the world of work. Students are immersed into a process that they can take charge of and direct their learning to better meet their needs. Most important, the technology of career development, as it has done for many disciplines, removes the mundane and time-consuming aspects of career education from the client-counselor relationship so that the participants can interact at a level that characterizes our discipline and continues to be the humanistic hallmark of our profession.

KEY WORDS

eDiscover: An online website that provides information and guidance to help students make career and education decisions.

Choices: An online website that helps students explore career and educational options and track their progress as they create successful plans.

Real Life 101: An innovative television program available nationally that assists children and teens in career awareness. It also has an accompanying website that provides students with a variety of career development tools.

STEM: An interdisciplinary approach to learning which focuses on the four key areas of Science, Technology, Engineering and Math.

FAFSA (Free Application for Federal Student Aid): An online form that can be prepared annually by current and prospective college students to determine ability to receive federal aid for continuing education.

REFERENCES

ACT, Inc. (2007). *DISCOVER. Homepage.* Web-based computer guidance system. Retrieved December 13, 2007 from https://actapps.act.org/eDISCOVER/Index.jsp

ACT, Inc. (2007). *DISCOVER. Internet Version. Occupations.* Web-based computer guidance system. Retrieved December 13, 2007 from https://actapps.act.org/eDISCOVER/Index.jsp

ACT, Inc. (2007). *DISCOVER. Internet Version. Majors.* Web-based computer guidance system. Retrieved December 13, 2007 from https://actapps.act.org/eDISCOVER/Index.jsp

ACT, Inc. (2007). *DISCOVER. Internet Version. Schools.* Web-based computer guidance system. Retrieved December 13, 2007 fromhttps://actapps.act.org/eDISCOVER/Index.jsp

ACT, Inc. (2007). *DISCOVER., Internet Version. Job Search.* Web-based computer guidance system. Retrieved December 13, 2007 from https://actapps.act.org/eDISCOVER/Index.jsp

ACT, Inc. (2007). *DISCOVER. Internet Version. My Portfolio.* Web-based computer guidance system. Retrieved December 13, 2007 from https://actapps.act. org/eDISCOVER/Index.jsp

Bowers, J. (2002). Using technology to support comprehensive guidance program operations: a variety of strategies. In P. Henderson & N. Gysbers (Eds.), *Implementing comprehensive school guidance programs: Critical leadership issues and successful responses* (pp. 115–120). Greensboro, NC: CAPS Publications.

Bridges Transitions Inc. (2007). *Choices Planner. Student Homepage.* Retrieved December 10, 2007 from Bridges Web site: https://access.bridges.com/portal/student/landingPage.do

Bridges Transitions Inc. (2007). *Exploring Careers.* Retrieved December 10, 2007 from Bridges Web site: https://access.bridges.com/portal/student/topic/exploringCareers

Bridges Transitions Inc. (2007). *Planning Your Future.* Retrieved December 11, 2007 from Bridges Web site: https://access.bridges.com/portal/student/topic/planningyourfuture

Bridges Transitions Inc. (2007). *College and Post Secondary.* Retrieved December 11, 2007 from Bridges Web site: https://access.bridges.com/portal/student/topic/collegePostsecondary

Brown, D. (2003). *Career information, career counseling, and career development* (8th ed.). Boston: Allyn & Bacon.

Brown, D. (2007). *Career information, career counseling, and career development* (9th ed.). Boston: Allyn & Bacon.

Buboltz, W. C., Miller, M., & Williams, D. J. (1999). Content analysis of research in the *Journal of Counseling Psychology* (1973–1988). *Journal of Counseling Psychology, 46,* 496–503.

Casey, J. (1995). Developmental issues for school counselors using technology. *Elementary School Guidance & Counseling, 30,* 26–34.

Corporation for Public Broadcasting. (2007). Public Broadcasting Act of 1967, as *Amended.* Retrieved December 10, 2007 from http://www.cpb.org/aboutpb/act/text.html

Coy, D., & Minor, C. (1997). Technology and the school counselor. In B. Evraiff & L. Evraiff (Eds.) *Caring in an age of technology: Proceedings of the international conference of counseling in the 21st century, 6.* Beijing: Publisher.

D'Andrea, M. (1995). Using computer technology to promote multicultural awareness among elementary school-age students. *Elementary School Guidance & Counseling, 30,* 45–54.

Dollarhide, C. T., & Saginak, K. A. (2008). *Comprehensive school counseling programs.* Boston MA: Pearson Education Inc. 290.

Elias, M. J., Hoover, H. V. A., & Poedubicky, V. (1997). Computer-facilitated counseling for at risk students in a social problem solving "lab". *Elementary School Guidance & Counseling, 31,* 293–310.

Gerler, E. R. (1995). Advancing elementary and middle school counseling through computer technology. *Elementary School Guidance and Counseling, 30,* 8–15.

Glover, B. L. (1995). DINOS (Drinking is not our solution): Using computer programs in middle school drug education. *Elementary School Guidance & Counseling, 30,* 55–62.

Hardesty, G., & Utesch, W. E. (1994). Counselors and computers: A survey of compatibility and use. *Reports-Research, 143,* 16.

Harris-Bowlsbey, J. (1990). Role of the counselor with computers. In E. R. Gerler, J. C. Ciechalski, & L. D. Parker (Eds.), *Elementary school counseling in a changing world* (pp. 207–217). Ann Arbor, MI: American School Counselor Association.

Herr, E. L., Cramer, S. H., & Niles, S. G. (2004). *Career guidance and counseling through the lifespan* (6th ed.). Boston, MA: Allyn and Bacon.

Katz, M. R., & Shatkin, L. (1983). Characteristics of computer-assisted guidance. The *Counseling Psychologist, 11,* 15–31.

Marland, S. P. (1974). *Career education* (p. 100). New York: McGraw-Hill.

PBS. (2007). *PBS Financial Report 2005.* Retrieved December 10, 2007 from http://www.pbs.org/aboutpbs/content/annualreport/2005/PBSCFS0504.pdf

PBS. (2007). *About PBS.* Retrieved December 13, 2007 from http://www.pbs.org/aboutpbs/

Moore, R. L. (1992). Computer applications by Arkansas school counselors in conducting K-12 guidance and counseling programs. *Dissertation Abstracts International, 52,* 2824 (UMI No. 9204727).

PBS Kids. (2007). *Mister Rogers Neighborhood. Appreciating the World.* Retrieved December 12, 2007 from http://pbskids.org/rogers/parentsteachers/series/summary.html

PBS Kids. (2007). *Mister Rogers Neighborhood. Weekly Themes.* Retrieved December 12, 2007 from http://pbskids.org/rogers/parentsteachers/theme/

PBS Kids. (2007) *Zoom.* Retrieved December 13, 2007 from http://pbskids.org/zoom/

Scholastic Kids. (2006). Magic *School Bus. Theme Index.* Retrieved December 28, 2006 from http://www.scholastic.com/magicschoolbus/theme/index.htm

PBS Teachers (2013). Engineer with Design Squad. Retrieved April 3, 2013 from http://www.pbs.org/teachers/designsquad/

PBS Teachers (2013). SciGirls: Educational philosophy. Retrieved April 3, 2013 from http://www.pbs.org/teachers/scigirls/philosophy/

Pennsylvania Higher Education Assistance Agency. (2011). Education Planner. *Counselor Homepage.* Retrieved April 3, 2013 from http://www.educationplanner.org/counselors/index.shtml

Pennsylvania Higher Education Assistance Agency. (2011). Education Planner. *Parent Homepage.* Retrieved April 3, 2013 from http://www.educationplanner. org/students/index.shtml

Pennsylvania Higher Education Assistance Agency. (2011). Education Planner. *Student Homepage.* Retrieved April 3, 2013 from http://www.educationplanner. org/parents/index.shtml

Rogers, E. (1983). *Diffusion of innovation.* New York: Macmillan.

Scholastic Kids. (2012). Magic *School Bus. Kicks Up A Storm.* Retrieved January 28, 2012 from http://www.scholastic.com/magicschoolbus/tv/episodes/kicks_ up_a_storm.htm

Scholastic Kids. (2012). Magic *School Bus. Homepage.* December 28, 2012 from http://www.scholastic.com/magicschoolbus/home_2.htm

Shulman, H.A. (1995). A computer-assisted approach to preventing alcohol abuse: Implications for the middle school. *Elementary School Guidance & Counseling, 30,* 63–77.

The Television Syndication Company. (2013). *Real Life 101.* Retrieved February 16, 2013 from http://www.rl101.com/

Trilling, B., & Hood, P. (1999). Learning, technology, and education reform in the knowledge age or "we're wired, webbed, and windowed, now what?" *Educational Technology, 39,* 5–18.

Van Horn, S., & Myrick, R. (2001). Computer technology and the 21st century school counselor. *Professional School Counseling, 5,* 124–131.

Linking Career and Mental Health Concerns through Technology

DEBRA S. OSBORN, JACQUELINE BELLE, AUSTIN GONZALEZ, AND SHAE C. MCCAIN

INTRODUCTION

Career decision-making is a complex process that often times is accompanied by mental health concerns (Betz & Corning, 1993; Krumboltz, 1993; Walker & Peterson, 2012; Zunker 2008). For example, long-term unemployment is often accompanied by depression (Rottinghaus, Jenkins, & Jantzer, 2009; Saunders et al. 2000; Walker III, & Peterson, 2012), and anxiety (Gati, Asulin-Peretz, & Fisher, 2012; Nauta, 2012; Saka & Gati, 2007). In addition, negative or dysfunctional career thinking has repeatedly been shown to predict career indecision (Bullock-Yowell, Peterson, Reardon, Leierer, & Reed, 2011; Saunders, Peterson, Sampson, & Reardon, 2000). Interventions to address these concerns often involves cognitive restructuring (Sampson, Peterson, Lenz, Reardon, & Saunders, 1996), which often occurs within face-to-face sessions with a client. However, today's technologies offer career practitioners unique tools to address these concerns both within and outside of the traditional office setting. In the sections that follow, we offer practical suggestions on how to transform traditional tools via technology, using online applications (apps) to strengthen the link between career and mental health, and how to take advantage of social media to address this connection.

Debra S. Osborn, Jacqueline Belle, Austin Gonzalez, and Shae C. McCain, "Linking Career and Mental Health Concerns Through Technology," *Career Planning and Adult Development Journal*, vol. 32, no. 1, pp. 151-160. Copyright © 2016 by Career Planning and Adult Development Network. Reprinted with permission. Provided by ProQuest LLC. All rights reserved.

TRANSFORMING TRADITIONAL TOOLS

The fields of mental health and career counseling are constantly changing with the additions and innovations regarding technological advancements (Osborn, Dikel, & Sampson, 2011). In 2000, the National Career Development Association (NCDA) and the Association for Counselor Educators and Supervision (ACES) emphasized the need for counseling students to know not only about existing technologies, but how to integrate them into career service delivery. As such, career practitioners are being required to attain competence with the new technologies available to them while also being able to display their competence in a counseling setting. Although much of the focus resides on new technological advancements, it is of the authors' opinions that career counselors should strike a balance between being technologically savvy and preserving client welfare with regards to incorporating technology into their practice. While maintaining an open mind towards new technologies is recommended, it is also essential for practitioners to consider more traditional technologies and their practical capabilities for counseling purposes.

Utilizing traditional tools such as a video camera can be truly beneficial in a counseling setting. Video recording capabilities are now readily available in many formats such as phones, tablets, and traditional video recorders, and as such are commonly accessible by a wide audience. Transforming the traditional tool of a video camera to be utilized in the creation of video diaries has been successful when attempting to discover more of a client's life outside the counseling session and identifying a client's thoughts, feelings, and personal experiences (Iivari, Kinnula, Kuure, & Molin-Juustila, 2014). Utilizing an even simpler tool, an ordinary camera, could also provide alternative methods to traditional counseling interventions. A counselor often provides homework or activities in session which involve creating art of some kind, such as a collage or a genogram. Encouraging a client to create the assignment and capturing that product with a camera's photograph creates a visual that can be referred to in later sessions.

The simple tool of a camera or video camera can revolutionize, expand and enhance the clinical benefits of completing diaries in a career counseling setting. A traditional career counseling role-play could include performing a mock interview or elevator speech, with the counselor providing a situation in which the client and counselor will role-play together. Afterwards the counselor and client will review their thoughts and feelings on their memories of the role play. By using a video camera to record the session, counselors and clients can instantly review the video recorded role-play in session, even stopping it at certain points, and identify positive aspects of the session as well as areas for improvement. A career counselor can now focus more attention on the role play itself and be "more in the moment" and spend less time making mental notes of points to discuss after the role play. Video cameras can also provide opportunities for clients to record video statements for themselves, such as positive statements about themselves (such as, "I can make effective decisions," or "Remember when you get tongue-tied to slow down and monitor your breathing. You are in control."), remind themselves of previous commitments ("I can do this. I told myself to apply to three jobs today."). Another option would be for the counselor to record instructions on activities such as relaxation techniques and deep breathing exercises, how to access career information and monitor negative self-talk (e.g., "So here you can see the description of the occupation—remember you're not going to eliminate the option until you read about the job tasks, salary, and education or training requirements.") These in-session experiences can then be shared with the client electronically for review and further practice. These are a few of the many ways to address and integrate career and mental health concerns utilize a technology tool that is more commonplace today.

Note-taking during sessions is a common practice of career practitioners. These notes may be of words that a counselor hears the client repeating, a resource that the counselor thinks of while the client is sharing, follow up questions the counselor may want to ask, or specific questions a client wants addressed. Applying note-taking technology, such as Livescribe Smartpens, can significantly impact a practitioner's counseling. The use of a Smartpen allows a counselor to automatically and wirelessly transfer notes written in a session to a device such as a tablet or computer, thus collecting notes electronically. This allows session notes to be included in the modern process of maintaining electronic medical records. In addition to taking client notes, a practitioner could use this when co-creating an intervention plan with a client. Livescribe Smartpens can also record the audio of a counseling session and synchronize the notes with the audio of the session. Career and mental health practitioners no longer need to hurriedly write notes in a session, but instead write a single word during the session and replay the audio at a later time. Or, as a client is sharing career beliefs, the counselor can make note of accompanying emotions or non-verbal expressions the client is indicating. Or, if a counselor makes use of diagrams or models to explain career and mental health connections (e.g., how negative career thoughts impact other areas of career decision making), the client could draw arrows demonstrating that connection while describing it for future reference. Another option would be for the career practitioner, especially those in training, to write down a symbol or a word for when they feel stuck in a session. During supervision, this would allow them to pinpoint the exact moment in the dialogue where this occurred. Clients can also utilize these tools in or out of session, as they can write their goals or ideas along with their own voice recordings. Smartpens allow both the client and the counselor to enhance their contributions to the session in order to maximize their time and efforts.

Hipaachat is another tool which transforms the constant need for co-worker communication into a modern technological success. This tool utilizes basic messaging and video-communicating technology but provides safe, secure, and confidential protection. Hippachat is a mobile tool that allows practitioners to send typed or audio recorded messages, and also allows the practitioner to send attachments (such as photos and videos), thus providing a simpler and safer method of communicating confidential information. This software can assist with providing mobile consults, supervisions, and group communicating, all while maintaining compliance with the federal Health Insurance Portability and Accountability Act (HIPPA) compliance. VSee is a similar online chat tool that claims HIPPA compliancy.

Career practitioners might also use automatic reminder systems to inform clients of upcoming sessions, relevant workshops, unexpected cancellations, and so forth. As email becomes less popular with the current generation, finding a non-intrusive way to share these reminders that works with the technology of today's client is necessary. Secure text messaging is one such means. TigerText is an example of such a system, in which the sender's phone number is obscured and a return option is not allowed (i.e., individuals cannot reply to the text that is send). In addition, it is possible to restrict the message from being copied and forwarded. The messages are encrypted and will disappear or "self-destruct after a period of time sent by the sender." Another example used by teachers to reach a group of students at one time is remind101. Any type of reminder is possible, including an encouragement to keep working on goals, or a client-developed mantra for the week such as "I can make effective career decisions" or "I am a worthwhile person." The career practitioner should consult with the client on if and how often they would like to receive such messages.

Technology also provides organizational options for client information. Over the course of a few sessions, a career practitioner may have provided multiple resources such as decision-making guides, career information, resume critique, a plan for addressing multiple questions, stress-busters, links and contact information specific to a clients' needs. If hard copies are given out at each session, there is the risk of that information being lost. Similarly, if information is sent via email, a client might need to search through several emails to access the desired information. Traditionally, client information would be stored in a folder that is accessed during each session. Technology provides options for shared electronic folders or files between the client and the practitioner that can be accessed by both during and between sessions. Evernote, Dropbox and Google Drive are examples of such sharing programs. Care should be taken to ensure that client privacy is maintained. One way to accomplish this would be to password protect each folder.

Whiteboards are a tool that career practitioners might use during session as a brainstorming activity that can be helpful when addressing career and mental health concerns. For example, a client in the job search process might want to identify possible places of employment and relevant job titles. On a whiteboard, they might create a mindmap by listing out various settings, and within those settings, expand out to list job titles and even potential contacts within those settings. Another example might be brainstorming stress management techniques a client might employ when preparing for an interview. A picture could be taken to capture the whiteboard image. Or, a counselor might use a virtual whiteboard or mindmapping tool such as spiderscribe.com, bubbl.us, or padlet.com, or even online stickies such as stickr.com or onlinestickies.com. While using these virtual tools can be at times cumbersome, especially when two (or more) people are working on it at the same time, there is an added benefit in that links can be included and easily accessed, which isn't the case with a picture. The Mindmap pictured below **[Figure 12.1]** shows an example of how a career practitioner operating form Cognitive Information Processing theory (Sampson, Reardon, Peterson, & Lenz, 2004), might use with a client to brainstorm activities to address self and options knowledge, as well as managing the anxiety that this client is experiencing due to negative career thoughts.

Virtual Reality (VR) technology is also a topic of great interest to career and mental health counselors, clients, and the general public. Virtual realities expand roleplaying by immersing individuals into an environment, rather than just asking them to imagine that they are in a given environment. The new advancements with VR technology have allowed companies such as Oculus to develop programs that allow individuals to visually immerse themselves in a pre-determined and artificial environment. These

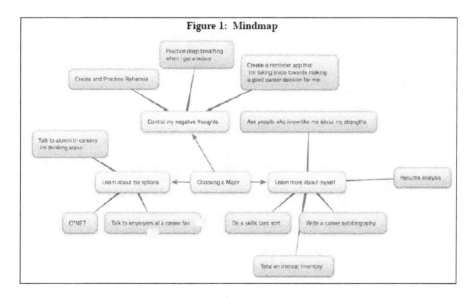

Figure 12.1 Mindmap

environments could include simulations such as roller coasters, tall buildings, airplanes, or even worlds populated with dinosaurs! Counselors could utilize this technology to allow individuals to transform the traditional role-play and systematic desensitization techniques. By using VR technology, a counselor could create a virtual situation where a client could practice public speaking to a virtual audience, or become desensitized to their fear of spiders by watching a virtual spider crawl in front of them. One example of a company creating and providing virtual reality therapy can be found at virtuallybetter.com, who offer virtual reality experiences in a clinical setting to address issues such as anxiety and depression. Many people express stress over making a public presentation or giving a speech, and often times, individuals are asked to do this as part of a job search interview. Having a virtual environment in which avatars are the audience allows a client to experience the anxiety, and try different approaches, where the cost and practicality of creating a similar experience in real life would be prohibitive.

THE POWER OF APPS

The wide range of computer and smartphone applications made readily available today offer ample opportunities for practitioners to connect with clients, and enhance service delivery beyond the office setting (Osborn, Kronholz, Finklea, & Cantonis, 2014). According to Bloomberg Business (2014), individuals in the United States with access to a smartphone or tablet spend an average of two hours and fifty-seven minutes on them daily, surpassing the average time spent watching television. Given the amount of time spent on mobile devices and tablets, and the popularity of these products, practitioners might examine how to ethically and responsibly incorporate the use of relevant applications as part of the counseling process. Researchers (Gati & Austin-Peretz, 2011; Osborn, Dikel, & Sampson, 2011) have shown that technology is a useful tool in assisting clients with the career-decision making process. As mentioned earlier, negative or dysfunctional career thinking has repeatedly been shown to predict career indecision (Bullock-Yowell, Peterson, Reardon, Leierer, & Reed, 2011; Saunders, Peterson, Sampson, & Reardon, 2000). In the field of career counseling, there are many apps that can be used to explore and address negative thinking and improve decision-making skills in regards to making a career choice. Negative metacognitions can influence a client's outlook on his or her self-knowledge, career options, and career-decision making skills (Peterson, Sampson, Reardon, & Lenz, 2002). Additionally, the process of decision-making may be confusing or overwhelming for some clients.

The following discussion will include examples of applications that can be used to assist clients in these two areas of concern.

Negative emotions and maladaptive thoughts, such as those that occur when a client feels depressed, anxious, or heavily stressed, can delay or block the career decision-making process (Osborn et al., 2014). Apps such as Headspace, FlipHead Thought-Stopping, and Moodkit—Mood Improvement Toolscan be useful in helping clients to understand and combat negative thinking. Headspace is a mindfulness app that provides a series of guided meditations ranging in time from 10–20 minutes. The FlipHead Thought Stopping app offers users insight into the effects of negative thoughts, and thought-replacement functions based on cognitive reframing strategies that can help individuals incorporate more positive language into their thinking, such as using positive affirmations (Osborn et al., 2014). Additionally, Moodkit—Mood Improvement Tools takes this a step further by having clients check and record their moods and thoughts throughout the day, helping clients and practitioners to see and discuss negative thinking patterns that could be impacting the career-decision making process.

When clients are feeling puzzled or distraught by the decision-making component of a career issue, apps like Unstuck®, iThoughts, and Sheepadvisor Decision Maker may be useful (Osborn et al., 2014). Unstuck® is a decision-making app that guides users through questions created to help individuals identify factors that influence the problem, such as other people, feelings regarding the decision, and what kind of decision the user is making. iThoughts may be useful in helping clients and practitioners to illustrate and conceptualize the decision at hand by creating decision trees. The Sheepadvisor Decision Maker app expands on the decision tree technique by providing a series of questions related to the decision, and producing a percentile breakdown of the options (Osborn et al., 2014).

The apps discussed above are just a few of the many applications that may be helpful when incorporated into the career counseling process. Practitioners are encouraged to explore the "world of apps" to see which might best fit their practice as well as their individual client's needs and preferences. As with all interventions involving the use of technology, practitioners should keep in mind the client's level of competency, access to devices with apps, and the cost (if any) to purchase the apps. If a client is paying for sessions, the practitioner needs to consider the time it takes to orient the client to an app and whether that time should be billable.

TAKING ADVANTAGE OF SOCIAL MEDIA

Twenty-first century career counseling offers clients technological resources that can be utilized during the career decision-making process (Osborn, Dikel, & Sampson, 2011). Specifically, social media sites afford clients a means of exploring and addressing negative career thought processes in addition to forms of depression and anxiety that often accompany it. With the surge of technology in the past decade, many clients have easy access to social media sites such as Pinterest, Facebook, Twitter, and Instagram. As a result, clients are able to peruse thousands of inspirational posts, quotes, photographs, and memes, reposting those they deem to be helpful in combating negative thoughts associated with career decision-making.

Online support groups also offer clients a way of gaining peer support from those who are experiencing similar issues during the career decision-making process (Shepherd, Sanders, Doyle, & Shaw, 2015). Some companies are combining the idea of social media with the concept of traditional support groups. For example, an individual battling depression attributed to negative thought patterns may benefit from sites such as Panopoly designed by Robert Morris.

The premise of Panopoly is multifaceted in that it provides clients an opportunity to develop a network of support that, in addition to regular counseling services, can aid the client in dealing with depression and other mental diagnoses. Emerging social media sites such as Panopoly are focused on providing individuals with tools to help in cognitive restructuring. Pinterest offers clients access to numerous cognitive restructuring tools including: journal templates to encourage clients to write positively about themselves and their experiences, index card projects that help clients create reminders of positive attributes they possess, and memes that are focused on helping clients develop positive patterns of thinking. However, social media sites dedicated to mental health are in their infancy, and thus, additional research is needed in determining how these resources may be used in an effective and ethical manner.

With the emergence of online support groups and mental health social media sites, researchers are beginning to examine how human communicational exchange via the Internet is able to involve human communicational characteristics such as empathy. Siriaraya et al., 2011 conducted a study on the expression of empathy through communication exchange in online discussion forums. The study found that empathy was expressed in great detail in online communication, among young people in particular, as compared to older generations. Therefore, it seems that a shift in communication styles with younger generations is setting the scene for social media sites such as Panopoly to become a mainstay in the field of mental health and career counseling.

Sites that offer mental health resources and networking should make it clear to their users that their services are not to take the place of professional mental health services, but rather to supplement traditional counseling and mental health treatments. As a cautionary procedure, users should always check the validity of the social media site and/or support group to ensure safety. Unfortunately, it should be noted that mainstream social media sites are sometimes used to promote unhealthy alternatives for mental issues. For example, sites that promote anorexia, bulimia, and other dangerous lifestyles or lifestyle choices should be avoided. Still, closed online group options can provide an option for individuals who cannot or do not wish to meet face-to-face. With any social media, career practitioners should ensure that their own privacy settings are appropriate, and encourage the same of all group members, and remind group members that all information and conversations that take place in the online setting are considered confidential. Other ethical standards such as group screening, personal disclosure, and boundaries also apply in these online environments.

SUMMARY

Recently, practitioners and researchers have been highlighting the connection between career and mental health concerns (Zunker, 2008). Previously, technology provided tools to address career and mental health concerns individually. Websites, apps and social media provided options for making career decisions and job searching, or managing depression and anxiety. As career practitioners become more comfortable with addressing mental health issues, and mental health counselors increase their comfort in discussing career-related concerns, likely there will be a demand for technological tools that address both simultaneously. In this paper, we identified several tools that, while may not have been specifically designed to do both, have the capability to do so. Ultimately, a career practitioner considering integrating technology into practice must consider their own competence in using these tools balanced with the client's comfort and appropriateness of the tool for the need at hand.

REFERENCES

Association for Counselor Education and Supervision/National Career Development Association. (2000). *Preparing counselors for career development in the new millennium.* [ACES/NCDA Position Paper]. Retrieved September 10, 2015, from http://www.ncda.org/aws/NCDA/pt/sp/guidelines.

Betz, N., & Corning, A. (1993). The inseparability of "career" and "personal" counseling. *Career Development Quarterly* 42, 137–143.

Brustein, J. (2014). *We now spend more time staring at phones than TVs.* Retrieved from http://www.bloomberg.com/bw/articles/2014-11-19/we-now-spend-more-time-staring-at-phones-thantvs

Bullock-Yowell, E., Peterson, G. W., Reardon, R. C., Leierer, S. J., & Reed, C. A. (2011). Relationships among career and life stress, negative career thoughts, and career decision state: A cognitive information processing perspective. *The Career Development Quarterly* 59, 302–314.

Gati, I., Asulin-Peretz, L., & Fisher, A. (2012). Emotional and personality-related career decision-making difficulties: A 3-year follow up. *The Counseling Psychologist* 40, 6–28. DOI: 10.1177/0011000011398726

Iivari, N., Kinnula, M., Kuure, L., & Molin-Juustila, T. (2014). Video diary as a means for data gathering with children—Encountering identities in the making. *International Journal of Human-Computer Studies* 72 (5), 507–521. doi:http://dx.doi.org/10.1016/j.ijhcs.2014.02.003

Krumboltz, J. D. (1993). Integrating career and personal counseling. *Career Development Quarterly* 42, 143–148.

Nauta, M. M. (2012). Temporal stability, correlates, and longitudinal outcomes of career indecision. *Journal of Career Development* 39, 540–558. DOI: 10.1177/0894845311410566

Osborn, D. S., Dikel, M. R., & Sampson, J. P., Jr. (2011). *The Internet: A guide to using the Internet in career planning* (3rd Ed.). Broken Arrow, OK: National Career Development Association.

Osborn, D., Kronholz, J. F., Finklea, J. T., & Cantonis, A. M. (2014). Technology-Savvy Career Counselling. *Canadian Psychology* 55 (4), 258–265. doi:10.1037/a0038160

Peterson, G. W., Sampson, J. P., Reardon, R. C., & Lenz, J. G. (2002). *Core concepts of a cognitive information processing approach to career development and services.* Retrieved from http://www.career.fsu.edu/Tech-Center/Designing-Career-Services/Basic-Concepts

Rottinghaus, P. J., Jenkins, N., & Jantzer, A. M. (2009). Relation of depression and affectivity to career decision status and self-efficacy in college students. *Journal of Career Assessment* 17, 271–285. DOI: 10.1177/1069072708330463

Saka, N., & Gati, I. (2007). Emotional and personality-related aspects of persistent career decision-making difficulties. *Journal of Vocational Behavior* 71, 340–358. DOI: 10.1016/j. jvb.2007.08.003

Saunders, D. E., Peterson, G.W., Sampson, J. P., & Reardon, R. D. (2000). Relation of depression and dysfunctional career thinking to career indecision. *Journal of Vocational Behavior* 56, 288–298. doi:10.1006/jvbe.1999.1715.

Sampson, J. P., Jr., Peterson, G. W., Lenz, J. G., Reardon, R. C., & Saunders, D. E. (1996). *Career Thoughts Inventory: Professional manual.* Odessa: FL: Psychological Assessment Resources.

Shepherd, A., Sanders, C., Doyle, M., & Shaw, J. (2015). Using social media for support and feedback by mental health service users: thematic analysis of a twitter conversation. *BMC Psychiatry* 15 (1), 1–9. doi:10.1186/s12888-015-0408-y

Siriaraya, P. P. (2011). A comparison of empathic communication pattern for teenagers and older people in online support communities. *Behaviour & Information Technology* 30 (5), 617–628. doi: 10.1080/0144929X.2011.582146.

Walker III, J. V., & Peterson, G. W. (2012). Career thoughts, indecision, and depression: Implications for mental health assessment in career counseling. *Journal of Career Assessment* 20, 497–506. DOI: 10.1177/1069072712450010

Zunker, V. G. (2008). *Career, work, and mental health: Integrating career and personal counseling.* Thousand Oaks, CA: SAGE.

ABOUT THE AUTHORS

Debra Osborn, PhD, is an Associate Professor in the Educational Psychology and Learning Systems Department at the Florida State University, and a Nationally Certified Counselor. She is Past President of the National and Florida Career Development Associations, and currently serves on the NCDA and ACA boards as a governing council representative. She is a Fellow of the National Career Development Association and of the American Counseling Association. She earned the PhD in Combined Counseling Psychology and School Psychology at Florida State University in 1998. Her program of research covers three foci: (a) the design and use of technology in counseling, (b) innovation and effectiveness in counselor education; and (c) the design and use of assessments in career services. She has authored 25 peer-reviewed articles, 7 books, 8 book chapters, and over 55 national presentations on these topics. As a counselor educator, she is passionate about teaching career development, and is the author of Teaching Career Development: A Primer for Instructors and Presenters (2008). She was the guest editor of special issues of the Career Planning and Adult Development Journal entitled The Education of Career Development Practitioners (2009) and Career Assessments (with Seth Hayden, 2014). She has been honored with several awards, including the Robert M. Gagné Faculty Research Award (2015), the JoAnn Harris-Bowlsbey Award for Excellence in the Field of Technology in Career Development (2010), Outstanding Practitioner Award (National Career Development Association, 2009), Counselor of the Year (Florida Counseling Association, 2006), and the American Counseling Association's Emerging Leader Award (2005). Contact her as follows: *Debra Osborn, PhD, Associate Professor, Educational Psychology and Learning Systems Department, Florida State University, 3205-E Stone Building, Tallahassee, FL 32306 USA. 850-644-3742. e-mail: dosborn@fsu.edu*

Jacqueline Gabbard Belle is a second year graduate student in the combined M.S./ Ed.S Career Counseling program at Florida State University (FSU). She currently works as a co-instructor and career advisor at the FSU Career Center, providing career services to college students, alumni, and Tallahassee community members. Her professional and research interests include: the connection between career and mental health, career development in student athletes, development and delivery of career-related services for high school students, and student resiliency factors.

Austin Gonzalez is a doctoral student in Florida State University's Combined Counseling and School Psychology program, where he works at the Career Center as a Career Advisor. He earned the MS/EdS in mental health counseling at Florida State University. He is interested in exploring the relationship between technology and counseling, specifically the effect of Virtual Reality and distance technology on traditional counseling. He hopes to expand his research towards working with a military population in order to ease the transition from deployment to civilian life.

Shae McCain is a doctoral student in the Combined Doctoral Program in Counseling Psychology and School Psychology at Florida State University. He earned the Master of Science in Marriage and Family Therapy and the Bachelor of Science in Psychology, both at Valdosta State University. He works at the Florida State University Career Center as a career advisor and is also one of the instructors for Introduction to Career Development. His research and clinical interests include utilizing technology in clinical work, the use of assessment in clinical work, and the intersection of mental health and career development.

DISCUSSION QUESTIONS

1   As you engage in your normal activities (today or this week), spend some time thinking about and looking for "career information" while you are using any type of technology that accesses the Internet. You don't have to do any research to intentionally look for information, simply observe what is already around you. Report on what you have observed: What kind of career information did you observe (e.g., social media), receive (e.g., email), or come across while using technology?

2   The use of social networks is important when it comes to career programming, career counseling, and your own personal career development. It can be one of the primary methods of networking for your clients and yourself. What types of social networks do you use, and how do you use them? If you don't currently use any social media networks, then consider this a request to at least use LinkedIn. *Note: Please do not confuse the statement regarding "networking for your clients and yourself" to mean that you should network with your clients (or future clients). This is a breach of confidentiality and a potential dual relationship.*

3   In what ways do you plan on using technology in your future work with clients? How will you be sure to use the technology ethically and responsibly?

CONCLUSION

Advances in technology and the Internet have enhanced the career counselor's ability to provide a wealth of resources and information. These same advances have allowed anyone to develop a global network of contacts. Although there are drawbacks to using technology (e.g., reducing face-to-face contact) and potential ethical issues (e.g., confidentiality and social networking), the benefits of using technology are worth it, but it is essential for the career counselor to understand the technology—and to eliminate or limit the potential risk toward a client.

INDEX OF KEY TERMS

- choices
- computer-assisted career guidance systems (CACGS)
- DISCOVER
- education planner
- Health Insurance Portability and Accountability Act (HIPAA)
- social media/social networks
- System of Interactive Guidance and Information (SIGI)

REFERENCES

Internet World Stats. (2018). *World Internet Users Statistics and 2018 World Population Statistics*. Retrieved from http://www.internetworldstats.com/stats.htm

Statista. (2018). *Number of month active Facebook users worldwide as of 4th quarter 2017*. Retrieved from https://www.statista.com/statistics/264810/number-of-monthly-active-facebook-users-worldwide/

SUGGESTED PUBLICATIONS FOR FURTHER READING

Jencius, M., & Rainey, S. (2009). Current online career counseling practices and future trends. *Career Planning and Adult Development Journal, 25*(3), 17–28.

National Career Development Association. (2018). *Internet Sites for Career Planning*. Retrieved from https://ncda.org/aws/NCDA/pt/sp/resources

Osborn, D., & LoFrisco, B. (2012). How do career centers use social networking sites? *Career Development Quarterly, 60*(3), 263–272.

CAREER COUNSELING RESOURCES

INTRODUCTION

We all need resources! One of the goals I set for my students is for them to start collecting as many counseling-related resources during their time in our program. These resources include counseling techniques, developing relationships with local agencies, and other community services that are available for their clients. Career counseling is no different. Career counseling can utilize a plethora of career counseling resources to best guide clients in their career exploration. Resources can include the Bureau of Labor Statistics, the *Occupational Outlook Handbook*, O*Net, and any state or national occupational information system

(OIS). Most public schools in the United States use some type of OIS in their work with students. This chapter will review some of the career counseling resources that are available to career counselors.

Occupational Classification Resources

MATTHEW W. ISHLER

"What careers are suited for me? What careers are related to my interest in math, science, writing, or helping people?" Career counselors frequently hear requests for career information. These requests may be explicit, such as, "what is an actuary", and some of these requests may be embedded within a client's process of career exploration, "What careers are related to my interest in leading groups of people and organizing events?" Some of the earliest theories of career development focused upon assisting clients as they learn information—information about the self and information about the world of work. This chapter will highlight some of the tools that are related to career information, including their link to career counseling theory and models.

Career information plays a vital role in the career development process. Clients will present with varying degrees of knowledge about their values, interests, skills, and personality. As clients reflect on these factors and increase their self-knowledge, they present questions about how to identify or learn more about careers related to these self-characteristics. Clients are seeking accurate and timely information about careers, in order to make decisions about possible career paths. National Career Development Association (NCDA) identifies Information/Resources as one of the core competencies that individuals in a career counseling role should possess

Matthew W. Ishler, "Occupational Classification Resources," *Career Counseling Across the Lifespan: Community, School, and Higher Education*, ed. Grafton T. Eliason, Jeff L. Samide, John Patrick, and Trisha Eliason, pp. 127-135. Copyright © 2014 by Information Age Publishing. Reprinted with permission.

and implement with clients (NCDA, 2009). Specifically, this competency outlines that individuals should have information related to: "Education, training, and employment trends, labor market information, and resources that provide information about job tasks, functions, salaries, requirements, and future outlooks related to broad occupational fields and individual occupations" (NCDA, 2009). The Council for the Accreditation of Counseling and Related Educational Programs (CACREP) includes specific learning objectives related to information resources within career counseling process (CACREP, 2009):

INFORMATION RESOURCES

1   Understands education, training, and employment trends, as well as labor market information and resources that provide information about job tasks, functions, salaries, requirements, and future outlooks related to broad occupational fields and individual occupations.

2   Understands the resources and skills clients use in life-work planning and management.

3   Knows the community/professional resources available to assist clients in career planning, including job search.

SKILLS AND PRACTICES

1   Demonstrates the ability to manage career, educational and personal-social information resources.

2   Demonstrates the ability to evaluate and disseminate career and educational information.

Information alone can not make career decisions or address the career satisfaction of clients, but as clients have access to career information, and begin to learn about careers, clients can more effectively connect their self-characteristics with career titles, industries, career settings, and career tasks. Career counselors rely on sources of information in order to assist clients with career exploration, with decisions regarding further education or training, as well as to understand current trends in industries and careers. Career information resources also assist counselors and clients in expanding career possibilities by grouping similar careers into sections and themes. This chapter will introduce information resources including the Occupational Outlook Handbook, The Dictionary of Occupational Titles, and the Standard Occupational Classification Manual. These resources were developed and are applied within the context of specific theoretical models of career development. As you read this chapter, you should take away an understanding of these resources and knowledge of their connection to established career theories.

STANDARD OCCUPATIONAL CLASSIFICATION MANUAL

The Standard Occupational Classification (SOC) is developed and used by federal agencies to create occupational categories for the purpose of standardizing the collection and communication of occupational data. "SOC defines an occupation as a category of jobs that are similar with respect to the work performed and the skills possessed by the incumbents. A job is defined as the set of skills possessed by an individual worker." (http://www.bls.gov/soc/soc_2010_user_guide.pdf, date). "The organizing principle of the SOC is work performed rather than job title so there are many fewer occupation codes in the SOC than there are jobs in the economy. There are four tiers (levels) of detail of categories within SOC, enabling career counseling clients to quickly identify occupations that are similar in terms of work performed, which could increase the array of possible careers related to an individual client's pattern of values, interests, and skills. The four tiers include: Major Groups, Minor Groups, Broad Occupations, and Detailed Occupations. The following example of the four tiers is directly from the SOC user guide:

Major Group: 29–0000: Healthcare Practitioners and Technical Occupations
Minor Group: 29–1000: Health Diagnosing and Treating Practitioners
Broad Occupation: 29–1060: Physicians and Surgeons
Detailed Occupation: 29–1062: Family and General Practitioners

This tiered system permits the counting of occupational and career participation at multiple levels—from the detailed occupations to the major groups. SOC is comprised of 840 detailed occupations, 461 broad occupations, 97 minor groups, and 23 major groups. It is important to note that SOC is strictly a statistical category and counting system, it does not rank or group occupations by education, credentials, or earnings. O*NET or Occupational Outlook Handbook would be examples of places to find this information. SOC was first developed in 1980, and its most recent revision was completed in 2010. This 2010 revision contains 24 new occupations and codes, including fundraisers, web developers, community health workers, genetic counselors, and wind turbine service technicians. The next revision of the SOC is scheduled to begin in late 2013 and is expected to be released in 2018. Federal government agencies that apply the Standard Occupational Collection Manual's system of categorizing occupations include the Department of Commerce, Department of Labor, Office of Personnel Management, Equal Employment Opportunity Commission, and Department of Education, among others.

Each SOC listing provides readers with the SOC code for the occupation, a title of the occupation, a definition of the occupation, a statement of required duties, and several illustrative examples designed to offer examples of specific career titles that individuals within this category may hold. To enhance clarity of categories, SOC codes could possibly include "May statements", "Includes statements", or "Excludes statements". "May statements" are intended to provide examples of tasks that may be included in this occupation (where applicable), an "Includes statement", which offers example of an occupational title and description that would be included in this category, and an "Excludes statement" which highlights occupations that would not be included in this occupational category, http://www.bls.gov/soc/soc_2010_user_guide.pdf.

What is the utility of the SOC for career counselors and their clients? The SOC provides concise and clear occupational descriptions. Clients and counselors can identify major groups of occupations related to the client's interests, values, and skills, and then can highlight minor groups, broad occupations, and ultimately, detailed occupations which the client can explore around a central interest, value, or ability area. For example, a client interested in healthcare could reference SOC major group 29–0000 Healthcare Practitioners and Technical Occupations. This major group is comprised of minor groups of: Health Diagnosing and Treating Practitioners (29–1000); Health Technologists and Technicians (29–2000); and Other Healthcare Practitioners and 29–9000). A client with interest in the Health Diagnosing and Treating Practitioners occupations (29–1000), would further see a broad occupation of Dentists (29–1020) and would further see a detailed occupation of Orthodontists (29–1023). Other careers that could be part of the career counseling discussion or exploration could include General Dentists (29–1021), Oral and Maxillofacial Surgeons (29–1022), Prosthodontists (29–1024) and Dentists, All Other Specialists (29–1029). The benefit of this information resource is that the client could learn about multiple aspects of dentistry in one location, and could clearly see occupational distinctions between these fields, such as

Orthodontia and General Dentistry. However, please note when using the SOC that there is no data available through this source regarding educational preparation for these careers, average salary levels of professionals in this field, or anticipated growth or decline in the availability of careers in this category. Other sources such as O*NET or Occupational Outlook Handbook should be consulted for this information. Also, SOC does not contain any self-assessment or career assessment exercises, it is strictly a categorization system which groups similar occupations together within its structure based upon the work performed and skills possessed by the people who hold those occupations.

DICTIONARY OF OCCUPATIONAL TITLES

The Dictionary of Occupational Titles (DOT) correlates career titles with the Holland occupational classification system developed by John Holland (1985/1992). Holland's theory strives to classify a person's interests and abilities among six themes of personality, and further connects those same six themes to occupations. Through examining similarities and differences between an individual's interests and abilities, and the opportunities afforded through a specific occupation, career choice, persistence, and job satisfaction can in part be predicted or anticipated. Holland's theory posits that the likelihood of career satisfaction is enhanced when an individual understands: values, preferred activities, image of the self, how others view me, and what activities I choose to avoid. Occupational environments are classified according to the competencies that they require, the values and behaviors that are rewarded or challenged, and the tasks involved in these occupations. Specifically, occupations were rated among seven scales:

1   Worker Functions (Data-intensive, People-intensive, or Things-intensive)

2   Education and Training (General Education or Specific Vocational Preparation)

3   Aptitudes (Intelligence, Verbal aptitude, Numerical aptitude, Spatial perception, Motor coordination, among others)

4   Temperaments (Direction, control and planning; Feelings, ideas or facts, Influencing, Sensory/Judgmental criteria, Dealing with people; and Variety and change, among others)

5 Bipolar Interests (Communication of data vs. activities with things; Scientific and technical activities vs. business contact; abstract and creative vs. routine and concrete activities; Activities involving processes and machines versus social welfare; and Activities resulting in tangible productive satisfaction vs. prestige and esteem

6 Physical Demands (lifting, carrying, climbing, balancing, crawling, stooping, talking, hearing, and seeing)

7 Working conditions (outside, extreme heat, extreme cold, and noise, among others)

Holland applies a six-dimensional model to understand differences along these categories. The six dimensions are: Realistic, Investigative, Artistic, Social, Enterprising, and Conventional. An assumption underlying this theory is that individuals select careers that are congruent with their picture of their own self. For example, an individual possessing interests, abilities, and values consistent with the Social theme, would find a complementary opportunity to express, enact, and be rewarded for these Social elements, in a work environment that requires skills, interests, and values consistent with the Social theme (Gottfredson & Holland, 1996).

The DOT organizes its listing of careers in two main sections. The first section is organized among the Holland themes, and lists careers according to 3-theme combinations such as AIR or SEC. The second section lists occupational titles alphabetically and then provides the Holland theme. Counselors working with the DOT to assist clients with career planning should be familiar with the meaning of the nine-digit DOT codes. The first digit represents the primary occupational category, ranging from low level to high level work. The second and third digits reflect the broader group that this occupation represents. The middle three numbers represent the degree of complexity involved in working with data (4th digit), people (5th digit), or things (6th digit). The final three digits provide a unique ordering system, to distinguish one number from another, and provide no other meaningful data. Although these numerical identifiers are unique to the occupations, it is important to keep in mind that within any occupation, and within every person, there is often overlap among the Holland categories, and that each occupation simply an extension of one of the themes. Similarly, there is overlap among the occupations contained in the DOT. The set of skills, expectations, and values will be shared and will overlap among careers within the same Holland themes. Counselors will undoubtedly be called upon by clients to highlight distinctions when these distinctions between occupations may be very slight, if they exist at all.

DOT benefits from the strengths of the Holland theory, its clear categories and the research that supports the application of this theory with a wide range of clients, diverse in age, country of origin, and level of educational achievement. Research supporting

Holland's theory and its application to career development include evidence linking congruence to career satisfaction. This includes studies of simulated work experiences and studies of employed workers which found that career choice is connected to the pursuit of congruence between personality, interests, and ability, and occupational environment. Examining personality, interests, and abilities with clients who possess work experience can also provide insight into factors that may lead to dissatisfaction with current or former employment (a lack of congruence between the person and the work environment, for example).

OCCUPATIONAL OUTLOOK HANDBOOK

The Occupational Outlook Handbook (OOH, 2006) is a career information resource used within career counseling and career development contexts to gather information about careers. Within career counseling, the descriptions of occupations found within OOH often forms a foundation of knowledge about careers, which career counseling clients will use to develop strategic application materials (resume, cover letter, application), conduct networking activities (attend industry or organizational events, conduct occupational information interviews), and may make decisions regarding attaining further education or training in preparation for entering or advancing in a selected field. OOH is one of the most comprehensive sources of information about occupations, and counselors will find themselves returning to this resource frequently as a means of supporting the work of their clients.

Occupational descriptions are categorized into groups within the Occupational Outlook Handbook. These groups include: Management and business and financial operations occupations; Professional and related occupation; Service occupation; Sales and related occupation; Office and administrative support occupation; Farming, fishing and forestry occupation; construction trades and related workers; Installation, maintenance and repair occupation; Production occupation; Transportation and material moving occupations; and Job Opportunities in the Armed Forces. Occupational descriptions within OOH contain multiple sections of career information: "Significant points" offers highlights about the occupation, including job market trends and often, educational requirements. "Nature of the Work" offers information about the tasks that workers in this occupation do, and what tools they may use. "Working Conditions" describes the workplace environment and often the typical hours of work for this occupation. "Training, other qualifications, and advancement" contains information about typical entry level expectations regarding education, experience, or other forms of training. This section also contains information that describes what type of experience or education is necessary to advance within this occupation. "Employment" presents the number of people employed in this occupation, and where possible, divides this into specific settings or work titles that comprise this occupation. "Job Outlook" is a projection of the increase or decrease in demand for this occupation anticipated over a certain number of years. Factors impacting this projection, such as changes in technology, state or federal laws, or anticipated retirement data are usually outlined in this section. "Earnings" outlines the average compensation, a national median, for members of this occupational group. If the setting or a specific subcategory of an occupational title impacts wages significantly, then this distinction is usually listed. "Related Occupations" outlines occupations that are similar to the occupation that is profiled in the OOH. This is useful in helping clients expand career options, explore different occupational settings, and relate a core set of interests or abilities to multiple occupations. "Sources of Additional Information" includes resources such as professional associations, unions, and other networks where individuals share information or opportunities related to this occupation. This could be a starting point for finding individuals to discuss the occupation with, to observe or shadow in the workplace, or to build experience in the occupation. OOH also contains one picture of each occupation.

The OOH also contains information about population demographics and participation in the workforce. This demographic data includes projections regarding the expected fastest growing occupations, and jobs expected to decline over the next ten years. Counselors are encouraged to use caution when interpreting these national projections with clients, and to always introduce more geographically specific employment projections wherever possible, depending upon the client's geographic preferences.

SUMMARY

With the volume of information available to career counselors and their clients through OOH, it can be tempting to rely exclusively on information resources in the OOH and through other sources, in career counseling. Counselors should approach the use of this resource with an understanding of their client's decision making process, including motivations, perceived barriers, and desired outcomes. Clients and counselors should exercise caution in relying on only one source of career information, and should seek opportunities to enhance decision making by discussing career goals with professionals in desired occupations, and wherever possible, through direct experience as a volunteer, an intern, or as a form of professional development from within one's current role. Career decision making is influenced by factors such as perception of one's self, self-concept, self-esteem, motivation to learn new skills and enact life changes, and is influenced by our picture of a client's definition of success. Information is only one piece of what a career counselor provides to a client. When over-emphasized, information resources can shift the control of career decision making from the individual to what the information says. Some clients are pleased to rely upon external sources to make career decisions. Other clients may be hesitant to look at information for fear that it will discourage or present barriers to achieving goals. Counselors will rely upon their interpersonal skills and the relationship that they have established with clients to introduce career information and along with the client, will place career information in the context of a process of career and life exploration.

KEY WORDS

Standard Occupational Classification: U.S. government occupational classification system used primarily by federal government agencies involved in collecting and communicating employment and career data.

SOC code: SOC Codes refer to the numerical categorization of careers within the standard Occupational Classification. The purpose of SOC Codes is to provide for the collection and communication of employment data by specific occupational categories. The 2010 SOC included 840 occupational types.

Dictionary of Occupational Titles (DOT): Occupational classification system that correlated occupational titles with the occupational classification system developed by John Holland (Gottfredson & Holland, 1996).

The Occupational Outlook Handbook (OOH): A career information resource published by the U.S. Department of Labor's Bureau of Labor Statistics and is used within development contexts to identify occupational information such as the nature of work tasks, working conditions, training, occupational trends and outlooks, and earning statistics.

Occupation: A category of jobs that are similar with respect to the work performed and the skills possessed by the incumbents.

Job: A job is defined as the set of skills possessed by an individual worker.

REFERENCES

2009 Standards of the Council for Accreditation of Counseling and Related Educational Programs (CACREP). 2009. Retrieved on June 10, 2012 from http://www.cacrep.org/doc/2009%20Standards%20 with%20cover.pdf

Gottfredson, G. D., & Holland, J. L. (1996). Dictionary of Holland Occupational Codes (3rd Ed). Psychological Assessment Resources, Inc.

Occupational Outlook Handbook (2006). Indianapolis, IN: JIST Publishing.

Standard Occupational Classification Policy Committee (2010). 2010 SOC User Guide. Retrieved July 6, 2012 from http://www.bls.gov/soc/soc_2010_user_guide.pdf

National Career Development Association. (2009). Career counseling competencies: Revised version, 1997. Retrieved June 12, 2012 from http://www.ncda.org/aws/NCDA/pt/sd/news_article/37798/_self/ layout_ccmsearch/true

The NOICC/SOICC Network
Policy, Programs, and Partners, 1976–2000

JULIETTE N. LESTER, JAMES WOODS, AND BURTON L. CARLSON

This historical and reflective account of the National Occupational Information Coordinating Committee's (NOICC) and the State Occupational Information Coordinating Committees' (SOICCs) significant development of a national infrastructure that shaped career development policy, practice, and training from 1976 to 2000 offers key lessons for future development practice and potential in the United States and beyond. The establishment of the NOICC/SOICC network marked a turning point in the systematic development and delivery of standardized occupational information and supporting resources designed to meet the needs of career development, education and training program design, and employer information requirements. NOICC's core occupational information activities and national career development guidelines and programs are discussed. Public policy that supports career information and counseling services is suggested.

Keywords: NOICC/SOICC network, public policy

Juliette N. Lester, James Woods, and Burton L. Carlson, "The NOICC/SOICC Network: Policy, Programs, and Partners, 1976-2000," *The Career Development Quarterly*, vol. 61, no. 2, pp. 186-192. Copyright © 2013 by National Career Development Association. Reprinted with permission. Provided by ProQuest LLC. All rights reserved.

The National Occupational Information Coordinating Committee (NOICC) was a federal interagency coordinating committee whose members eventually represented 10 agencies involved in various aspects of the U.S. economy. Member agencies included key offices of five federal departments: *Labor:* Employment and Training Administration and the Bureau of Labor Statistics; *Education:* National Center for Education Statistics, Office of Vocational and Adult Education, Rehabilitation Services Administration, Office of Postsecondary Education, and Office of Bilingual Education and Minority Language Affairs; *Commerce:* Economic Development Administration; *Defense:* Office of Force Management and Personnel; and *Agriculture:* Office of Small Community and Rural Development.

State Occupational Information Coordinating Committees (SOICCs), NOICC's state partners, represented state agencies concerned with job training, vocational and technical education, employment security, vocational rehabilitation, economic development, higher education, and more. Together, NOICC and SOICCs formed an integrated network of developers and users of occupational and labor market information and career development initiatives. Established by Congress in 1976, with subsequent legislative amendments, the NOICC/SOICC network was a unique federal-state partnership that provided a framework for addressing workforce development and career preparation issues and opportunities.

The work of the NOICC/SOICC network was based on the idea that if people were guided on how to make informed choices about education, training, jobs, and careers, this would improve the skills and productivity of the workforce, the match between workers and the needs of the labor market, and the competitiveness of the U.S. economy. This meant making sure people had the skills and information they needed to make informed choices. To accomplish this mission, the NOICC/SOICC network developed and implemented occupational, labor market, career information, and career development systems and programs that could be adapted for use at the state and local level. NOICC provided the leadership, technical assistance, and training to carry out this ambitious agenda. SOICCs developed, adapted, distributed, and encouraged use of the systems and programs in their states.

Training was a vital and fundamental component of all NOICC/SOICC initiatives. NOICC's train-the-trainers workshops and other training programs for SOICCs and members of the broader network crosscut all program areas, including information development, delivery, and use, as well as youth and adult career development. SOICCs conducted state and local train-the-trainers workshops in their states. Several professional associations, including the National Career Development Association (NCDA), were NOICC's partners at many joint conferences and in training programs.

Congress established the NOICC/SOICC network in the Vocational Education Amendments of 1976 and subsequent regulations. Later legislation that reinforced and expanded the primary mission and objectives of the national and state committees included the Career Education Incentive Act of 1977, Youth Employment and Demonstration Projects Act of 1977, Comprehensive Employment and Training Act Amendments of 1978, Job Training Partnership Act of 1982, Carl D. Perkins Vocational Education Act of 1984, Carl D. Perkins Vocational and Applied Technology Education Act Amendments of 1990, and Job Training Reform Amendments of 1992.

In addition to technical assistance and training provided to the SOICCs, more than 85% of NOICC's overall budget directly supported state career development activities. Funding was channeled through grant programs that helped sustain SOICC operations and supported their participation in special projects that addressed network priorities. NOICC's basic operations were supported by the U.S. Departments of Labor and Education. NOICC's annual budget was approximately $8 million to $10 million. The U.S. Office of Education became the Department of Education in 1980. The Defense, Labor, and Education departments provided additional funds for special projects.

Russell Flanders was NOICC's executive director from 1976 to 1986. In 1988, he wrote about the NOICC/SOICC structure:

> The innovations of the state committees reduce costs to other states and add to NOICC's capability to lead. Similarly, NOICC provides leadership and funds to decrease costs to states. Working together, efficient computerized delivery systems have been installed in most states. Planners and counselors have more and accurate information at their fingertips including information in formats never before available. (Flanders, 1988, p. 158)

CORE OCCUPATIONAL INFORMATION ACTIVITIES

When NOICC began operations in 1977, one of its first tasks was conceptualizing a workable nationwide occupational information system (OIS) designed to meet the needs of education and workforce training program planners, employers, and individual career development and planning. A series of projects in partnership with the state committees were undertaken to identify existing labor market information; delivery systems; user needs, sources, and resources; gaps in data; and means for bringing data together from a wide range of sources. In 1979, NOICC published The *Framework for Developing an Occupational Information System*, providing initial guidance to states and federal partners on the structure and elements of an OIS. This was followed up by Volumes 1 and 2 of the *Occupational Information System (OIS) Handbook* (NOICC, 1981a, 1981b), providing detailed guidance to implement national and state OISs in coordination with each committee's member agencies. Over the next several years, a number of key initiatives were undertaken to support OIS development and user-friendly application and access. A few of these are discussed below.

A critical need was a capability to link data among various systems, including occupational projections, education program data, and military occupational data. Data were developed using different classifications systems available at different geographical levels and representing different measures. A major challenge was how to bring data together from these various sources, for example, how to link education program data to occupational data. NOICC (1982) issued the *Guide to Forming Units of Analysis*, which provided a method to group and link related educational program data and occupational data. These clusters proved useful to both program planning and career development. In 1983, NOICC established the National Crosswalk Service Center (NCSC) in Iowa to automate and update occupational, industry, and educational program files as various classification systems were changed and new ones implemented. The NCSC continues to operate in 2012, supported by U.S. Department of Labor funding, and remains an important resource to many career development initiatives and products. NCSC crosswalk and related data files may be accessed at http://www.xwalkcenter.org.

Automating OISs was an important aspect of the NOICC/SOICC network to improve user accessibility. From 1979 to 1983, a number of states developed OISs on mainframe computers with hard-copy reports provided to users. Some states experimented with user access to mainframe systems as well. Innovations by states were shared and adopted by other states. These innovations also informed national developments and guidance and, most importantly, provided the foundation for efforts to develop microcomputer-based information systems. Recognizing the difficulty of adapting mainframe-based systems across states, in 1984 NOICC released the first version of the Micro-OIS operating on microcomputers. By 1987, nearly 40 states had selected and implemented the Micro-OIS to support program-planner needs in their states. In 1994, a totally redesigned Micro-OIS was released, providing greater flexibility and ease of use, along with a greatly enhanced set of outputs.

Under the leadership of James Woods, NOICC played a key role in working with federal agencies and SOICCs to encourage greater standardization across systems and data sources. The crosswalk provided one means of standardizing relationships across systems. The Micro-OIS encouraged standardization of data files to the extent that they populated the Micro-OIS. However, one of the most significant efforts undertaken by NOICC toward standardization was the Occupational and Labor Market Information Database (OLMID). The purpose of OLMID was to create a comprehensive database structure for occupational, labor market, and training data with data sets and defined file structures. OLMID provided a means for each state to bring together data from different sources in its state and incorporate them in its OLMID. This permitted easy sharing of data across states and easier implementation of new delivery systems, because any state that adopted the OLMID structure would have data in the same format as other states, no matter the original source. NO ICC also worked to fill some data gaps, including development of the Licensed Occupational Information System (LOIS). The OLMID and LOIS efforts have had a lasting legacy, being adopted by U.S. Department of Labor information systems and many state labor market information units, as well as supporting data incorporated in career information delivery systems (CIDS).

NOICC undertook several cooperative efforts with the Department of Defense (DOD). One of the first was working with DOD to develop a crosswalk between military and civilian occupations. These files are updated periodically and maintained at the NCSC. They are an important resource to DOD and to career information delivery systems, among other users. From 1983 to 1988, NOICC awarded state grants for the Military Occupational and Training Data initiative, which supported integration of military information into CIDS. Working with the Navy Reserve, NOICC developed the Civilian Training Inventory, a computerized database to assist Naval Reserve personnel in identifying civilian training programs that would provide training in skills required by the Reserves. NOICC also worked with the Veterans' Employment and Training Service to develop and implement the Civilian Occupational Labor Market Information System to support military personnel who were moving to the civilian sector.

The above-mentioned efforts, along with many others implemented by NOICC and SOICCs between 1978 and 2000, supported important information needs for education/training planning and employer workforce planning, and they provided a foundation for data supporting career development. The lasting legacy is that many of the features and innovations by the NOICC/SOICC network provided some foundation and lessons for developing the robust delivery systems available throughout the United States today.

NATIONAL CAREER DEVELOPMENT GUIDELINES AND PROGRAMS

Starting in 1991, Burton L. Carlson oversaw the editing and updating of NOICC's *Improved Career Decision Making (ICDM) in a Changing World* (NOICC, 1996). Judy Ettinger did the primary work. In 1994–1995, Carlson oversaw the first revision of *The National Career Development Guidelines*, which NOICC had first released in 1989; Linda Kobylarz was the primary editor (NOICC, 1989). By then, the guidelines were widely known and recognized as the basis for all career development tools and publications and the standard against which career development products published by private providers were expected to conform. Indeed, very early on, such products carried a statement to that effect.

A second aspect of NOICC's guidelines activities was developing and delivering training in the content and uses of the guidelines to counselors, teachers, and school administrators at the state and local level. SOICCs generally organized local activities. Eventually, through NCDA, a training network was established through which trainers were certified. Carlson coordinated those activities within the SOICC network.

A third aspect of NOICC guidelines activities was promulgating guidelines knowledge, training, and use among other countries, including Canada, the United Kingdom, Japan, and Australia. Canada led the way by creating its *Blueprint for Life/ Work Designs* (National Life/Work Centre, Human Resources and Skills Development Canada, & Canada Career Information Partnership, n.d.). Canada then became the primary international purveyor of guidelines knowledge in coordination with the marketing of *The Real Game Series* (Barry, 2001).

The fourth aspect of NOICC's guidelines activities was developing career development products for use by counselors and teachers in schools. Primary among these was *The Real Game Series* (Barry, 2001), a set of career development activities directed to elementary, middle, and high school students and their parents. Canada and NOICC jointly developed these products. NOICC distributed them through its network, while Canada helped implement their use in many other countries.

Other NOICC products that supported guidelines use included SOICC publications such as career information tabloids, comic books, pamphlets, and bookmarks that were distributed by the thousands throughout the states. These documents included detailed economic and employment statistics such as employment trends, job descriptions, and educational requirements. States conducted extensive training with teachers, school counselors, and other career resource agencies and personnel. In this effort, NOICC also supported the Career Development Facilitator Program at Oakland University in Rochester, Michigan.

The NOICC Training Support Center, which the Oklahoma SOICC operated under an NOICC grant, coordinated NOICC's training programs and conferences nationwide. NOICC also established the Career Development Training Institute to design career development training programs for states.

GALLUP NATIONAL SURVEYS

In 1989, NCDA, in collaboration with NOICC, commissioned the Gallup Organization to conduct a national survey to, among other objectives, "develop more precise information about the perceptions held by minority groups with regard to career planning, occupational information, problems experienced on the job, and the need for career development activities in public schools" (Brown & Lester, 1992, p. 2). In 1993, NCDA, in cooperation with NOICC, commissioned another Gallup poll that focused on the career preparation of adults age 18 and older. This was the third national survey NCDA had commissioned (Hoyt & Lester, 1995).

One of the key findings of the 1993 poll was that the American public expected high schools to help all students make a successful transition from school to work. Although the poll did not ask that question directly, answers to a number of questions revealed both a need for career development assistance among young adults who have recently left school and an expectation that high schools should provide more jobs and career assistance to their students.

> One half of all adults said high schools were not doing enough to help students with choosing careers, developing job skills, learning job-finding skills, and job placement. In most of the categories, the percentages were well above 50%. Among students, they were well above 60%.(Hoyt & Lester, 1995, p. 19)

In the 1993 Gallup poll, the needs of this "neglected majority" were evident. Although the neglected majority requires much more attention, one should not overlook the needs of those who went to college, especially those who went but who have not earned a degree. The Gallup poll found that a majority of adults with 4-year degrees or higher were faring well in the workplace, liking their jobs very much, and expected to stay in them over the next few years. Making connections and maintaining them take time, "but the investment will be worthy of the voyage" (Hoyt & Lester, 1995, p. 22).

Kenneth B. Hoyt (Hoyt & Lester, 1995) wrote:

> The emerging information-oriented high-technology occupational society seems sure to complicate the career decision-making process for both youth and adults in America. ... Helping persons decide, plan, ready themselves for, and enter into occupations they have chosen must be a strong priority in any national transition from schooling to employment effort. (p. 96)

THE NECESSARY ART OF CONNECTIONS

"In a turbulent workplace, public needs for information about opportunities in employment and education are broad-based and persistent. One federal response to the demand for such information was the creation of the national and state co-ordinating committees" (Lester, 1996, p. 201). For 24 years, NOICC and the SOICCs worked together in a unique federal-state partnership that provided a framework for addressing workforce development and career preparation issues and opportunities. The network evolved and expanded dramatically over the years, involving a broad network of partners in a wide range of endeavors. Products, services, and resources grew and multiplied. The focus expanded from coordinating occupational and labor market information to a concern with its delivery and use. And new paths were forged into areas of career development for both young people and adults.

But success does not always breed success. It is often said that change is the only constant. And change indeed came to the NOICC/SOICC network. In 2000, legislation transferred NOICC's OIS functions to the Department of Labor and its career development functions to the Department of Education. Herr and Gysbers (2000) wrote,

> For more than two decades, the NOICC has been the one federal organization charged with integrating career guidance and counselling services for children, youth and adults across the federal departments of Education, Labor and Defense. Unfortunately, in the past several months, the NOICC has been dismantled as a federal co-ordinating unit. (p. 271)

Support for career development remains a worthy investment, in good economic times and bad. Ultimately, it stands to benefit the country, by empowering citizens to navigate effectively in the complex, ever-changing labor market that we now are experiencing.

REFERENCES

Barry, B. (2001). *The Real Game series* (Rev. ed.). St. John's, Newfoundland, Canada; The Real Game.

Brown, D ., & Lester, J. N. (1992). Introduction to and overview of the 1989 survey. In D. Brown & C. W. Minor (Eds.), *Career needs in a diverse workforce: Implications of the NCDA Gallup survey* (pp. 1–11). Alexandria, VA; National Career Development Association.

Career Education Incentive Act of 1977, Pub. L. No. 95–207 (1977).

Carl D. Perkins Vocational and Applied Technology Education Act Amendments of 1990, Pub. L. No. 101–392, 104 Stat. 753 (1990).

Carl D. Perkins Vocational Education Act of 1984, Pub. L. No. 98–524 (1984).

Comprehensive Employment and Training Act Amendments of 1978, Pub. L. No. 95–524, § 2, 92 Stat. 1909 (1978).

Flanders, R. (1988, Spring). The evolution of the NOICC-SOICC programs: 1977–1987. *Journal of Career Development, 14,* 145–159.

Herr, E. L., & Gysbers, N. C. (2000). Career development services and related policy issues: The U.S. experience. In B. Hiebert & L. Bezanson (Eds.), *Making waves: Career development and public policy—International symposium 1999, papers, proceedings, and strategies* (pp. 264–276). Ottawa, Ontario, Canada: Canadian Career Development Foundation.

Hoyt, K. B., & Lester, J. N. (1995). *Learning to work: The NCDA Gallup survey.* Alexandria, VA: National Career Development Association.

Job Training Partnership Act of 1982, Pub. L. No. 97–300, 29 U.S.C. § 1501, et seq. (1982).

Job Training Reform Amendments of 1992, Pub. L. No. 102–367, 106 Stat. 1021 (1992).

Lester, J. N. (1996). Turbulence at the (Gallup) polls. In R. Feller & G. Walz (Eds.), *Career transitions in turbulent times: Exploring work, earning, and careers* (pp. 193–204). Greensboro, NC: ERIC/CASS.

National Life/Work Centre, Human Resources and Skills Development Canada, & Canada Career Information Partnership. (n.d.). *Blueprint for life/work designs.* Retrieved from http://www.blueprint4life.ca

National Occupational Information Coordinating Committee. (1979). *The framework for developing an occupational information system.* Washington, DC: Author.

National Occupational Information Coordinating Committee. (1981a). *The occupational information system (DIS) handbook: Vol. 1. Occupational information development.* Washington, DC: Author.

National Occupational Information Coordinating Committee. (1981b). *The occupational information system (OIS) handbook: Vol. 2. Occupational information analysis presentation and delivery.* Washington, DC: Author.

National Occupational Information Coordinating Committee. (1982). *Guide to forming units of analysis.* Washington, DC: Author.

National Occupational Information Coordinating Committee. (1989). *The national career development guidelines.* Washington, DC: Author.

National Occupational Information Coordinating Committee. (1996). *Improved career decision making (ICDM) in a changing world.* Garrett Park, MD: Garrett Park Press.

Vocational Education Amendments of 1976, Pub. L. No. 94–482 (1976).

Youth Employment and Demonstration Projects Act of 1977, Pub. L. No. 95–93, 91 Stat. 627 (1977).

DISCUSSION QUESTIONS

1 Discuss the role of career counseling resources in career counseling.

2 How could you use some of the most popular career counseling resources in your work with an adult client?

3 How could you use career counseling resources in your work with school-aged clients?

4 Do you think you could use web-based resources with all your clients? Are there limitations to using web-based services?

CONCLUSION

Career counseling resources play a vital role in our work with clients. Connecting clients to community resources can help them expand their career network, allowing them to have more options as they make career-related decisions. There are numerous resources that career counselors can use, as many of them are web-based and free of charge. Resources to use will be decided on after discussing options with the client. This collaboration encourages clients to learn more about available career resources as well as take action in their career development. This chapter provided an overview of career counseling resources and where to find some of the most popular.

INDEX OF KEY TERMS

- Bureau of Labor Statistics
- career resources
- National Career Development Association
- occupation information systems
- *Occupational Outlook Handbook*

SUGGESTED PUBLICATIONS FOR FURTHER READING

Martin, R. R. (2011). A review of the literature and important resources concerning career development in higher education. In J. Samide, G. T. Eliason, & J. Patrick (Eds.), *Career development in higher education* (pp. 3–24). Charlotte, NC: Information Age.

U.S. Bureau of Labor Statistics. (2018). *Occupational outlook handbook*. Washington DC: Author. Retrieved from:https://www.bls.gov/ooh/home.htm

Bureau of Labor Statistics. (n.d.). July jobless rates down in 11 states, up in 2; payroll jobs up in 6 states, down in 1. Retrieved from https://www.bls.gov/home.htm

CAREER CHOICES ACROSS THE LIFESPAN

INTRODUCTION

A person's career develops over time and can include positions held, jobs worked, and occupations changed. Our careers begin early in life (in our adolescence), and, more often than not, we transition from one position, job, or occupation to another position, job, or occupation. The choices that we make across our life shape our overall career. Changes are part of nearly everyone's career path, and rarely do people follow the same path as one another.

As counselors, we need to be aware of and understand these changes. Sometimes, we are called on to help people make decisions about their career choices (initial choices or later choices). Other clients may need assistance and information regarding searching for (or securing) a job. And even other clients need counseling to help with adjusting to a job or coping with a work stressor. This doesn't nearly describe every situation in which you will find yourself as a counselor, but they are good examples of situations that can occur for most clients at specific points in their life. Career counselors need to have a basic understanding of career choices across the lifespan.

Career Choice

SARAH SIFERS, JULENE NOLAN, AND DANIEL HOULIHAN

Career choice is part of identity development, and it can be a lifelong process that begins in adolescence and may extend into adulthood. In fact, youth of today will likely have had numerous careers by the time they are ready to leave the working world, and may have to re-tool their skills and education a number of times throughout their lives. In today's technologically rich and ever-changing society, many of the occupations that young people will eventually settle on do not even exist yet. This requires innovation at high schools and post-secondary institutions to prepare young people to be successful in the world of work.

Some theorists claim that the current generation of adolescents are unlike those of previous generations in that they demonstrate less independence and require more concrete supports like direction, structure, and feedback than did previous generations (Feiertag & Berge, 2008). They also claim that post-secondary educators and post-high school employers must learn to work with young people who are not particularly adept at communicating in person and require access to technology to assist in performance and aid learning. Because it encompasses such a vast period, it may be helpful to conceptualize adolescent development in stages, with early adolescence defined as ages 10 to 14, middle adolescence from 15 to 17, and late adolescence from 18 to 20.

Sarah Sifers, Julene Nolan, and Daniel Houlihan, "Career Choice," *Real World, Real Challenges: Adolescent Issues in Contemporary Society*, pp. 180-191. Copyright © 2016 by Cognella, Inc. Reprinted with permission.

Early adolescence may be a time for exploring careers by learning about the world in general and what is meant by words like occupation, career, job, and vocation. While occupation and job indicate paid employment for specific tasks, career refers more to a pattern of jobs or occupations that are within the same category. **Vocation** refers to a feeling that one is well suited to a career, or is "meant" to devote their time to a certain occupational pursuit.

By middle adolescence, teens and their families may begin to explore specific educational options that would aid in narrowing career choices while providing access to the training needed to pursue a variety of career interests. It is during this time (often in high school) that adolescents usually take career inventories, investigate college or technical programs, and seek the advice of career guidance counselors. By late adolescence, often teens have made a choice about which post-secondary training they will pursue (Porfeli & Skorikov, 2010). Psychological and social factors influence career choice. This includes individual factors (e.g., gender, socioeconomic status [SES], and ethnicity), the microsystem (e.g., parents and peers), and the exosystem (e.g., social policy, media, cultural trends, and trends in valuing money versus valuing service).

PSYCHOLOGICAL DIMENSIONS

Understanding which career path may be suitable for a particular adolescent begins with identity development and self-awareness. During high school, adolescents may take different personality or aptitude tests to determine where they fall on a number of personality constructs. One common way to conceptualize personality is the Big 5 approach, which rates the personality characteristics of openness, conscientiousness, extraversion, agreeableness, and neuroticism (Goldberg, 1990). The theory is that when people understand where their personality falls on different constructs, they will be better able to find a career that offers opportunities that are harmonious with their personality, leading to better job performance and satisfaction.

John Holland (1973) also created a theory of career suitability, which was eventually adopted into the Strong Interest Inventory. This tool rates the individual on constructs including realistic, investigative, artistic, social, enterprising, and conventional, and suggests career fields based on how one scores on these factors (Harmon, DeWitt, Campbell, & Hansen, 1994).

Today, there are several personality and interest scales used in career search and employment selection. A few more popular assessments include Myers-Briggs Type Inventory, Enneagram of Personality Types, NEO Personality Inventory–Revised, DiSC, and Strengths Finder. Career counseling agencies and private coaching firms use these or develop their own tools. The reader is cautioned to understand the validity (limited in most cases) of these assessments before investing too much faith in test results. This is particularly true of the free online "personality" tests. It is sufficient to say that these tools can be helpful in self-discovery and as an avenue to begin learning about potential careers. While personality is considered a relatively constant construct, life events such as trauma and education can change how a person responds on personality assessments over their lifetime, and thus may change the personality profile that is generated from these assessments.

Success in and satisfaction with a career may depend upon suitability of personality characteristics for a particular career. It may also depend on achievement orientation, which is a theory based on the work of David McClelland (1961) about what drives an individual to perform. **Mastery orientation** is the desire to practice a task to become very good at it. It is based on a belief that success in a task has more to do with practice and hard work than innate competencies. **Performance orientation** is the desire to practice a task to become better than everyone else at it. It is based on a belief that success in a task has more to do with innate competencies. Performance orientation theory contends that job performance and satisfaction depend on a match between job requirements and benefits. It also depends on mastery versus performance orientation, and the suitability of that orientation for a particular job (Janssen & Van Yperen, 2004).

Other theorists propose that motivation has an important influence on matching people to jobs. **Motivation** is an internal feeling of desire to do something, and people are thought to be predominately extrinsically or intrinsically motivated. Those with predominately **extrinsic motivation** will perform better and enjoy a job more when there is an ample supply of external motivators like pay, prestige, praise, and opportunity. Those with **intrinsic motivation** find pleasure in the job itself. Performance and satisfaction for these people depend on autonomy and freedom in the workplace (Amabile, Hill, Hennessey, & Tighe, 1994).

Additional psychological factors that may impact job performance and job satisfaction include **competence**, or the ability to perform a job completely and successfully, **initiative**, which is the internal drive to complete some task or reach some goal, and **work ethic**, which is valuing hard work and finding it to be a self-satisfying and worthy pursuit.

There is also evidence that career selection begins with individual identity development, and is successful when a teen makes a commitment to an occupational identity. Adolescents who receive help in preparing for this transition demonstrate better outcomes in terms of mental health and career attainment (Malanchuk, Messersmith, & Eccles, 2010). Developing occupational goals during high school as well as a plan to achieve those goals also leads to better outcomes.

Career choice and job satisfaction is included within the field of industrial/organizational psychology and a complete investigation of theories of career choice is beyond the scope of this chapter. The reader is directed to texts in this field for a comprehensive look at theories of career selection and job performance, as well as a wider explanation of the psychological factors that affect career selection (see, for example, Patton & McMahon, 2014).

COGNITIVE FACTORS

Intelligence is strongly correlated with academic achievement, but does not necessarily predict career choice. One study of 1,326 Swedish adolescents found that, in adulthood, those with an IQ greater than 119 were ten times more likely to have a Master's degree than those with an average IQ (90–110), indicating that high IQ is related to advanced education (Bergman, Corovic, Ferrer-Wreder, & Modig, 2014). There is also evidence that cognitive ability may predict the field an adolescent will choose, and considering an adolescent's ability within a field makes this prediction more accurate (Lubinski & Benbow, 2006; Robertson, Smeets, Lubinski, & Benbow, 2010). For example, adolescents with strong science, technology, engineering, or math skills (STEM), who have even stronger verbal skills, are more likely to choose a non-STEM track career (Lubinski, Webb, Morelock, & Benbow, 2001). Research indicates that career choice is influenced by a variety of factors, including both person-specific and environmental factors. These factors in turn influence an adolescent's behavior and shape their progression through planning, exploring, and pursuing career goals (Lent, Brown, & Hackett, 1994).

There has also been disagreement about whether intelligence predicts career success. A number of studies indicate there is a relationship between intelligence and career success, as measured by external factors (income, position, et cetera). In fact, in a meta-analysis of studies on intelligence and career success, the research indicated that intelligence does predict education, occupation, and income, but it is not a considerably better predictor than grades in school or socioeconomic status of parents (Strenze, 2007). Other studies indicate the importance of emotional intelligence in career choice, career success, and satisfaction (see, for example, Coetzee & Beukes, 2010; Di Fabio & Kenny, 2010; O'Boyle, Humphrey, Pollack, Hawver, & Story, 2011).

Finally, the social cognitive theory of career development (Lent et al., 1994) attributes career development to an adolescent's self-efficacy, effectiveness, and ability to create and achieve personal goals, as well as factors outside of the adolescent that either bolster or thwart career aspirations. For example, in adolescence it is common to feel that one is the center of attention (termed the "imaginary audience").

This perception can lead to **self-handicapping** behavior. For example, adolescents self-handicap by not engaging in tasks to avoid failing. Behaving this way helps to manage both self-esteem and other peoples' impressions of the adolescent. When adolescents engage in self-handicapping, they also may demonstrate a **competence-performance gap**, which is the difference between ability and performance. An example is when one's true ability is different from how one performs a given task. This may happen when adolescents are embarrassed about being skilled in an area that they think others will ridicule (e.g., being a good singer, artist, mathematician) because it is perceived by others as a nerdy, gender-specific, or strange activity.

SOCIAL DIMENSIONS

Career choice in adolescents is profoundly influenced by factors within the microsystem, including gender, ethnicity, SES, work experience, parents, and peers. It is also influenced by factors in the exosystem, including social policy, culture, media, and trends in valuing money versus service to society. These will be examined in the following sections.

MICROSYSTEM FACTORS

Gender and career paths. Historically, males and females have chosen careers that conform to a traditional view of gender roles and, although these norms are changing, research demonstrates that gender may continue to be a factor in career choice. For example, currently women are more likely to pursue higher education than men, yet they are not as well represented in leadership in education as men (Abele & Spurk, 2011). Additionally, among those pursuing graduate degrees, women are still more likely than men to pursue degrees in social sciences, law, and medicine, whereas men are more likely to study STEM fields (Robertson et al., 2010; Su, Rounds, & Armstrong, 2009).

One study of 3,829 students found that females feel less connected to real-world context in the STEM field. For example, there are fewer female role models within STEM occupations and fewer collaborative tasks required (Hazari, Sonnert, Sadler, & Shanahan, 2010). Other researchers claim that the difference lies within the interests of males versus females, with females demonstrating interests in social and arts activities, whereas males demonstrate interest in realistic pursuits (using Holland's paradigm of career interest; Turner, Conkel, Starkey, & Landgraf, 2010). Further, these researchers indicated that while females demonstrate more adaptability and use their skill set to determine their career choice, males tend to be more assertive and manipulate their environment to generate occupational opportunities for themselves.

Other researchers claim that cultural and gender norms unduly influence career decisions by leading males and females to feel pressure to pursue traditional career paths and bias the results of self-assessments of career interest (see, for example, Correll, 2001; Thébaud, 2010). Gender (or gender bias) may have an influence in career choice, but whether it affects career investigation or exploration remains unclear. Some researchers report that there is no gender difference in career search and selection, while others claim the opposite (Rogers & Creed, 2011).

The relationship between gender and career outcomes has also been investigated. One 10-year longitudinal study found that having children negatively affected female career success (work hours, pay), especially for those who had their children early in their careers, but the same effect was not seen for men (Abele & Spurk, 2011). Gender also predicts extrinsic career rewards in adulthood, with women achieving less reward than men (Cochran, Wang, Stevenson, Johnson, & Crews, 2011). There has long been a debate about pay inequity between males and females, the underrepresentation of females in top-tier leadership, and the inequity in distribution of home and family responsibilities for females, and how this affects career success. While in the past high career aspirations were the domain of males, the research shows that this is no longer the case, and females aspire to higher educational achievement (Howard et al., 2011). Research in this area is vast and quickly evolving, and the reader is directed to the industrial/organizational literature for expanded coverage.

Ethnicity/SES and career paths. There appears to be less evidence for ethnic differences in career choice. One study of a national sample of eighth-grade students indicated that gender, but not ethnicity, impacts career interest. White and Latino females were 50% less likely than White males to have interest in employment in the field of math. Black and Latino males were equally likely to have interest in science and math careers as their White counterparts (Hirschi, Niles, & Akos, 2011). Other researchers found that, in a national sample of college graduates, males were overrepresented in science and engineering majors compared to females, but White males were not more numerous than Black and Latino males in STEM majors. Further, biology attracted across gender and ethnicity in equal measure (Riegle-Crumb & King, 2010). Researchers have found no ethnic difference in career interest; however, they have found differences in perceived barriers to opportunity, such that White students perceived fewer barriers than students of color (Fouad & Byars-Winston, 2005).

One study demonstrated that SES is related to expectations of educational achievement of adolescents (Trusty, 1998) and the literature has demonstrated at least a small effect of family SES on career ambitions, with those from higher SES having career aspirations towards higher-paying careers (Cochran et al., 2011; Howard et al., 2011).

Working adolescents. Many adolescents begin entry into the working world by holding part-time jobs. While there are some positive outcomes associated with adolescent employment, including job experience, practice functioning with adult responsibilities, learning a skill, increased household income, and less time spent in front of screens (Kalenkoski & Pabilonia, 2012), there are also negative outcomes associated with adolescent employment. These include less time engaged in homework, less sleep on non-work days, and worse school performance. Students who work more than 20 hours per week demonstrate poorer school performance than those who work fewer hours (Staff, Schulenberg, & Bachman, 2010).

Parent and peer influences. Parents have always had an influence on the career choice of adolescents; however, this influence has changed over the decades. In the early 1900s, an adolescent's career path was often dictated by the jobs held by elder relatives. At age 12, a young person went to work with an elder in an **apprenticeship**, which is a training program for a profession or trade in which the student works on the job with the teacher to develop job skills. Today, apprenticeships are most often professional relationships within trade occupations, such as plumber, electrician, construction worker, and so on. During this training, the apprentice is often provided supports to help learn a task and then these supports are gradually removed. This is called **independence training**. Currently it is common for young people to find a **mentor**, who is a person with higher-level skills and more experience in the field. In fact, mentor programs are frequently used within organizations for new hires throughout a company, regardless of an individual's age.

Research demonstrates that peers and parents both influence career exploration, preparation, and career choice (Metheny & McWhirter, 2013; Tynkkynen, Nurmi, & Salmela-Aro, 2010). These members of the microsystem have been shown to increase adolescents' engagement in the career search, which is associated with better career outcomes. This may include everything from words of encouragement to making connections for teens so that they may job shadow, participate in informational interviewing, discover interesting new career avenues, explore more post-secondary options, locate mentors, and so on. Parenting styles may even play a role in influencing career decisions, with authoritarian parenting style associated with poorer career decision-making abilities (Koumoundourou, Tsaousis, & Kounenou, 2010).

EXOSYSTEM FACTORS

Social policy. The jobs available to adolescents often are influenced by exosystem factors such as social policies, culture, media, and trends in society. Social policy includes norms, rules, legislation, and customs around how people are treated within a society. When laws are passed that provide services for people without resources, this can create jobs for people interested in working to help people. As the leaders in government change, social policy can change to provide more or fewer career opportunities for adolescents to pursue (Ashby & Schoon, 2010).

Culture. The culture of the United States has changed tremendously with regard to career choice. For example, today young people are free to choose whatever career they have an interest in and the resources to pursue, whereas 50 to 100 years ago, adolescents were expected to continue in occupations held by their parents. Additionally, where once women were expected to stop working as soon as they married or had children, they are now working in lifelong careers and choosing not to marry or have children. It is illegal to use discriminatory hiring practices based on gender or race; still, institutional discrimination has kept women and minorities from securing some occupations and advancement within some fields. The culture of the United States also dictates that it is typical and expected for adolescents to make career choices early and to secure a career path by the time they graduate from high school. However, due to rapid technological advances, it is likely that young people entering the job market today will end up in careers that do not even exist yet.

Media. Media can influence career choice for adolescents, and as instant access to worldwide information becomes commonplace, adolescents are exposed to local, national, and global issues that may impact their career choice. Movies, Internet videos, television shows, websites, broadcast media, and so on can influence career choice through popularization of certain careers or exposing unpopular, dangerous, or illegal facets of some careers.

Trends. Just as social policy, culture, and media change to influence career choice in adolescence, so do trends in valuing money versus service to society. The research is not conclusive on this point; however, one study of 16,000 Baby Boomers (born between 1946 and 1964), Generation Xers, (born in the early 1960s to early 1980s), and Generation MEs (born late 1980s to 2000; a.k.a. Gen Ys, or Millennials) found a steady increase in the value of leisure time from one generation to the next, as well as a decrease in the importance of work (Twenge, Campbell, Hoff man, & Lance, 2010). Gen X demonstrated the highest proportion of respondents who endorsed status and financial reward as important. There were fewer people in Gen ME who endorsed these extrinsic rewards, but still more Gen MEs than Boomers who endorsed the importance of status and financial rewards. Most interesting was the finding that Gen ME did not report valuing service to society, friends, and intrinsic reward as much as popular press has indicated. In fact, Boomers were rated the highest in these areas.

CONCLUSION

Adolescence is a time of identity development, including career identity development and career choice. Technology is rapidly changing, and it is difficult to prepare adolescents of today for careers because, for many adolescents, the career they will choose as adults does not exist yet. It is important to prepare adolescents to better understand themselves, their personalities, values, and goals, and then help them to explore careers that will be a good fit. Parents, teachers, and peers have powerful influence on adolescent career choice, and those who prepare, explore, set goals, and work toward achieving those goals demonstrate better career outcomes as adults.

CRITICAL THINKING QUESTION

How can high schools best prepare students for post-secondary education or the world of work?

KEY TERMS

Apprenticeship—A training program for a profession or trade in which the student works on the job with the teacher to develop job skills

Competence—Ability to perform a task completely and successfully

Competence-performance gap—When one's ability is different than their performance on a task, generally in the direction of high ability and low performance

Extrinsic motivation—Using external rewards (e.g., money, prizes, recognition) to induce a person to behave a certain way or complete a task

Independence training—Using supports to help a person learn a task and then gradually removing the supports

Initiative—Internal drive to complete some task or reach a goal

Intrinsic motivation—Internal rewards (e.g., pride, self-satisfaction, feeling of competence) from performing a task that induce a person to behave a certain way

Mastery orientation—The desire to practice a task to become very good at it, based on a belief that success in a task has more to do with practice and hard work than innate competencies

Mentor—A person with higher-level skills and more experience who guides and advises some-one with lower-level skills and less experience

Motivation—Internal feelings of desire to do something

Performance orientation—The desire to practice a task to become better than everyone else at it, based on a belief that success in a task has more to do with innate competencies than practice

Self-handicapping—Avoiding performing a task to avoid failing and manage both self-esteem and others' perceptions of one's competence and worth

Vocation—Feelings of particular suitability for a job or occupation

Work ethic—Valuing hard work and finding it to be self-satisfying and a worthy pursuit

ADDITIONAL RESOURCES

Online Big 5 Personality Assessment: http://www.outofservice.com/bigfive/

Holland Personality Assessment: http://www.truity.com/test/holland-code-career-test

Gender and Career Choice: The Role of Biased Self-Assessment https://sociology.stanford.edu/sites/default/files/publications/gender_and_the_career_choice_process-_the_role_of_biased_self-assessments.pdf

Gender and Entrepreneurship: http://w.asanet.org/images/journals/docs/pdf/spq/Sept10SPQFeature.pdf

REFERENCES

Abele, A. E., & Spurk, D. (2011). The dual impact of gender and the influence of timing of parenthood on men's and women's career development: Longitudinal findings. *International Journal of Behavioral Development, 35*, 225–232.

Amabile, T. M., Hill, K. G., Hennessey, B. A., & Tighe, E. M. (1994). The work preference inventory: Assessing intrinsic and extrinsic motivational orientations. *Journal of Personality and Social Psychology, 66*, 950–967. doi:http://dx.doi.org/10.1037/0022–3514.66.5.950

Ashby, J. S., & Schoon, I. (2010). Career success: The role of teenage career aspirations, ambition value and gender in predicting adult social status and earnings. *Journal of Vocational Behavior, 77*, 350–360.

Bergman, L. R., Corovic, J., Ferrer-Wreder, L., & Modig, K. (2014). High IQ in early adolescence and career success in adulthood: Findings from a Swedish longitudinal study. *Research in Human Development, 11*, 165–185.

Cochran, D. B., Wang, E. W., Stevenson, S. J., Johnson, L. E., & Crews, C. (2011). Adolescent occupational aspirations: Test of Gottfredson's theory of circumscription and compromise. *The Career Development Quarterly, 59*, 412–427.

Coetzee, M., & Beukes, C. J. (2010). Employability, emotional intelligence and career preparation support satisfaction among adolescents in the school-to-work transition phase. *Journal of Psychology in Africa, 20*, 439–446.

Correll, S. J. (2001). Gender and the career choice process: The role of biased self assessments. *American Journal of Sociology, 106*, 1691–1730.

Di Fabio, A., & Kenny, M. E. (2010). Promoting emotional intelligence and career decision making among Italian high school students. *Journal of Career Assessment, 19*, 21–34. doi:10.1177/1069072710382530

Feiertag, J., & Berge, Z. L. (2008). Training Generation N: How educators should approach the Net Generation. *Education and Training, 50*, 457–464.

Fouad, N. A., & Byars-Winston, A. M. (2005). Cultural context of career choice: Meta-analysis of race/ethnicity differences. *The Career Development Quarterly, 53*, 223–233.

Goldberg, L. R. (1990). An alternative "description of personality": The Big-Five factor structure. *Journal of Personality and Social Psychology, 59*, 1216–1229.

Harmon, L. W., DeWitt, D. W., Campbell, D. P., & Hansen, J. I. C. (1994). *Strong Interest Inventory: Applications and technical guide: Form T317 of the Strong Vocational Interest Blanks.* Redwood City, CA: Stanford University Press.

Hazari, Z., Sonnert, G., Sadler, P. M., & Shanahan, M. C. (2010). Connecting high school physics experiences, outcome expectations, physics identity, and physics career choice: A gender study. *Journal of Research in Science Teaching, 47*, 978–1003.

Hirschi, A., Niles, S. G., & Akos, P. (2011). Engagement in adolescent career preparation: Social support, personality and the development of choice decidedness and congruence. *Journal of Adolescence, 34*, 173–182.

Holland, J. L. (1973). *Making vocational choices: A theory of careers.* Upper Saddle River, NJ: Prentice Hall.

Howard, K. A. S., Carlstrom, A. H., Katz, A. D., Chew, A. Y., Ray, G. C., Laine, L., et al. (2011). Career aspirations of youth: Untangling race/ethnicity, SES, and gender. *Journal of Vocational Behavior, 79*, 98–109. doi:10.1016/j.jvb.2010.12.002

Janssen, O., & Van Yperen, N. W. (2004). Employees' goal orientations, the quality of leader-member exchange, and the outcomes of job performance and job satisfaction. *Academy of Management Journal, 47*, 368–384.

Kalenkoski, C. M., & Pabilonia, S. W. (2012). Time to work or time to play: The effect of student employment on homework, sleep, and screen time. *Labour Economics, 19*, 211–221.

Koumoundourou, G. A., Tsaousis, I., & Kounenou, K. (2010). Parental influences on Greek adolescents' career decision-making difficulties: The mediating role of core self-evaluations. *Journal of Career Assessment, 19*, 165–182. doi: 1069072710385547.

Lent, R. W., Brown, S. D., & Hackett, G. (1994). Toward a unifying social cognitive theory of career and academic interest, choice, and performance. *Journal of Vocational Behavior, 45*, 79–122.

Lubinski, D., & Benbow, C. P. (2006). Study of mathematically precocious youth after 35 years: Uncovering antecedents for the development of math-science expertise. *Perspectives on Psychological Science, 1*, 316–345.

Malanchuk, O., Messersmith, E. E., & Eccles, J. S. (2010). The ontogeny of career identities in adolescence. *New Directions for Child and Adolescent Development, 130*, 97–110.

McClelland, D. C. (1961). *The achieving society*. Princeton, NJ: Van Nostrand.

Metheny, J., & McWhirter, E. H. (2013). Contributions of social status and family support to college students' career decision self-efficacy and outcome expectations. *Journal of Career Assessment, 21*, 378–394.

O'Boyle, E. H., Humphrey, R. H., Pollack, J. M., Hawver, T. H., & Story, P. A. (2011). The relation between emotional intelligence and job performance: A meta-analysis. *Journal of Organizational Behavior, 32*, 788–818.

Patton, W., & McMahon, M. (2014). *Career development and systems theory: Connecting theory and practice*. Rotterdam, The Netherlands: Sense Publishers.

Porfeli, E. J., & Skorikov, V. B. (2010). Specific and divisive career exploration during late adolescence. *Journal of Career Assessment, 18*, 46–58.

Riegle-Crumb, C., & King, B. (2010). Questioning a white male advantage in STEM: Examining disparities in college major by gender and race/ethnicity. *Educational Researcher, 39*, 656–664.

Robertson, K. F., Smeets, S., Lubinski, D., & Benbow, C. P. (2010). Beyond the threshold hypothesis even among the gifted and top math/science graduate students, cognitive abilities, vocational interests, and lifestyle preferences matter for career choice, performance, and persistence. *Current Directions in Psychological Science, 19*, 346–351.

Rogers, M. E., & Creed, P. A. (2011). A longitudinal examination of adolescent career planning and exploration using a social cognitive career theory framework. *Journal of Adolescence, 34*, 163–172.

Staff, J., Schulenberg, J. E., & Bachman, J. G. (2010). Adolescent work intensity, school performance, and academic engagement. *Sociology of Education, 83*, 183–200.

Strenze, T. (2007). Intelligence and socioeconomic success: A meta-analytic review of longitudinal research. *Intelligence, 35*, 401–426.

Su, R., Rounds, J., & Armstrong, P. I. (2009). Men and things, women and people: A meta-analysis of sex differences in interests. *Psychological Bulletin, 135*, 859–884.

Thébaud, S. (2010). Gender and entrepreneurship as a career choice: Do self-assessments of ability matter? *Social Psychology Quarterly, 73*, 288–304.

Trusty, J. (1998). Family influences on educational expectations of late adolescents. *The Journal of Educational Research, 91*, 260–271.

Turner, S. L., Conkel, J., Starkey, M. T., & Landgraf, R. (2010). Relationships among middle-school adolescents' vocational skills, motivational approaches, and interests. *The Career Development Quarterly, 59*, 154–168.

Twenge, J. M., Campbell, S. M., Hoffman, B. J., & Lance, C. E. (2010). Generational differences in work values: Leisure and extrinsic values increasing, social and intrinsic values decreasing. *Journal of Management, 36*, 1117–1142.

Tynkkynen, L., Nurmi, J. E., & Salmela-Aro, K. (2010). Career goal-related social ties during two educational transitions: Antecedents and consequences. *Journal of Vocational Behavior, 76*, 448–457.

Beyond Self Actualization
Voluntary Midlife Career Transitions and Implications for Career Counselors

BETH HUEBNER AND CHADWICK ROYAL

ABSTRACT

Voluntary career change during the midlife stage of the lifespan can sometimes be attributed to self-actualization concerns. Midcareer adults realize the reasons that brought them into a career no longer apply. Those in midlife often seek meaning in life, and some can attain this meaning through finding a calling. Choosing to change careers in midlife is not always a rational decision, and emotions play a strong role. Career counselors are encouraged to employ creative approaches such as the Transtheoretical Model of Change, the Life-Span Life-Space approach, as well as narrative techniques to help middle-aged clients find increased happiness in their work.

Career change can occur at any time during one's career. This change can be voluntary or involuntary. Workers in midlife may choose to evaluate different careers in order to fulfill self-actualization concerns. After someone achieves job security and prestige in a career, the need to find meaning in one's work may emerge. Midcareer adults seeking a calling require guidance beyond the standard trait and factor. These individuals make emotions-based decisions and need assistance discovering their calling and then weighing the risks and rewards to achieve their new goals. The

Beth Huebner and Chadwick Royal, "Beyond Self Actualization: Voluntary Midlife Career Transitions and Implications for Career Counselors," *Career Planning and Adult Development Journal*, vol. 29, no. 4, pp. 37-44. Copyright © 2013 by National Career Development Association. Reprinted with permission. Provided by ProQuest LLC. All rights reserved.

purpose of this paper is to provide additional insight into the population of midcareer adults who are seeking self-actualization and beyond in a career. It will also explore the unique ways in which these individuals make career choices and changes, as well as the implications for counselors.

MIDLIFE CAREER CHANGE

Zemon (2002) provided the factors that typically influence one's initial career choices, such as youthful dreams, interests, talents, market availability, geographic preferences, and the likelihood that a career would support one's lifestyle. She argues that these are all forward-looking factors. Middle-age individuals review where they are in life and what they want to have in the future. Some mid-career adults find that the reasons they began in their current career are no longer valid or applicable. Someone new to the world of work may desire job security and then prestige. A new graduate may be more willing to work long hours and sacrifice personal time to gain recognition at work. Some older workers may not be willing to sustain the personal sacrifice that they endured in their twenties and thirties. Middle-aged people change careers because of occupational dissatisfaction, lack of career identity, job insecurity, workplace bullying, or conflicts between work and other life roles (Barclay, Stoltz, & Chung, 2011).

Barclay and colleagues (2011) pointed out that career change is a frequent occurrence. As many as 1 in 3 are currently in the process of changing jobs. Career change typically occurs in the maintenance stage of lifespan development, between the ages of 35–65 (Super, Savickas, & Super, 1996). Super (1980) has illustrated that this recycling process can happen at any stage in a career. During the maintenance stage, a worker evaluates what he or she has accomplished, and then explores alternatives by seeking new information about the world of work (Super, 1980). Some report satisfaction in their current roles at midlife and do not require a career change. They can derive workplace satisfaction by growing in their current role. Others become dissatisfied, and seek out career change to help fulfill their needs and values (Zemon, 2002). Midlife career changes are a reaction to both experience and mortality (Zemon, 2002).

An example of this reflection on experience and mortality is the case of a 40 year old Caucasian male who recently experienced a mild heart attack. He had been working long hours and signing up for additional projects at work in order to achieve the title of Vice President. He knows he is still on track for that promotion, but has begun questioning his motivation for the promotion. When he was younger, he was concerned for his new family. He wanted to make sure he had a reliable job and could save enough to put his two children through college. His children are now out of college, yet he is still working the long hours. In the recovery process from his heart attack, this client discovered his love for Yoga and meditation. He has expressed a desire to become certified in Yoga instruction so that he can assist others in relaxation techniques to help ward off the stressors that can increase risk for heart attack.

FINDING MEANING THROUGH A CALLING

Steger and Dik (2009) discussed how important it is for people to find meaning in life. Some find it in their children, volunteering, being good at what they do at work, or a combination of factors. This meaning can be achieved through multiple paths such as goal directedness, a sense of coherence in life, the pursuit and attainment of goals, and the need for purpose, values, and self-efficacy in life (Cohen & Ciarns, 2012). People who have their psychological needs met at work report higher self-esteem and less anxiety. Steger and Dik (2009) described having one's psychological needs met at work as a calling.

Duffy and Sadlacek (2007) reviewed the available literature to attempt to further define the construct of a calling, and determined that it is an external pull that individuals feel toward a certain career path. A calling means that one's career provides meaning and purposeful experiences, and also contributes to the greater good. Those who experience a calling tend to report having meaning in life (Steger & Dik, 2009). Dik and Duffy (2009) summarized available definitions of a calling into three parts: an externally-driven transcendent summons, deriving a sense of purpose or meaningfulness from one's work, with the primary sources of motivation coming from other-oriented values and goals. Using these definitions, one who seeks a calling is searching for meaning in life, which is derived from fulfilling one's own sense of purpose and helping others.

SELF-ACTUALIZATION AND BEYOND

Maslow's hierarchy of needs theory is based on the premise that human beings are motivated to acquire things they do not have, and once they have them, those needs are no longer a motivator (Maslow, 1943). Applying Maslow's hierarchy to the workplace, employees first desire job security. After job security, employees seek social needs. These needs can be met outside the workplace, such as with religious or other groups, but work can also be viewed as a social setting. After social needs, employees seek ego needs, such as being recognized at work for a job well done. The final level in Maslow's hierarchy when applied to the workplace is self-actualization or self-fulfillment (Greene & Burke, 2007).

Maslow later suggested there was a level beyond self-actualization. This level can be described as selfless-actualization, because to achieve peak experience, people need to move from concerns of the self to concerns of others. These workers are less concerned about personal prestige, and are now focused on how they can help others succeed. One characteristic of an employee who is working beyond self-actualization is that he or she tends to feel that everyone should be allowed the opportunity to develop to their highest potential. Another characteristic is being attracted to unsolved or difficult problems (Greene & Burke, 2007). Workers that find self-actualization and beyond tend to thrive. These workers also understand how their work impacts others, and how it contributes to the bigger picture (Spreitzer, Sutcliffe, Dutton, Sonenshein, & Grant, 2005).

An example is a client who entered into a career dialogue because he was feeling unsatisfied in his long-time career as a project manager in a large metropolitan area. This client had become aware of the amount of animals that are euthanized because of overpopulation. He wanted to find a way to help these animals and was contemplating quitting his lucrative job in order to serve the greater good. He saw animal overpopulation as an unsolved problem that he felt would give him fulfillment in life if he could work on the solution. This client was driven by these external, other-oriented forces, to pursue a calling in an area mostly unknown to him. Traditional trait-and-factor approaches and rational decision-making are not adequate to address this client's career concerns.

CAREER DECISION-MAKING

Rational decision-making involves exploring options and then choosing the option that would provide the highest outcome possible. These rational models have been labeled as the logical way to make career decisions. Murtagh, Lopes, and Lyons (2011) stated that there are too many instances in which people do not make the decision based on the highest yield, and there are other factors at play.

The authors stated that systematic decision-making is not possible in the realm of careers (Murtagh et al., 2011). There is a great deal of chance at work in career decision-making, and emotions also play a large role. The results of Murtagh and colleagues' (2011) research demonstrated that there were two major themes among individuals who change careers voluntarily. The first was planless actions and positive emotions. The majority of individuals in this category began learning a new skill for the enjoyment of it, without planning for a new career in that area. Others changed careers based on a gut feeling that the new occupation felt right to them. The second decision-making model that appeared was what the researchers referred to as "constructing the decision". These individuals knew what they wanted, and took time to make the career change happen. Those who constructed careers were often middle-aged, and saw a better version of themselves in the new occupation (Murtagh et al., 2011).

IMPLICATIONS FOR COUNSELORS

Those individuals who display characteristics of self-actualization have the highest levels of happiness, which makes helping a mid-career client find a calling even more prudent for career counselors. Cohen and Ciarns (2012) suggest that clinicians could assess a client's level of self-actualization to determine the distress level caused by the search for meaning in life. Clinicians can also work with clients to determine the client's need for meaning. If it is high, and they have not found it, distress levels could be high and the client could be clinically depressed (Cohen & Ciarns, 2012).

Sackett (1998) describes what Maslow meant by self-actualization and how it shows up in the career counseling setting. Some people never strive for self-actualization at work because they are concerned with more foundational goals such as prestige or even security. Those who have attained the first four levels will strive for self-actualization and beyond, and may report dissatisfaction with their current career or job in terms of lacking meaning or fulfilling a calling. The earlier examples of clients both began to feel a sense of disappointment in their current roles after having discovered their calling. In both cases, these clients had discovered their calling, but did not know how to begin the career transition and were unsure if they were ready and willing to take the risk necessary to make the change.

Sackett (1998) described clients who are closed off to initiating the necessary steps for a job search because they are presently concerned about prestige and security and choose not to risk change. Clients who strive for self-actualization choose new jobs that promote growth. The opposite of growth is sometimes fear. Some clients who are at the point of wanting to change careers may fear change to the point that they are unwilling or not ready to change jobs. Another way forward is shutting out the voices of others and listening to one's own voice (Sackett, 1998). Meeting the client where he or she is, is essential to the counseling process.

In a career counseling setting, clients who are honest about their accomplishments and desires are most apt to be successful in their career change. If the path to self-actualization is the priority, and other needs are met, then one may choose what one enjoys over what pays the most. Self-actualization can occur as a process rather than an end state. It can also come from peak experiences. These peak experiences are moments when someone realizes they have a unique gift or skill. In the case of the project manager who wanted to open an animal rescue organization, he was able to realize peak experiences by volunteering at a local animal shelter. A hurdle in achieving self-actualization is identifying defense mechanisms and overcoming them (Sackett, 1998). For the project manager client, we concentrated on discovering his fears related to career change, and developed a plan to face and overcome those fears.

Barclay and colleagues (2011) posited that little research has been done to show the cognitive, behavioral, and affective progression middle-aged individuals go through in a career change. They suggested using the Transtheoretical Model of Change (TTM; Prochaska, DiClemente, & Norcross, 1992) with the Life-Span Life-Space approach to career development (LSLS; Super, 1980) to measure clients' growth with career decision-making. TTM is used to measure readiness of change in clients. LSLS describes the major career and life role stages of development, which include growth, exploration, establishment, maintenance, and disengagement. Integrating TTM and LSLS can help counselors assess where the client is in their life stage, and then their stage of, and readiness for, change (Barclay et al., 2011).

Barclay and colleagues (2011) suggested that career counseling is most important for midlife clients because these clients should make the most of the change, to align with their life-stage development. The midlife career change decision is not as simple as a trait-and-factor match, and often involves many aspects of the client's life and sense of self. A career counselor can help a client through the emotional, cognitive, and behavior processes as well as traditional career assessments and interventions.

Chen (2003) provided further evidence for the need for career counselors to integrate theories in career counseling. Trait and factor must be integrated with other theories for the best counseling outcomes. The sense of self is imperative to any career journey—career is a process for self-realization. Self-concept, personal disposition, self-efficacy, and contextual meaning making can be combined into a career counseling process that helps clients achieve self-realization. Chen (2003) describes how narrative techniques can help clients find meaning in traditional career assessments. Each client has a story to tell about his or her career, which helps clients with self-realization.

DISCUSSION

Voluntary midlife career changes occur for many different types of reasons. Seeking self-actualization and beyond is just one such reason. Clients in this category are striving for meaning in life, and thus are looking to pursue a calling. Typical career assessments are not adequate when working with this population. Those seeking a calling do not always make decisions based on the analysis of assessment results and available data. These clients often make decisions based on emotions or other non-rational factors. Integrating standard trait-and-factor counseling with other constructivist or narrative theories will help draw out the client's story and assist them on their career journey.

In working with midcareer adults, it is important to listen to the client's story. Clients will often reveal peak experiences when asked to reveal what they are most proud of from their career. A counselor can then help the client find meaning in these experiences. Based on the client's readiness for change, a counselor can also assist the client to find more ways to achieve these experiences, be it through volunteer work, additional projects, or a career change. Some clients will be willing to follow their gut feeling and jump into a new career, whereas others require time and more experiences to construct a new career.

REFERENCES

Barclay, S., Stoltz, K., & Chung, Y. B. (2011). Voluntary midlife career change: Integrating the transtheo-retical model and the life-span life-space approach. *Career Development Quarterly, 59*, 386–399.

Chen, C. (2003). Integrating perspectives in development theory and practice. *Career Development Quarterly, 51*, 203–216.

Cohen, K., & Ciarns, D. (2012). Is searching for meaning in life associated with reduced subjective well-being? Confirmation and possible moderators. *Journal of Happiness Studies, 13*, 313–331.

Dik, B. J., & Duffy, R. D. (2009). Calling and vocation at work: Definitions and prospects for research and practice. *Counseling Psychologist, 37*, 424–250.

Duffy, R., & Sadlacek, W. (2007). The presence of and search for a calling: Connections to career development. *Journal of Vocational Behavior, 70*, 590–601.

Greene, L., & Burke, G. (2007). Beyond self-actualization. *Journal of Health and Human Services Administration, 30*, 116–128.

Maslow, A. H. (1943). A theory of human motivation. *Psychological Review, 50*, 370–396.

Murtagh, N., Lopes, P., & Lyons, E. (2011). Decision making in voluntary career change: An other-than-rational perspective. *Career Development Quarterly, 59*, 249–263.

Prochaska, J., DiClemente, C., & Norcross, J. (1992). In search of how people change: Applications to addictive behaviors. *American Psychologist, 47* (9), 1102–1114.

Sackett, S. (1998). Career counseling as an aid to self-actualization. *Journal of Career Development, 24*, 235–244.

Spreitzer, G., Sutcliffe, K., Dutton, J., Sonenshein, S., & Grant, A. (2005). A socially embedded model of thriving at work. *Organization Science, 16*, 537–549.

Steger, M., & Dik, B. (2009). If one is looking for meaning in life, does it help to find meaning in work? *Applied Psychology: Health and Well-Being.* 1 (3), 303–320.

Super, D. (1980). A life-span life-space approach to career development. *Journal of Vocational Behavior,* *16,* 282–298.

Super, D., Savickas, M., & Super, C. (1996). The life-span, life-space approach to careers. *Career Choice & Development, 3,* 121–178.

Zemon, C. (2002). Midlife career choices: How are they different from other career choices? *Library Trends, 50,* 665–672.

ABOUT THE AUTHORS

Beth Huebner is a Masters student in the Counselor Education program at North Carolina Central University in Durham, North Carolina. She plans to graduate in December 2013 with a Master of Arts in Career Counseling and Placement, and pursue licensure as a professional counselor (LPCA). She earned the MBA in Management at Strayer University in 2006. She currently works at Cisco Systems, where she has held multiple leadership roles in her 17-year tenure. After a successful career as a Technical Services Manager and Director, she realized her best days at work were those spent helping employees understand their own potential and assisting them to find ways to do more of what they love in their careers. She made a voluntary midlife career change in 2012 when she moved from Technical Services to Human Resources at Cisco. After graduation in December, she plans to continue working with mid-career adults in their career journeys. Contact her as follows:

Chadwick Royal, PhD, is Associate Professor in the Counselor Education Program at North Carolina Central University. He is the coordinator of the Career Counseling and School Counseling Programs. He earned the PhD in Counselor Education at North Carolina State University in 1999, and the MS in Community Counseling at the University of North Carolina, Greensboro in 1996. In addition to his work as a counselor educator, he has worked as a mental health counselor in public and private settings, as a school counselor, and as a non-profit director. He has authored several peer-reviewed articles, and has recently co-authored a text book on Consultation (in production at SAGE). Contact him as follows:

DISCUSSION QUESTIONS

1 Spend some time thinking about your own career development. When you were five, six, or seven years old, what did you want to be when you grew up? What about when you were 11 or 12 years old? How about when you were 18? Do your early choices match what you want to do now? What happened to your childhood dreams of your career?

2 If you were writing a book about your life (specifically about your career), what would be your chapter titles?

3 How did you decide to enter your field/career? What factors are (or were) important to your decision? How do you think your reasons for your decision compare to others' reasons?

CONCLUSION

Occupations, jobs, and positions are bound to change for our clients over time. All changes are part of their (overall) career. Although certain changes could be considered developmentally appropriate, it doesn't mean that they would not benefit from a career counselor's efforts. It is important for counselors to understand the developmental context of their clients and to select developmentally appropriate interventions.

INDEX OF KEY TERMS

- career
- career decision-making
- career transition
- cognitive factors
- job
- midlife career change
- occupation
- position
- self-actualization

- social dimensions
- voluntary/involuntary career change

SUGGESTED PUBLICATIONS FOR FURTHER READING

Hartung, P. J., Porfeli, E. J., & Vondracek, F. W. (2008). Career adaptability in childhood. *Career Development Quarterly, 57*(1), 63–74.

Royal, C., Wade, W., & Nickel, H. (2015). Career development and vocational behavior of adults with attention deficit/hyperactivity disorder. *Career Planning and Adult Development Journal, 31*(4), 54–63.

Tracey, T., & Sodano, S. (2008). Issues of stability and change in interest development. *Career Development Quarterly, 57*(1), 51–62.

CAREER COUNSELING SETTINGS

INTRODUCTION

If someone asked you to name locations where career counseling takes place, how many could you name? Most of you would probably say career counseling takes place in local high schools across the country. Did you know that career counseling takes place in college career centers, private practices, mental health centers, and government-supported career centers in almost every community? This chapter will discuss several of the settings where career counseling takes place.

Career Development in Schools
An Historical Perspective

BRIAN HUTCHISON, SPENCER G. NILES, AND JERRY TRUSTY

S chool counselors represent a historical cornerstone of the counseling profession, and career development represents a longstanding core focus of the work performed by school counselors. Professional school counselors provide career interventions to address the developmental needs of their students and to maximize students' potential for success as workers and citizens. Moreover, the evolution of school counseling and, by extension, the career counseling strategies used by school counselors reflect a symbiotic relationship with societal developments. Urban migration, Sputnik, technological advances, a global economy, and exploding cultural diversity serve as examples of societal factors influencing the values emphasized and the career interventions used by school counselors. For example, the flight of Sputnik led to the National Defense and Education Act that led to increased efforts at moving talented students toward more involvement in science-related course work. The point is that career interventions do not occur in a vacuum. Understand the forces at work in society and there is an excellent chance that one will gain important insight into the career interventions being provided in schools (Herr, 2001).

Toward this end, [...] we outline four historical periods that have influenced career interventions in the schools. These periods contain

Brian Hutchison, Spencer G. Niles, and Jerry Trusty, "Career Development in Schools: An Historical Perspective," *Career Counseling Across the Lifespan: Community, School, and Higher Education*, ed. Grafton T. Eliason, Jeff L. Samide, John Patrick, and Trisha Eliason, pp. 167-188. Copyright © 2014 by Information Age Publishing. Reprinted with permission.

important information regarding national values and priorities. They reflect the link between how societal developments shape the school counseling profession. Each period underscores the pattern of various developments occurring followed by school counselors responding to the societal needs created by these developments. To aid in your understanding of each era, a sidebar has been inserted that will prompt deeper introspection. These side bars may be used for personal reflection, as goals for the reader to actively engage in understanding the material, or as course assignments.

THE PRE-PROFESSION ERA (1800s–1913)
HISTORICAL CONTEXT

American society in the late nineteenth and early twentieth century underwent dramatic change in reaction to fast-paced industrialization. Virtually the entire populace was affected as technological advancements in communications (the telegraph and telephone), travel (the railroad), and manufacturing (steam power and the development of factories) became commonplace. Workers from rural farming communities flocked to growing urban areas in search of plentiful jobs in mines and factories. Immigrants, mostly from Eastern and Southern Europe, were also attracted to the burgeoning American markets (McCormick, 1997). Between 1870 and 1914 approximately 23 million immigrants arrived at the doorstep of a nation whose population was a mere 76 million in the year 1900 (Divine et al., 2007). In retrospect, it was probably inevitable that the nation's first ghettos arose as cities strained to cope with the influx of new residents during this time.

In 1890, almost half of residential buildings in New York City were over-crowded tenement buildings housing up to 334,000 people per square mile in some wards. City ghettos at the turn of the century were dangerous, stench-smelling, crime-riddled areas more conducive to cultivating diseases than raising families. Waste was dumped into the same bodies of water from which drinking water was drawn. Smoke and pollutants hung in the air from the factories that provided the meager livelihood that trapped families in the ghettos. With the rise of cities came a steady rise in the national homicide rate, suicide rate, and incidence of alcoholism (Divine et al., 2007). Given the environmental conditions in which many children were growing up, it is hardly surprising that families were forced to send their children to work in order to survive and have any hope of making a better life for themselves.

Concern grew during this time over work conditions specifically the health and integrity of workers and the abuse of child labor (Herr, 2001). Prior to 1900, the average worker spent approximately sixty hours per week on the job taking home between $400 and $500 per year in an economy that required a $600 annual income for a family of four to "live decently" (Divine et al., 2007, p. 477). Divine et al. (2007) paints an even bleaker picture for the children that were often forced to work in this economic environment. Child labor was so common place in the early 1900s that using the term in reference to boys at that time typically meant males under the age of 14 who worked. In 1900, 20% of all boys between the ages of 10 and 15 years held jobs while the same could be said for about 10% of girls. Children were employed in textile mills, coal mines, family farms, and as home-based piecemeal workers paid for the number of items (such as costume jewelry or clothing) they produced until after 1908 when the first national child-labor law was passed (Bernert, 1958). The conditions in which these children, and most industrial workers for that matter, worked were abysmal by today's standards. Not only were children paid much less than adults, an incentive to employers for hiring children over adults, but the environments in which they worked were rife with dust, chemicals, and other pollutants that often led to chronic illnesses (Divine et al., 2007).

In this milieu, the demand for more highly skilled workers grew, challenging the educational system to better prepare students for the demands of the new world of work and eventually leading to the development of the vocational guidance programs in schools, the precursor to school counseling (Herr, 2003).

IMPORTANT CONTRIBUTORS

Brewer (1918) identifies several texts that pre-date 1900 as contributing to the field of vocational guidance. Plato's *Republic* and MacKenzie's (1795) *Man of Feeling* both highlighted the need for vocational guidance long before any efforts were made to develop actual career guidance interventions. Lysander S. Richards (1881) book *Vocophy* is the first, according to Brewer (1918) that identifies the need for career guidance as well as providing an intervention plan, the use of phrenology, for accomplishing the task of guiding persons into appropriate careers. It was not until the late 1800s and early 1900s that systematic efforts were first implemented into schools.

In 1898, Jesse B. Davis worked as a guidance counselor for 11th grade boys and girls at Central High School in Detroit, Michigan where he served as a "counselor on educational and career problems" (Pope, 2000, p. 198). This experience provided the foundation for an organized program of vocational and moral guidance that Davis implemented upon becoming the principal of a high school in Grand Rapids, Michigan in 1907. This program included counseling with respect to courses and extracurricular activities and the incorporation of vocational related assignments into English and other curricula (Brewer, 1918; Herr, Cramer, & Niles, 2004; Pope, 2000). In addition to Davis, several others were experimenting with career interventions during the same time frame including George Merrill in San Francisco, Eli W. Weaver in New York City, Meyer Bloomfield in Boston, and Frank Goodwin in Cincinnati, OH (Tang & Erford, 2004).

Frank Parsons, often called the "Father of Vocational Guidance" founded the Breadwinner's College (or Institute), part of the Civil Service House to provide educational opportunities for immigrants and young persons needing employment in 1905 and The Vocational Bureau in 1908. The Vocational Bureau trained young men to become counselors in YMCA affiliated schools, colleges, and businesses. Within a few years, the school system of Boston had created the first counselor certification program which eventually was adopted to become the first university based counselor education program at Harvard University in 1911. These programs provided training for many of the 100 elementary and secondary teachers in Boston who became vocational counselors in the Boston School System as part of the Boston Plan. School districts across the country soon followed suit, training and appointing vocational counselors to meet the growing demands for vocational intervention in schools (Borow, 1964; Brewer, 1918).

KEY EVENTS, DEVELOPMENTS, ORGANIZATIONS, AND LEGISLATION

Less than five months before he died, Frank Parsons presented a lecture that described what was to become the trait and factor theory of career decision. In this lecture, he provided data on the results of using this theory at The Vocational Bureau to counsel 80 men and women. Parson's seminal work, *Choosing a Vocation*, was published posthumously in May of 1909 providing the framework for systematic vocational intervention to the growing cadre of school counselors. The death of Parsons left a void that was quickly filled by leaders of the vocational guidance movement such as David Snedden, Frank Thompson, and Meyer Bloomfield who led the first national conference on vocational guidance in Boston (1910). Bloomfield also succeeded Frank Parsons as administrator of The Vocational Bureau and taught the first vocational guidance course at Harvard College (Brewer, 1918).

While the seeds of the vocational guidance movement were being planted in the United States, a French psychologist, Alfred Binet working with a collaborating psychiatrist named Theophilus Simon, was developing and refining the first modern

SIDEBAR 9.1

Visualize yourself as a recent immigrant living in Boston, MA in the early twentieth century. It is October 4, 1906 and you are reading the Boston Evening Transcript, a local newspaper when you see the following advertisement in the classified section (advertisement is excerpted). How would you respond to the ad? What questions would you have? What would be the impediments to your attendance?

THE BREADWINNERS' COLLEGE

Along with the opening of the great institutions of learning about us comes the announcement of the second year's lectures at the Civic Service House in old Salem street at the North End, a sort of "university extension" which constitutes the Breadwinners' College. Beyond the public-school period of the life of the youth of the North End, which is usually a very brief one, comes the life of labor and wage-earning. All the members of the family are usually breadwinners. Perhaps the primary and grammar school courses have been supplemented, in some cases, with the evening school advantages. It requires a good deal of character and a genuine taste for study, together with a habit of devotion to duty, to turn from amusements into a schoolroom immediately after supper at the end of a long day's confinement at work; but many there be who make these sacrifices for education, as the full ranks of the evening schools attest. And beyond the evening school classes, even, the ambition and actual thirst for culture spurring on the brighter members of this community of toilers, press them forward to higher planes of coordinated knowledge and thought. It is not enough to declaim the speeches of great orators: they wish to think and speak themselves.

Employers of labor who are interested in their employees would do well to call their attention to the prospectus of the Breadwinners' College. Whatever they get there is certain to make them more efficient "help," if only the selfish interest of the employer be thought of. But there is a large number of wage-earners, especially among the young generations of Russian Jews and Italians recently thronging hither, who need, besides the specific training for greater efficiency in some industrial or mercantile pursuit,.the broader outlook depending on certain large elements of culture and training along intellectual lines. To supply such needs for this class of young people is the aim of the Breadwinners' College. The courses for 1906–7 include lectures by an excellent staff of instructors, some of them well-known professors at our leading institutions of learning, upon general history and biography, principles of economics, biology, English composition, English literature, civics, the art of expression, geology, practical psychology, industrial history and law for laymen.

Mr. Meyer Bloomfield is the visible head of this latest expression of that well-known intelligent and untiring philanthropy which has ever made education of the deprived classes its main and special object, with a truly far-seeing sagacity and the highest of public alms. All preceding efforts are crowned by this purpose to discover and develop the special endowments of each individual among those who frequent the Civic Service House, in order to make them of use to him and his neighbor, and also bring him into active contact with the life and progress of the city, State and nation, and secure his contribution thereto. The studies are so selected and arranged as to go directly to the heart of each subject, so that these evening collegians, with always a first call upon them for their six o'clock breakfast the next morning, may make the most of their limited time and grasp what is most worthy of their attention.

(*Boston Evening Transcript*, October 4, 1906; retrieved March 26, 2013 from http://news.google.com/newspapers)

intelligence test. The Binet-Simon intelligence scale was designed in 1905 to help identify students who were struggling with the school curriculum. In 1916, after Binet's death in 1911, the first widely accepted American revision of the Binet-Simon test was published by Lewis M. Terman, a Stanford University professor. This revision measured a person's Intelligence Quotient (IQ) and became the Stanford-Binet IQ test that is commonly used today (Keyser & Sweetland, 1987).

KEY CONCEPTS THAT AROSE FROM THE ERA

The advantage of formal vocational preparation and guidance in schools was first recognized in the late 1800s and early part of the twentieth century. Brewer (1942) as cited in Borow (1964) identified four societal conditions spurred on by the Industrial Revolution that led to the rise of the vocational guidance movement. The four conditions were:

1   The division of labor

2   The growth of technology

3   The spread of modern forms of democracy

4   The extension of vocational education.

These conditions created the need for ways of providing vocational guidance and counseling. In 1908, Frank Parsons introduced the first systematic framework for addressing vocational needs in a counseling setting. The Parsonian framework would later grow to become the trait/factor approach to career decision-making that is still used to this day. This framework includes three steps in the career decision-making process:

1   Develop a clear understanding of yourself, aptitudes, abilities, interests, resources, limitations, and other qualities.

2   Develop knowledge of the requirements and conditions of success, advantages and disadvantages, compensation, opportunities, and prospects in different lines of work.

3   Use "true reasoning" on the relations of these two groups of facts. (Parsons, 1909, p. 5)

THE EARLY PROFESSIONAL ERA (1913–1945)
HISTORICAL CONTEXT

The Industrial Revolution was the fire in which worldwide technological innovation was forged in the first half of the twentieth century. In 1913, Henry Ford developed the moving assembly line which led to the mass production of goods and American global economic supremacy during the remainder of the twentieth century. In the years between 1913 and 1945, Americans saw the electric engine replace steam power; the automobile replace other means of personal transportation; personal appliances such as ranges, washing machines, and vacuum cleaners ease the burden of household chores; and an increase in marketing and advertisements as the economy became consumer driven (Divine, et al., 2007).

The United States was surprised by the onset of World War I in 1914 and for almost three years continued its attitude of isolation and neutrality before entering the fray in April of 1917. Upon entering the war, the nation as a whole believed that the battle would lead to a stable world free of future wars. This optimism was further buoyed by the continued economic growth experienced throughout much of the 1920s. On a "Black Thursday" in 1929, the stock market, which had been built by over-speculation over the course of five years, crashed, affecting not only investors but the entire national economy as financial institutions and manufacturers took the brunt of the economic blow. During the Great Depression, unemployment rose to 25% while the gross national product declined by 67% over the course of three years. The impact on families was devastating as savings disappeared, possessions were sold off to survive, and many men and boys had to leave home in search of work to support their families (Divine, et al., 2007).

The backdrop for the early years of the vocational guidance profession was one of extreme technological advancement, social change, turmoil, and warfare. In less than 30 years, American society experienced several periods of tension between the needs of the newly industrialized society and the needs of the workforce. At the beginning of the century, the growing industrialized economy needed more skilled workers than the workforce could supply. Following World War I, the Great Depression was a time when industrialized society failed to provide the work desperately needed by the workforce to survive, forcing government to intervene with the New Deal in an effort to jump start the economy. Just as this course of action was beginning to work, World War II redefined the world of work yet again, introducing women into the workforce in numbers greater than ever before causing great societal change at the end of the conflict (Divine, et al., 2007). These often contradictory influences caused multiple, sometimes dichotomous, guidance movements to emerge in the relatively short period of time that the vocational guidance profession was being established.

IMPORTANT CONTRIBUTORS

In 1913, the National Vocational Guidance Association (NVGA), which would become the National Career Development Association in 1984, was formed in Grand Rapids, Michigan during the Third National Conference on Vocational Guidance. Founding members included Frank Leavitt, Jesse B. Davis, Meyer Bloomfield, and John M. Brewer, all who went on to become early presidents of the NVGA. The formation of the NVGA provided a forum for scholarly research publication and the sharing of the history and principles of vocational guidance profession through the *Vocational Guidance Bulletin*, the organization's first journal, published in 1915 and later to be renamed *Occupations: The Vocational Guidance Journal*. The NVGA formalized the profession's principles in 1921 by publishing "Principles and Practices of Vocational Guidance" which has been periodically updated since then. In 1942, founding member and fifth NVGA President John M. Brewer published *History of Vocational Guidance*, an early definitive history of the movement (Pope, 2000).

In 1917, few American scientists and psychologists had any faith in intelligence tests or their ability to benefit occupational placement. One believer in testing for this person was the president of the American Psychological Association, Robert M. Yerkes. Yerkes saw the onset of World War I as an opportunity to apply intelligence testing and lobbied hard for the inclusion of intelligence testing as part of the United States Army's personnel procedures. At the time, the military had no means of placing the multitude of incoming soldiers recruited for the war effort, identifying soldiers with special skills, or of meritoriously promoting officers instead relying only on seniority for determining promotion. In the midst of many obstacles to the implementation of intelligence testing, Yerkes joined forces with Walter Dill Scott who had developed a close relationship with the Secretary of War and was also a proponent of the use of intelligence tests in support of the war effort. On August 9, 1917, the Committee on Classification of Personnel under the Office of the Adjutant General was established with Scott as the chairperson and Yerkes as a member. This committee developed and tested the Army Alpha and Beta tests with the Beta designed for use with illiterate soldiers. During World War I, the Committee administered the Alpha and Beta tests to approximately 1,175,000 soldiers. The acceptance of testing for the military during the war created an environment of greater acceptance in the scientific community and the general public, leading to the advancement of intelligence testing in the field of career guidance (Kevles, 1968).

John Dewey was a professor of philosophy, psychology, and pedagogy at the University of Chicago and Columbia University in the early 1900s. His influence on the development of the progressive education movement still influences teaching and curriculum to this day. Dewey believed that a teacher's job is to use a student's inherent motivation and interests to guide their educational growth. Although this may not seem to be revolutionary today, it was a far departure from the rote training method of education incorporated in most schools in 1916 when Dewey published *Democracy and Education* (1916). One critical aspect of Dewey's philosophy was his opposition to vocational specific education. Instead, Dewey proposed that schools should educate all students to be citizens and that vocational studies should be part of the general curriculum for all students (Rose, 2004). In current terms, Dewey's philosophy is consistent with efforts aimed at closing achievement gaps for students of lower socioeconomic status and from racial-ethnic minority groups (see ASCA, 2012; Education Trust, 2007).

Placement and testing services were expanded with the onset of the United States involvement in World War II. At the same time a seminal shift was occurring in the field of psychotherapy and career counseling. The impetus of this shift was the publication of Carl Rogers' book, *Counseling and Psychology* (1942). Rogers' focus on the importance of the counselor sharing the client's view of the world as well as the resulting attendance to the client's verbalized feelings led to a shift in the theoretical viewpoint of career guidance (Borow, 1964). "Among the significant developments which resulted were a revamping of the older cognitive concept of the client in vocational guidance to include the dynamics of affective and motivational behavior, the increased emphasis on self-acceptance and self-understanding as goals of vocational counseling" (Borrow, 1964, p. 57). In summary, a shift in focus began to occur that went away from the external locus of finding one's fit in the world of work to a more humanistic approach that incorporated an understanding of one's internal world and its interaction with the meaning of work in one's life.

KEY EVENTS, DEVELOPMENTS, ORGANIZATIONS, AND LEGISLATION

Given the inextricable link between the early vocational guidance and the current school counseling movements, it might be said that both professions began in Grand Rapids, Michigan in 1913 with the formation of the National Vocational Guidance Association (NVGA) and the subsequent publication of *Vocational Guidance*, also known as Bulletin No. 14, the summarization of the papers presented at this organizational meeting (Herr, Cramer, & Niles, 2004). In this same year, the U.S. Department of Labor was founded and included the Bureau of Labor Statistics which was moved at this time from the purview of the Department of the Interior (Pope, 2000). While these professional and governmental organizations became the formal agencies of the new profession of vocational guidance, two important tools were also being developed at this time by The Army Committee on Classification of Personnel. These were the Army Alpha and Beta tests for occupational classification and selection (Herr, Cramer, & Niles, 2004). In one seminal year (1913), the first vocational guidance professional association was formed; the government created a department concerned with employment including a bureau for collecting relevant data; and two psychometric tests were developed specifically for vocational guidance measurement.

SIDEBAR 9.2

Think about a client you have had or might have in your counseling practice. Now imagine that they had a question or problem that would prompt them to use the Occupational Outlook Handbook (OOH). Pretending you are that client, visit the OOH online at *http://www.bls.gov/ooh/* and explore as if you were the client you have in mind. How useful is the OOH? What might you, as the counselor, wish to communicate to the client before they use this resource?

The formation of the NVGA, creation of the Department of Labor, and development of the Army Alpha and Beta tests created an environment in which vocational guidance and counseling could grow and become recognized as a profession. In 1926, New York became the first state to require certification for school guidance professionals (Tang & Erford, 2004), a practice that occurs today in all fifty states and the District of Columbia (State certification requirements). In 1939, the Bureau of Labor Statistics, part of the U.S. Department of Labor, published the *Dictionary of Occupational Titles*, the first comprehensive overview of work in the United States. This was followed nine years later by the first publication of *The Occupational Outlook Handbook* in 1948. In 1945, the General Aptitude Test Battery was initiated by the U.S. Employment Service (Herr, Cramer, & Niles, 2004). These resources are widely used still today by school and career counselors.

One scholar of note laid the foundation for future impact on the profession with a seminal work published during this time period. Carl Rogers published *Counseling and Psychotherapy* in 1942. Whereas the impact on the field of career and school counseling was not immediate, this work first introduced the idea of counseling as it is defined today. Up to this point, counseling was still looked at only through a medical/disease lens where the therapist or counselor was a directive authority figure in the counseling relationship.

KEY CONCEPTS THAT AROSE FROM THE ERA

In 1918, John M. Brewer wrote a book titled *Vocational-Guidance Movement: Its Problems and Possibilities*. The book focused on the current, at the time, problems and possibilities of vocational guidance, educational guidance, and vocational counseling. In this text, Brewer posed seven questions to aid in conceptualizing the "Guidance Problems in the School":

1   What can be done to give children vocational outsight, insight, and purpose—to widen each child's "vocational horizon"?

2   How can the individual discover his talents?

3   How may a person prepare for his occupation?

4   How shall we obtain and use occupational information?

5   What are some methods appropriate in guidance?

6   What may be learned from actual accomplishments, in this country and abroad?

7   How may a principal or superintendent inaugurate a plan for vocational guidance? (Brewer, 1918, p. 15–17)

In reading the synopsis of the questions posed by Brewer at that time, one might be struck by the similarity between the core issues facing the school counseling profession now and the guidance movement approximately ninety years ago.

The Early Professional Era may be best described as a time of great change and exploration that planted the seeds for the future growth of the vocational guidance and school counseling profession. Counselors during this era experienced a gradual shift in focus from a job placement perspective to one that incorporated personal counseling and academic advisement. Several movements throughout this era, including mental hygiene, childhood development, psychometric measurement, and progressive education, opened the door for counselors to begin to look at the clients through a wider lens that allowed for issues such as personality and human development to be acknowledged in a vocational guidance concept (Gysbers, 2001). In short, multiple life roles and the development of skills for living were now part of the vocational guidance movement.

THE PROFESSIONAL ESTABLISHMENT ERA (1945-1989)

HISTORICAL CONTEXT

Rising from the ashes of World War II, the Cold War was a major geopolitical force that would influence American foreign policy and education for more than forty years. At the end of the war, the United States emerged as the unquestionable strongest nation, both militarily and economically, on Earth. The war had boosted the economy aiding in the recovery from the Great Depression, women had gone to work in support of the war effort forever changing the demographics of the American workforce, the GI Bill opened doors to postsecondary education that had never before been open, and an entire generation of "Baby Boomers" was born during the time of postwar euphoria

---

SIDEBAR 9.3

Watch the 3 minute 25 second movie promo about Sputnik at *https://www.youtube.com/watch?v=TbAXkWPasYw* and imagine your reaction to the launch of Sputnik if you were your current age and living at that time. What would your emotional reaction be? What concerns about the future might you have had in reaction to this event?

---

and prosperity. Any feelings of goodwill following World War II were short-lived as another type of war, never before seen, quickly loomed on the horizon (Divine, et al., 2007).

The United States and Soviet Union, allies during the Second World War, suffered from deep ideological differences about the reconstruction of postwar Europe. This simmering conflict between the Soviet Union and the United States grew in the late 1940s, leading to the first of a series of proxy wars, conflicts and crises; the Korean War. In 1957, the Soviet Union launched Sputnik the first man-made satellite to orbit the Earth leading to nationwide concern in the United States that it lacked the scientific and technological might to win the Cold War. The United States' response to the Sputnik launch created a global competition between the two nations resulting in the space race, nuclear proliferation, the Vietnam War, and global economic competition. Technological advances were an inevitable by-product of the Cold War (Gaddis, 2005).

The United States government acted quickly in response to Sputnik, passing the *National Defense Education Act* (NDEA) in 1958 with the purpose of identifying and encouraging students talented in science and engineering. NDEA provided funding for schools and school counselors, counselor education programs, and for consultants to aid in developing career development services for students. The impact on the school counseling profession was dramatic (Herr, 2001).

IMPORTANT CONTRIBUTORS

Robert Mathewson published *Guidance Policy and Practice* in 1949. Mathewson outlined the first developmental framework for implementing guidance programs in schools. The impact of both of these important publications will be seen in the formation of the National Standards for School Counseling Programs (Campbell & Dahir, 1997) outlined in The Transition Era (1989–present).

The team of Ginzberg, Ginsburg, Axelrod, and Herma (1951 as cited in Herr, Cramer, Niles, 2004) speculated about occupational choice being a developmental process including a series of decisions made over a period of time culminating in one's twenties with an occupational choice. Ginzberg et al. proposed four interrelated factors that ultimately led to a final career choice: individual values, emotional factors, the amount and kind of education, and the effect of reality through environmental pressures.

In 1957, Donald Super offered empirical support to the idea of developmental career theory with the publication of initial findings from the *Career Pattern Study*. Super and his colleagues studied the career development of a group of adolescent boys, documenting their work history for 25 years, and identified a series of life stages for career development. These stages include Birth, Growth, Exploration, Establishment, Maintenance, Decline, and Death. Super's (1957) theory created a paradigm shift, moving the emphasis from vocational development (the single point-in-time event of making an occupational choice) to career development (the longitudinal expression of career behaviors including the precursors to achieving readiness for career decision-making). Super's theory also provided the theoretical foundation for the subsequent development of career education models aimed at infusing career content into the educational curriculum. Career education initiative (led by persons such as Kenneth Hoyt) blossomed in the 1970s as ways to help students develop their readiness for career and educational planning.

Building on Frank Parson's early trait and factor work, John Holland published his first book, *The Psychology of Vocational Choice: A Theory of Personality Types and Model Environments,* in 1966. Holland's theory provided counselors with an empirically based, user-friendly method of matching clients' personalities to environments using six interrelated personality characteristics: Realistic, Investigative, Artistic, Social, Enterprising, and Conventional. According to the theory, both persons and work environments can be described by combinations of these six characteristics. If a person's work environment matches their personality, they are likely to be more satisfied. The task of career counseling then is to assess the client's personality characteristics and then match it to the known work environments that fit those personality characteristics (Anderson & Vandehey, 2006).

KEY EVENTS, DEVELOPMENTS, ORGANIZATIONS, AND LEGISLATION

The George Barden Act of 1946 was passed at a time when there were only 80 institutions training counselors in the United States. This legislation addressed concerns about the quality of counselor preparation including the enhancement of certification and training requirements. This paved the way for the professionalization of school and vocational counseling by encouraging reimbursement of counselor training programs, state supervision and certification processes, and eventually the phase-out of most undergraduate counselor training programs by the early 1950s (Herr, 2001).

The passing of the National Defense Education Act of 1958 was a watershed moment for the school counseling profession. Created in response to growing concerns over the ability of the United States to remain competitive with the Soviet Union in the areas of technology and science, the act required states to test secondary school students so that those who were academically talented could be encouraged to pursue higher education in the sciences.

Title V-A provided funds for support and development of local school guidance programs. Title V-B appropriated funds for counseling and guidance institutes for the purpose of upgrading the qualifications of secondary school counselors. The act, which initiated an enormous increase in the number of school counselors across the nation in addition to the identification of academically talented students, also included provisions supporting the career development of students by counselors (Herr & Shahnasarin, 2001).

KEY CONCEPTS THAT AROSE FROM THE ERA

The 1950s may very well be the most dynamic decade in the history of career and school counseling. No decade of the twentieth century saw more activity that formed the profession as we experience it today. The emphasis on career development rather than vocational development paved the way for developmental career guidance programs in the schools. The development of computer-assisted career guidance systems connected technology and career guidance to provide efficient supplemental services to counselor interaction. In many ways, this era initiated the transition from the initial approaches to career development theory and practice that arose in the early part of the twentieth century to the current developments within the area of career counseling in the schools.

THE TRANSITION ERA (1989–PRESENT)

HISTORICAL CONTEXT

In 1989, the Berlin Wall was razed providing a vivid symbolic end to the Soviet Union and the Cold War (Gaddis, 2005). Instant communication with any location in the world was quickly becoming possible and more efficient through telephone, facsimile, and the Internet. This newfound ability to communicate globally, along with the collapse of the Soviet Union, allowed for the introduction of new economies in Eastern Europe and Asia (Pope, 2000).

The United States entered the twenty-first century with more power compared to the rest of the world than at any point in history, yet a feeling of vulnerability continued to pervade the American collective psyche like never before. Being the world's sole military superpower has increased the likelihood of being the target of terrorist attacks instead of lessoning it. The American economy also suffers the influence of foreign markets and global forces like never before (Divine, et al., 2007). "The fundamental challenge for Americans of the twenty-first century would be to balance their power against their vulnerabilities." (Divine, et al., 2007, p. 881).

IMPORTANT CONTRIBUTORS

One of the primary contributors to current directions in school counseling and career development in schools is Norman C. Gysbers of the University of Missouri. Gysbers's many publications and work with the Missouri Department of Elementary and Secondary Education have served as a major guide for important developments such as the American School Counselor Association (ASCA) National Model (ASCA, 2012) and the National Center for Transforming School Counseling. In particular, the Gysbers and Henderson (2000) book has had strong influence on the roles and activities of school counselors.

Reese M. House, the initial Director of the National Center for Transforming School Counseling (see Education Trust, 2007) has had a large impact on transforming school counseling efforts in various states, school districts, and counselor education programs around the United States. Additionally, House published several articles on the *new vision* of school counseling. These articles focused on emerging important roles for school counselors including leadership in school reform, advocacy, closing achievement gaps, and using data to improve school counseling programs.

John Krumboltz and his colleagues (Mitchell & Krumboltz, 1996) developed a social learning theory of career decision-making (SLTCDM) that provides a cognitive orientation to career development. Specifically, the SLTCDM provides counselors with a theoretical and practical framework for understanding how their students may artificially limit their career exploration. Irrational thinking can become an impediment to making career and educational plans. Krumboltz adapted Bandura's model of social learning to illustrate how these impediments arise and how they can be addressed in career counseling with students.

KEY EVENTS, DEVELOPMENTS, ORGANIZATIONS, AND LEGISLATION

Campbell and Dahir (1997) published the ASCA National Standards for School Counseling Programs. These Standards cover three developmental domains, namely, academic, career, and personal-social development. The Standards are further broken down in Competencies, and these are broken down into specific behavioral Indicators. The Standards, Competencies, and Indicators are a codification of the knowledge and skills that students, Pre-K through Grade 12, should gain. These National Standards were an important step toward the development of the ASCA National Model.

The ASCA National Model (ASCA, 2003) was a milestone in the profession of school counseling. This model is a useful framework for developing school counseling programs that address the academic, career, and personal-social needs of students. The model is built around the National Standards, but it goes beyond the Standards in offering a conceptual framework and practical tools for developing comprehensive school counseling programs. The National Model builds on the work of Gysbers and Henderson (2000), the Education Trust and National Center for Transforming School Counseling (Education Trust, 2007) and others in offering a system for assessing, designing, implementing, and evaluating comprehensive school counseling programs.

Four themes drive the current ASCA National Model, namely, (a) leadership, (b) advocacy, (c) collaboration and teaming, and (d) systemic change (ASCA, 2012). School counselors are leaders in the school reform process, focusing on closing achievement gaps and ensuring opportunity-to-learn of for all students. School counselors advocate for students, families, schools, communities, and their profession. They advocate at numerous levels to eliminate barriers to students' success (see Trusty & Brown, 2005). School counselors collaborate and team with various stakeholders to promote access, equity, and educational attainment for all students. Leadership, advocacy, and collaboration are effectively used to bring about systemic changes in schools. School counselors use data to make informed decisions that result in schools and programs that better serve students.

The themes of the ASCA National Model (ASCA, 2012) are very consistent with the goals of the National Center for Transforming School Counseling (Education Trust, 2007): School counselors (a) work as leaders to promote access and equity for all students, (b) use data to change educational policies and practices, (c) design school counseling programs to help all students attain high levels of academic achievement, (d) advocate for positive changes in educational systems, and (e) use outcome data to drive subsequent steps in developing school counseling programs. The National Center for Transforming School Counseling works with numerous state departments of education and several school districts across the United States to transform school counseling programs so they can better serve students. These efforts focus in particular on closing historical achievement gaps that separate lower socioeconomic status students and students of color from other students.

Long before the introduction of the ASCA National Model, the Education for All Handicapped Children Act (P.L. 94-142) was enacted in 1975 to meet the educational needs of students with disabilities. Amendments were passed in 1990 to change the name of the law to the Individuals with Disabilities Education Act (IDEA) thus making the name of the act more inclusive, 1991 to reauthorize the Early Intervention Program for Infants and Toddlers, and again in 1997 to clarify sections of the law and restructure the subchapters. As the law stands today, all youth ages birth to 21 whose disability impacts their education are covered to receive services so that they may attain a free and appropriate education (FAPE). All states must have policies to ensure FAPE for students with disability with those policies meeting at least the minimum requirements of IDEA (Leinbaugh, 2004).

School counselors will often be a member of the school-based team responsible for the implementation of IDEA for students with disabilities. As such, it is important that professional school counselors are knowledgeable about the implementation procedures for the state in which they work. While each state will have specific provisions, there are six general steps outlined below that school-based teams follow:

1   Screening—Often done through the administration of group tests, this step is not required but is good practice to help identify students who may need further testing.

2   Prerefferal—Many schools have prerefferal teams to ensure that students are not misplaced in special education or referred to further evaluation because of a lack of instruction or English proficiency limitation.

3   Referral—The preferral team may submit a request for a nondiscriminatory evaluation for students whom they deem this step appropriate.

4   Nondiscriminatory evaluation—This evaluation measures students' cognitive, behavioral, physical, and developmental ability to determine if the student has a disability and, if so, their need for specifically designed instruction and services.

5   Evaluation team—This team includes the student's parents and various members of the school staff, often including the school counselors because of their knowledge of the general education curricula, local resources, related services personnel, and interpreting evaluation results.

6   Developing the Individualized Family Services Plan (IFSP) and Individualized Education Plan (IEP)—The IFSP is required for infants and toddlers and may fall under the evaluation team's purview when a school provides preschool programs. An IEP is required for students with disability ages 3–21. In both cases, school counselors may be asked to provide case management to ensure that the student has an opportunity for a free and appropriate education. If a member of the evaluation team, the school counselor may also participate in the development of the IEP (Leinbaugh, 2004).

KEY CONCEPTS THAT AROSE FROM THE ERA

The recent and current efforts of ASCA and the Education Trust have placed a stronger focus on academic and career development in schools. Before these efforts, more school counseling programs were reactive, focusing more on crisis response, mental health, and personal-social development. Thus, many school counselors were providing services to only a small percentage of students in the school (e.g., students experiencing crises, students with mental health concerns), ignoring the important developmental domains of academic and career development, and not offering comprehensive programs to students. The ASCA National Model and the new vision of school counseling, in contrast, focus on all the students in the school, providing proactive and developmental services (e.g., career guidance, preventive programming) in addition to remedial and responsive services. This new vision places school counselors in leadership roles and it connects school counselors more closely to the academic and career development missions of schools. The net effect of these efforts is that career and academic development are now receiving increased, deserved attention in more schools. Reese House, presenting at the National Center for Transforming School Counseling 5th Annual Summer Academy in Norfolk, VA, noted that the new vision of school counseling is not wholly new (House, 2004). House related that the new vision is largely a return to the original vision of counseling—the proactive, developmental perspective presented by Frank Parsons.

SIDEBAR 9.4

Ask a practicing school counselor out for coffee or lunch, or schedule an appointment to meet them at their school for a brief conversation. After reading about the current era of school counseling, what questions do you have about counseling in schools? Prepare your questions ahead of time and informally interview the school counselor.

SUMMARY

The evolution of career counseling in the schools is closely tied to the economic, social, and political history of the United States. The work of the school counselor does not occur in a vacuum, instead the expectation of the work performed by a school counselor has been forged by industrialization, migration, economic changes, wars, technological advances, and many other forces. Assuming that this pattern of societal influence on the role of the professional school counselor will continue future trends in school counseling may be affected by globalization, the availability of energy, fear of terrorism, and a myriad of other foreseen and unknown forces.

Georges Santayana (Hirsch, Kett, & Trefi 1, 2002) is credited with saying, "Those who cannot remember the past are condemned to repeat it." While condemnation may not be the consequence of ignoring our profession's past, a counselor would be remiss to do so. There is much to learn from those who have tread the path of the profession before that can inform both current and future school counselors.

KEY WORDS

American School Counselor Association (ASCA) National Model: Building from the ASCA National Standards for School Counseling (Campbell & Dahir, 1997), ASCA has twice published national model frameworks (ASCA, 1999; 2003; 2005; 2012) for school counselors. The current model is written o provide schools counselors with a guide to organize their practice within four dimensions: foundation, delivery, management, accountability (ASCA, 2005) while focusing on students' personal/social, academic, and career development needs.

Frank Parsons: Known as the "Father of Vocational Guidance", Parsons founded the Breadwinner's College (or Institute) in 1905 to help immigrants and youth in need of employment and then The Vocational Bureau in 1908 to help train employment counselors. Known for his posthumous work *Choosing a Vocation* (1909), Parsons is known as the creator of the trait and factor theory of career decision which is the precursor to Holland's Person-Environment Fit Theory used still today.

George Barden Act of 1946: In 1946 there were only 80 colleges and universities in the United States that offered counselor training programs. By addressing concerns about training and certification, this act led to the professionalization of school and vocational counseling by eliminating undergraduate counselor training programs and focusing on quality, standards-based graduate training for counselors.

National Center for Transforming School Counseling: "In June 2003, The Education Trust and MetLife Foundation established the National Center for Transforming School Counseling to ensure that school counselors are trained and ready to help all groups of students reach high academic standards. Initiated at a critical time when states, districts, and schools were raising standards and implementing accountability systems, NCTSC works to ensure that counselors play a critical role in advancing the equity agenda. The National Center for Transforming School Counseling promotes a new vision of school counseling in which school counselors advocate for educational equity, access to a rigorous college and career-readiness curriculum, and academic success for all students. Our mission is to transform school counselors into powerful agents of change in schools to close the gaps in opportunity and achievement for low-income students and students of color." (Retrieved March 20, 2013 from http://www.edtrust.org/dc/tsc/vision)

National Defense of Education Act (NDEA; 1958): Following the launch of Sputnik by the Soviet Union on October 4, 1957, President Dwight D. Eisenhower signed NDEA on September 2, 1958 as a means of promoting technological development through investment in science education in elementary, middle, and high schools as well as post-secondary education institutions. The impact on the profession of counseling was dramatic as increased funding was used to hire school counselors and develop counselor education programs for the training of counselors.

Occupational Outlook Handbook: First published by the U.S. Department of Labor in 1948, the *Occupational Outlook Handbook* endures today as a biennial source of 10-year employment projections and information about work environments, education and training requirements, skills, and earnings.

Trait and Factor Theory: Parsons (1909) proposed an actuarial approach to career decision making that assumes that people possess certain patterns of personal traits that can be profiled or measured; occupational environments also have factors that can be profiled or measured; and a probable fit between individuals' trait and an occupations' factors can be determined which will lead to a best fit between both the individual and the occupation. The career decision-making process therefore becomes one where the individual learns to know themselves, learns about the world-of-work, and then makes a rational choice regarding their fit in the work world.

United States Child Labor Laws: During the period of industrialization in the United States, the hiring of children was common practice particularly for jobs where a child's size might be an asset including mining and textile manufacturing. Education progressives and child welfare advocates used information campaigns about working conditions and collaborations with compulsory education advocates to lobby for these laws. The Keating-Owen Act was signed by President Woodrow Wilson in 1916 was the first such law. It prohibited the interstate sale of goods produced in factories were child labor was employed. The Keating-Owen Act was later struck down by the Supreme Court in 1918 but it served as a precursor to the Fair Standards Labor Act signed by President Franklin D. Roosevelt in 1938 which prohibits the employment of children in oppressive work conditions.

REFERENCES

American School Counselor Association (ASCA) (2012). *The ASCA National Model: A framework for school counseling programs*. Alexandria, VA: Author.

American School Counselor Association (ASCA) (2005). *The ASCA National Model: A framework for school counseling programs*. Alexandria, VA: Author.

American School Counselor Association (ASCA) (2003). *The ASCA National Model: A framework for school counseling programs*. Alexandria, VA: Author.

American School Counselor Association (ASCA) (1999). *The ASCA National Model: A framework for school counseling programs*. Alexandria, VA: Author.

Anderson, P., & Vandehey, M. (2006). *Career counseling and development in a global economy*. Boston, MA: Houghton Mifflin.

Bernert, E. H. (1958). *America's children*. New York: Wiley.

Borow, H. (1964). Notable events in the history of vocational guidance, In H. Borow (Ed.), *Man in a world at work* (pp. 45–64). Washington, DC: Houghton Mifflin.

Brewer, J. M. (1918). *The vocational-guidance movement: Its problems and possibilities*. New York: The MacMillan Company.

Brewer, J. M. (1942). *History of vocational guidance*. New York: Harper.

Campbell, C. A., & Dahir, C. A. (1997). *The National Standards for School Counseling Programs*. Alexandria, VA: American School Counselor Association.

Dewey, J. (1916). *Democracy and education: An introduction to the philosophy of education*. New York: The MacMillan Company.

Divine, R. A., Breen, T. H., Fredrickson, G. M., Williams, R. H., Gross, A. J., & Brands, H. W. (2007). *The American Story* (3rd Ed.). New York: Pearson.

Education Trust (2007). Homepage. Retrieved April 27, 2007, from http://www2.edtrust.org/edtrust. Author.

Gaddis, J. L. (2005). *The cold war: A new history*. New York: Penguin Press.

Ginzberg, E., Ginsberg, S. W., Axelrad, S., & Herma, J. (1951). *Occupational choice: An approach to a general theory*. New York: Columbia University Press.

Gysbers, N. C. (2001). School guidance and counseling in the 21st century: Remember the past into the future. *Professional School Counseling, 5*, 96–105.

Gysbers, N. C., & Henderson, P. (2000). *Developing and managing your school guidance program* (3rd ed.). Alexandria, VA: American Counseling Association.

Herr, E. L., Cramer, S. H., & Niles, S. G. (2004). *Career guidance and counseling through the lifespan: Systematic approaches* (Sixth Ed.). Boston: Pearson.

Herr, E. L. (2003). Historical roots and future issues. In B. T. Erford (Ed.), *Transforming the school counseling profession* (pp. 21–38). Columbus, OH: Merrill/Prentice-Hall.

Herr, E. L. (2001). Career development and its practice: A historical perspective. *The Career Development Quarterly, 49*, 196–211.

Herr, E. L., & Shahnasarin, M. (2001). Selected milestones in the evolution of career development practices in the twentieth century. *The Career Development Quarterly, 49*, 225–231.

Hirsch, E. D., Jr., Kett, J. F., & Trefi l, J. (2002). *The new dictionary of cultural literacy.* (3rd ed.). Boston: Houghton Mifflin Company.

Holland, J. L. (1966). *The psychology of vocational choice.* Waltham, MA: Blaisdell.

House, R. (2004, June). Keynote address. National Center for Transforming School Counseling 5th Annual Summer Academy, Norfolk, VA.

Kevles, D. J. (1968). Testing the armies intelligence: Psychologists and the military in World War I. *The Journal of American History, 55*(3), 565–581.

Keyser. D. J., & Sweetland, R. C. (1987). *Test critiques compendium: Reviews of major tests from the test critiques series.* Kansas City: Test Corporation of America.

Leinbaugh, T. (2004). Understanding special education policies and procedures. In B. T. Erford (Ed.), *Professional school counseling: A handbook of theories, programs, & practices.* (pp. 647–654). Austin, TX: Pro-Ed.

Mathewson, R. H. (1949). *Guidance policy and practice.* New York: Harper & Bros.

McCormick, R. L. (1997). Public life in industrial America, 1877–1917. In Foner, E. (Ed.), *The new American history: Revised and expanded edition* (pp. 107–132). Philadelphia, PA: Temple University Press.

Mitchell, L. K., & Krumboltz, J. D. (1996). Krumboltz's theory of career choice and counseling. In D. Brown, L. Brooks, & Associates (Eds.), *Career choice development* (3rd ed., pp. 233–280). San Francisco, CA: Jossey-Bass.

Parsons, F. (1909). *Choosing a vocation.* Boston: Houghton Mifflin.

Pope, M. (2000). A brief history of career counseling in the United States. *The Career Development Quarterly, 48*(3), 194–211.

Rogers, C. R. (1942). *Counseling and psychotherapy: Newer concepts in practice.* Boston: Houghton Mifflin.

Rose, C. (Ed) (2004). *American Decades: Primary Sources 1910–1919.* Farmington Hills, MI: Gale.

State certification requirements. (n. d.). Retrieved April 26, 2007, from http://school-counselor.org/content.asp?contentid=242

Super, D. E. (1957). *The psychology of careers.* NY: Harper & Rowe.

Tang, M., & Erford, B. T. (2004). The history of school counseling. In B. T. Erford (Ed.), *Professional school counseling: A handbook of theories, programs, & practices.* (pp. 647–654). Austin, TX: Pro-Ed.

Trusty, J., & Brown, D. (2005). Advocacy competencies for professional school counselors. *Professional School Counseling, 8*, 259–265.

Career Counseling Centers At The College Level

GENE SUTTON AND RHONDA GIFFORD

The role of the career center has evolved over the years from being a placement center that places students into full-time jobs to a fully comprehensible college and career planning center catering to freshmen through alumni in all aspects of career development. From the early 1900s to the late 1970s, most offices fell under the name of career planning and placement (Herr, Rayman, & Garis, 1993). When it came to on-campus interviewing, students would be hand-selected to interview for positions, usually by one of their professors. "This was primarily a male activity, an old boys' network, by which a faculty member would speak on behalf of a student or persons of importance who might employ him as a favor to, or out of respect for, the professor" (Herr et al., 1993).

With the advent of the G.I. Bill, it became apparent that soldiers returning home from World Wars I and II needed support. As a result, career placement offices began to open up on campuses across the country. In addition, employment associations also began to open. The first placement organization was established in February 1924 in Chicago—the National Association of Appointments Secretaries, named after the British equivalent of a placement director in the United States (Giordani, 2006). The name of the organization has since changed and is now the American

Gene Sutton and Rhonda Ghifford, "Career Counseling Centers at the College Level," *Career Counseling Across the Lifespan: Community, School, and Higher Education*, ed. Grafton T. Eliason, Jeff L. Samide, John Patrick, and Trisha Eliason, pp. 529-545. Copyright © 2014 by Information Age Publishing. Reprinted with permission.

College and Personnel Association. The goals of the organization now place more emphasis on professional development and job placement.

There have been many regional placement offices throughout the United States over the years. In 1956, a group at Lehigh University approved a constitution for a new national advisory council and named it the College Placement Publications Council. In later years, the name changed to the College Placement Council and again changed to the National Association of Colleges and Employers (NACE) in 1995. The mission of NACE was to support the goals of equal employment opportunities at the college level.

The goal of the Equal Employment Opportunity Commission (EEOC), established in 1956, was eliminating illegal discrimination from the workplace. In 1972, Congress gave the commission the ability to litigate enforcement in their jurisdiction. As equal employment opportunities began to change with the times, it became evident that the placement process was unethical. In the 1980s, many offices began to change their name to "Career Services" and made the interviewing processes available to all students. Due to concern with the hiring process, NACE developed the Principles for Professional Practice:

> The principles presented here are designed to provide practitioners with three basic precepts for career planning and recruitment: maintain an open and free selection of employment opportunities in an atmosphere conducive to objective thought; maintain a recruitment process that is fair and equitable to candidates and employing organizations; and support informed and responsible decision making by candidates. Adherence to the guidelines will support the collaborative efforts of career services and employment professionals while reducing the potential for abuses. (NACE, 2010c)

In the late 1980s and early 1990s, the offices began to expand their services to work with students throughout their college careers. Today, career services work with students from their freshman year through graduation. Most schools refer to this as the "four-year plan" or the "four-year timeline." California University of Pennsylvania (CalU of PA) places a heavy emphasis on their four-year plan called the Career Advantage Program. This program specifies the activities that students should be doing each year to ensure that in addition to pursuing their degree, they also obtain the soft skills employers seek (e.g., communication, leadership) to successfully market themselves as job candidates (California University of Pennsylvania, 2010).

CAREER CENTER FRAMEWORK

College and university career centers on different campuses can vary in their structure. Some have centralized offices, others have decentralized offices, and some have both. Campuses with a centralized office tend to work with all majors in all aspects of career development, from working with undecided majors to helping soon-to-be graduates with the job search process. Decentralized offices tend to be located within a specific college or major and work solely with those students (e.g., business or pharmacy department). Some campuses, whether centralized or not, will have a separate office that works with undecided students. One such campus is Oregon State University that has the office of university exploratory studies program. This program advises all undecided students through their sophomore year to guide them in to the degree that will fit their interests and goals (Oregon State University, 2010).

The name and size of career centers vary depending on a number of factors. These might include the size of the school, the budget, and the belief of upper administration regarding the importance of a career center. There are many different names for a career center, including Career Services, Career Life Planning, and Career Development.

Staffing the career center also varies with each institution. In an ideal situation, the office will have the following staff members: director, associate director, career counselors/ advisors, alumni career counselor/advisor, employer development coordinator, employer relations coordinator, receptionist, and graduate assistant(s). In addition to these positions, some offices will also host graduate-level practicum and internship students. The office of Career Services at CalU of PA is one such office that offers these opportunities to graduate students. Most of these students come from the Community and Agency Counseling program with the goal of working in a career center at the collegiate level.

As for the roles of the positions, the director oversees all aspects of the center and typically reports to the dean of student affairs, the dean of academic affairs, or occasionally the provost. In addition to overseeing the department, some directors will also take student appointments, hold leadership positions with organizations related to the various industries at the state, regional, and national levels, and assist with employer development. The director also collaborates with various departments on campus to develop new programs, such as alumni relations and university development. The associate director assists the director in the operations of the center, takes student appointments, and takes on various leadership roles similar to the director. This position usually entails heading programs and events that occur on and off campus such as job fairs and conference planning. The career counselors generally work mostly with student appointment, from working with undecided students in their freshman and sophomore years to helping them find a full-time job as they near graduation. They also work with alumni who are seeking employment for a variety of reasons. Ideally, the career center would have a counselor specifically working with alumni.

The employer development and employer relations coordinators are ideally separate, yet often combined positions. The development coordinator is in charge of creating relations with various companies in the region as well as nationally, going on company visits and bringing those companies to campus. They will also attend the Association of Colleges and Employers Conference at the state, regional, or national level, job fairs, chamber of commerce events, industry events, and Human Resource Association events. The relations coordinator generally is in charge of handling the recruiters from established organizations that are working with that particular college. The responsibilities can include coordinating on-campus interviews for internships and full-time jobs, setting up classroom presentations, and assisting with job fairs. The receptionist generally answers the phone, schedules student appointments, and assists the director as needed. Graduate assistants' responsibilities can range from working with students on all career-related matters to taking on projects and, in some cases, supervising student interns.

MISSION

The mission of most career centers is to help guide students through their college career. This may include working with undecided freshmen and sophomores to ensure they find a career path that is a best fit for them. Additionally, career centers help juniors and seniors gain experience in their fields so that they develop all the soft skills employers seek such as communication and problem solving. They may also help seniors seek full-time employment by assisting them with resume and cover letter writing, interviewing skills, job search strategies, or with the application process for graduate school. The mission statement of the office of Career Services at CalU of PA is the following:

> The office of Career Services supports the mission of California University of Pennsylvania in building character and building careers by providing services and resources that facilitate the lifelong career development process. Using the Career Advantage Program as a framework, we partner with our stakeholders: students, alumni, employers, university faculty and staff, and parents to provide these mutually beneficial services. (CalU of PA, 2010)

CAMPUS AND COMMUNITY RELATIONS

Depending on the particular career service office, many different relationships will develop with employers, faculty and staff, and advisory boards. "Career planning and placement services must maintain relations with relevant campus offices and external agencies, which necessarily requires regular identification of the office with which such relationships are critical" (Herr et al., 1993). In addition to employers, CalU of PA has developed relationships with many of the faculty and staff, and has at least one professor from each department who serves as the Career Advantage Program liaison (CalU of PA, 2010). These individuals are responsible for keeping their department up to date with the CalU of PA Career Advantage Program.

CalU of PA has also created an advisory board with employers, faculty and staff, and students as part of the membership. The advisory board was set up with the intention of staying current with the field, as well as generating new ideas and programs to offer to both employers and students (CalU of PA, 2010). CalU of PA also works with the community members assisting them in all aspects of the job search. Developing relationships with all of the various stakeholders is a key component of a successful career center.

SERVICES PROVIDED AND DELIVERY METHODS

The services offered by a four-year college or university career center varies based on its mission, scope, structure (centralized vs. decentralized), and staff size. Many career centers are comprehensive, offering a full range of services that includes career development and career needs. Career center services are grouped into four broad categories:

1 Career counseling

2 Job search services

3 Career information

4 Programming and outreach

CAREER COUNSELING SERVICES

The core service of a career center is career counseling. Herr, Rayman, and Garis (1993) noted that providing counseling services enables the career center to emphasize the developmental process approach to career choice and empowers clients with the knowledge and skills to clarify and implement career plans throughout their lifetime. Career centers that do not provide individual or group counseling services run the risk of being seen as merely a job or placement center whose effectiveness is evaluated primarily by the number of organizations recruiting on campus and the number of students and graduates finding internships and jobs.

The most common ways to provide career counseling services include individual counseling sessions by appointment, intake or "drop-in" counseling, group counseling (including career classes for credit), assessment, and online counseling (NACE, 2010).

INDIVIDUAL COUNSELING APPOINTMENTS

Individual counseling sessions by appointment typically last from 30–60 minutes and may address any of the following career issues (Herr et al., 1993):

- Career indecision
- Choice of major
- Exploring career options related to the client's major, interests, skills, and values
- Assistance in identifying opportunities for experiential education (i.e., job shadowing, cooperative education, internships, etc.)
- Assistance with the job search and/or graduate or professional school application process.

Confidential individual counseling session notes should adhere to ethical standards for Career Services as outlined by the Standards and Guidelines for Student Services/ Student Development (Council for the Advancement of Standards, 1986).

Herr, Rayman, and Garis (1993) point out that client expectations of career counseling are varied and complex, requiring the career center to clarify its philosophy and practices regarding the following questions:

- To what extent does the counselor serve as educator or provide information in career counseling?
- How much follow-up and how many career counseling sessions are available to clients?
- To what extent is assessment used in the career counseling process?
- To what extent are personal issues addressed and dealt with in career counseling?

Some clients may expect, seek, and be satisfied with one or two visits to the career center; others may require multiple counseling sessions. Client expectations of the career counseling process should be clarified in the early stages of the counseling appointment (Herr et al., 1993).

Demand and use of individual career counseling typically varies depending on the type of client. For example, upperclassmen are typically more likely to seek out career center services because they need assistance in developing a resume or finding a job, whereas freshmen and sophomores may need to be encouraged to become engaged in the career planning process early in their college career. For example, all CalU of PA freshmen enrolled in the University's First Year Seminar complete the Strong Interest Inventory. Career services staff members then visit each class section to help students interpret their inventory results and plan next steps as part of the University's Career Advantage Program (CalU of PA, 2010).

Because the connection between academic programs and career options are less defined in the liberal arts and humanities, students in these majors may be less likely to seek out career counseling and other services than vocationally-oriented majors such as business or engineering (Herr et al., 1993). Career centers with a counseling component are better able to engage and serve these populations than career centers with a focus only on "placement."

INTAKE AND DROP-IN COUNSELING

Many clients prefer individual counseling but also want quick service and the convenience of dropping in the career center without an appointment. Increased demand for this type of service has prompted many career centers to provide intake or "drop-in" counseling services at least several hours per week or more often, depending on available staff. Most often, an appointment is not necessary for intake counseling, and the sessions are brief and information based (10–30 minutes maximum).

The primary purpose of the "drop-in" session is for the intake counselor to address client questions quickly and screen or refer clients to appropriate career center services or programs. Topics discussed during an intake counseling session include resume and cover letter reviews, brief interview, job search, or graduate school application questions, and questions about services or programs (Herr et al., 1993).

Full-time or part-time staff, graduate assistants, and/or peer counselors may serve as intake counselors. Because of the wide variety of career questions that clients attending intake sessions may have, all staff serving as intake counselors should be carefully trained and need to be familiar with all of the services provided by the career center, as well as able to refer clients to appropriate resources outside of the career center.

Two advantages of intake counseling are that it allows individual counseling appointments to focus on more in-depth career issues such as career choice or exploration while allowing the career center to provide immediate assistance to clients without an appointment. Intake counselors can also refer clients to other career center programs and services, potentially increasing the number of clients taking advantage of those programs and services (Herr et al., 1993).

GROUP COUNSELING

Group counseling is an alternative means to engage clients in career planning. Group counseling typically focuses on a specific topic common to all members such as self-assessment, career exploration, internship search, job search strategies, or graduate and professional school search and application. The most effective groups ideally range from five to fifteen clients, meet for multiple sessions, and are interactive in nature. They may be offered as a series of non-credit workshops or as a credit-bearing class (typically one credit, but sometimes up to three credits).

Advantages of group counseling include efficiency as well as opportunity for sharing and modeling among members of the group (Herr et al., 1993). Group sessions tailored to specific populations such as undecided freshmen, graduating seniors, minority students, returning adult students, academically at-risk students, or arts-related majors may be especially effective in creating an atmosphere of interaction and understanding. Disadvantages of group counseling, especially of non-credit offerings, are that group members may not feel compelled to attend and may not feel that their specific career concerns are adequately addressed in the group setting (Herr et al., 1993).

ASSESSMENT

Career assessment should be offered through the career center because it supports the broader counseling and career exploration mission of the career center, and when used appropriately, it provides an additional source of information as part of the career exploration process during individual counseling appointments (Herr et al., 1993).

Career assessments should not be used strictly as a diagnostic tool by clients or counselors (i.e., "tell me what I should be or do"), but rather as a launch pad for further reflection, discussion and exploration of the client's interests, values, abilities, personal qualities, or beliefs. Career counselors must be well versed in the effective use of career assessments and assist their clients in how to effectively interpret and use the information gleaned from the assessment in the career planning and exploration process.

Career assessments can be classified as follows: assessment of the client's personality type, interests, values, and abilities; computer-assisted career guidance systems (CACG); and diagnostic measures of the client's career maturity, progress, or satisfaction in the career planning process (Herr et al., 1993). Some common career assessments include:

- Myers Briggs Type Indicator (MBTI). I. G. Myers and K. C. Briggs.
- Consulting Psychologists Press, Inc. (personality type)
- Strong Interest Inventory (SII). E. K. Strong, Jr., J. C. Hansen, and D. P. Campbell, Consulting Psychologists Press, Inc. (interests)
- FOCUS (CACG)
- eDISCOVER (CACG)
- Career Development Inventory (CDI). D. E. Super, A. S. Thompson, R. H. Lindeman, J. P. Jordaan, and R. A. Myers. Consulting Psychologists Press. (career maturity)
- My Vocational Situation (MVS). J. L. Holland, D. C. Daiger, and P. G. Power. Consulting Psychologists Press. (career planning, knowledge and process)
- Career Beliefs Inventory (CBI). J. D. Krumboltz. Consulting Psychologists Press. (work-related behavior or beliefs)

ONLINE COUNSELING

Computer-assisted career guidance systems may be used effectively without the guidance of a career counselor (Garis & Bowlsbey, 1984; Sampson & Stripling, 1979).

Career assessments commonly used during an individual counseling appointment such as the MBTI and SII require professional interpretation by a career counselor. The assessments that provide diagnostic measures of client career maturity, progress, or satisfaction in the career planning process are not commonly used in the career exploration process, but may be used to evaluate career center services such as individual career counseling or credit career planning courses (Garis & Bowlsbey, 1984).

JOB SERVICES

Herr, Rayman, & Garis (1993) noted that job search services provided by a career center might vary widely depending on the following factors:

- College/university size and enrollment
- Geographic location (urban, rural)
- Centralized or decentralized model
- Academic programs offered

Regardless of these factors, job search services (historically referred to as "placement") should be considered part of a process. This process would include a range of services to assist clients in the implementation of career plans throughout their academic career, not just an event that occurs at the end of the senior year.

Job search services at the career center typically include the following:

- On-campus recruiting
- On-campus and regional job fairs
- Alumni career network
- Credential files

ON-CAMPUS RECRUITING

On-campus recruiting provides an opportunity for career centers to connect student and alumni clients with representatives of business, industry, and government. These services also keep the career center in contact with employers and create a high profile for the career center. Career centers should have a well-organized system in place to notify and provide clients access to opportunities for on-campus interviews (Herr et al., 1993). Many centers use computerized systems to manage the on-campus interview process, including employer information and candidate notification and selection. Interviews can be "open" (first-come, first-serve basis) or "pre-screened" (employer selects specific interviewees from the applicant pool). The physical setting for on-campus interviews should be quiet, private, and professional. The career center should maintain the professionalism of on campus recruiting by providing clients with adequate interview preparation and by providing an orientation to recruiters (Herr et al., 1993).

ON-CAMPUS JOB FAIRS AND REGIONAL JOB FAIRS

Career and job fairs may be sponsored by the career center or a combination of organizations (a consortium). Some larger colleges and universities host a number of career and job fairs on campus, while other smaller colleges and universities may be more likely to participate in regional consortium fairs, whereby a number of partners collaborate to coordinate and host the fair. For example, a group of 44 colleges and universities in western Pennsylvania collaborate to host the biannual WestPACS Job & Internship Fair.

Employer and organization attendance at fairs varies widely depending on a variety of factors that include size and location of the campus, range and quality of academic offerings, and the recruiting organization's budget. Because of declining recruiting budgets, the increase in online applications and other "virtual" recruiting mechanisms has forced employing organizations to be selective in the number of colleges and universities at which they choose to recruit.

One disadvantage regarding on-campus recruiting and job fairs is that the types of employers and positions for which they are recruiting may be narrow in scope and may not represent the wide variety of majors offered at the college or university. Therefore, in order to accommodate the career exploration and job search needs of all majors, it is best for the career center to host a job fair that provides a broad range of employment options.

ALUMNI CAREER NETWORK

Most career centers offer online job postings, referral of candidate resumes to employers, and resume books. A variety of vendors provides systems to manage these services electronically. Because it is widely held that at least 75% of job seekers find jobs through personal networking, many colleges and universities have established alumni career networks to assist their students and job-seeking alumni. These networks can be offered online for ease of access and may be sponsored through the career center or the alumni association.

CREDENTIAL FILES

Some employers (i.e., school districts) and graduate schools often prefer confidential recommendations to be managed and stored by the career center. With the increase of online portfolio management systems, many career centers have reduced or eliminated their credential file management service.

CAREER INFORMATION

The career center is well positioned to serve as a source of career information because it bridges the gap between academia and business, industry and government (Herr et al., 1993). Every career center should gather and maintain career information accessible to clients and stakeholders (including faculty, prospective students, and parents) for use in career exploration and planning. Because employment and organizational information is widely available on the Internet, many career centers have reduced or eliminated the traditional "career library" shelves of books and periodicals. Rather, they market their websites for easier access to resources. Career information offered by the career center could include:

- Academic information
- Self-assessment and career exploration information
- Internship and summer job information
- Career/occupational information
- Graduate/professional school information

- Job search information regarding resumes, cover letters, interviewing, networking, etc.
- Company/organization information
- Career-related periodicals and web sites
- Job posting sites

PROGRAMMING AND OUTREACH

Because it is not mandatory in most cases for clients to use the services of the career center, programming and outreach efforts are crucial. Career outreach programs typically are brief (one to three hours) and are primarily information-oriented. The goals of career outreach programs may be to provide an opportunity for the career center to promote its services and programs, to introduce clients to the career planning or job search process, and to provide information about a specific career planning issue to a group (Herr et al., 1993). Tailored to each audience, outreach program topics may include:

- Career center orientation
- Self-assessment of skills, interests, and values
- Exploring linkages between majors and careers
- How to find an internship or cooperative education position
- Resume and cover letter preparation
- Interview skills
- Job search strategies, including networking
- Professional business etiquette
- Orientation to on-campus recruiting
- Graduate/professional school admission
- Transition from school to work

Herr, Rayman, & Garis (1993) noted that outreach programs allow the career center to gain access to students and can be offered in a variety of settings, including:

- Academic classes
- Student clubs and organizations, including Greek organizations
- Residence halls
- Campus events (i.e., orientation, activity fair)

- Faculty and student leader training/orientation programs (i.e., new faculty orientation; or training sessions for campus tour guides, peer mentors, and resident assistants)
- Community organizations

Outreach programs can be more successful when the career center partners with specific offices and groups on campus such as the student orientation office, alumni relations, international student services, support centers for student athletes, returning adult student services, disabled student services, admissions, honors program, and so on. For example, CalU of PA's office of Career Services is partnering with the student orientation office to host a "Major Dilemma" fair where both prospective and current students can speak with upperclassmen and faculty to explore academic majors and career options (CalU of PA, 2010).

Some colleges and universities offer a career planning and implementation course for credit, taught by career center staff or a faculty member. Such courses offer several advantages, including enhancing the professional credibility of the career center and its staff, enhancing decision-making skills, and facilitating the student career-planning progress (Bartsch & Hackett, 1979; Garis & Niles, 1990). Some career courses are focused on freshmen and sophomores, with the goal of facilitating the self-assessment and career exploration process, while other courses are focused on juniors and seniors, with the goal of facilitating the career implementation process.

ADDITIONAL SERVICES

With the increased focus on the value of experiential learning, many career centers provide support services to clients interested in obtaining professionally relevant experience. These services may range from assistance with resume preparation and interview skills, to assistance in identifying and applying to appropriate internship sites.

Herr, Rayman, and Garis (1993) noted that experiential education programs may include any of the following:

- Internships—semester or summer experience; typically includes academic credit; may be paid or unpaid
- Cooperative education—typically an alternating work-study program where students rotate semesters in the classroom and in the work environment; includes both credit and pay
- Externships/job shadowing—brief exposure (one day to two weeks); usually not for credit and not paid

Table 9.1

Trend	% Ranked 1 or 2	% Ranked #1
Budget changes	49.6%	32.5%
Technology	46.3	23.0
Assessment metrics	37.7	15.4

- Summer jobs

Benchmark studies show a steady increase in the number of career centers providing students with internship and co-op assistance. In 1975, just 26% of offices said they provided this service. In 2004, more than 85% of offices said they did so (NACE, 2005).

ALUMNI SERVICES

Students are the primary clients of career centers; however, some colleges and universities are experiencing increased demand from their alumni for assistance with career change or job search assistance. This requires that a career center develop a well-defined policy regarding response to alumni inquiries, including service content and fees, if applicable (Herr et al., 1993).

Due to decreased funding for higher education, some colleges and universities facing budget cuts have realized that an investment in providing career services to alumni may result in alumni engagement with the university. For example, CalU of PA, as part of the "CAL U for Life" initiative, provided funding for an alumni career counselor and an employer development coordinator, housed in the office of Career Services, to provide lifelong career services at no cost to alumni (CalU of PA, 2010).

Some career centers have expanded their services to alumni by collaborating with the alumni office or by charging alumni for services. Career services for alumni typically may be provided through the alumni office, through the career center, or through a combination of offices. Herr, Rayman, and Garis (1993) noted that alumni career services can include:

- Individual counseling
- Career planning and job search workshops offered on-site, regionally, or online
- Online job postings, career planning, and job search resources
- Newsletters
- Computer-based networking and resume referral

- On-site and regional career and job fairs and networking opportunities

TOP TRENDS AND ISSUES

According to the Future Trends Survey conducted by the National Association of Colleges and Employers (NACE) Future Trends Committee in 2009, career services professionals reported that they believe budget changes will be the most influential trend in the near future. Table 9.1 is a summary of the top three trend rankings by college and university career centers (NACE, 2009).

Responses differed among respondents from private versus public colleges and universities, and four-year versus two-year colleges. Private colleges ranked technology as the highest-ranking trend, while public universities ranked budget changes as the highest-ranking trend.

BUDGET CHANGES

According to the NACE (2009), more than half of career centers faced a decrease in their 2009–2010 operating budgets. Career centers are finding they need to do more with less. In response to funding cuts, many career centers have adopted fees for employers (i.e., for career fairs or advertising). A minority of centers have adopted fees for students and alumni (i.e., for administration of assessments).

TECHNOLOGY

According to career services practitioners who responded to the NACE 2009 Future Trends survey, social networking sites such as Facebook® and LinkedIn®, and communication media such as YouTube® and Twitter®, are the most important technologies that will affect career centers in the near future.

Technology can be used to reach alumni who are outside the campus' geographic reach. For example, the University of Illinois Alumni Association's Alumni Career Center uses e-mail and the phone for advising, conference calls, and webinars for workshops; it has also enhanced an online virtual career center for alumni (NACE, 2010b).

Online and virtual recruiting will grow in popularity, especially in the early stages of recruiting, resulting in direct interaction between employers and students (NACE, 2009). There is not a clear consensus regarding how this will affect college recruiting and the role of the career center. Some respondents are concerned that career centers will be by-passed in the recruiting process and that there will be fewer employers recruiting on campus and at job fairs, while others see a continued need for high-touch, face-to-face recruiting after the initial interview (NACE, 2009).

Balancing high-tech and high-touch methods is perhaps the most challenging issue related to technology. It is important for career services professionals to stay abreast of changes in technology and to understand the sophisticated use of electronic tools and resources.

ASSESSMENT METRICS

Assessment metrics, or measuring the results of career center programs and services and demonstrating the value of the career services function, is a critical issue for career centers. It can be challenging for career services professionals to identify and implement measures that demonstrate their value because there is no simple way that will accurately demonstrate the value of the career center's services.

For example, placement statistics (i.e., the number of new graduates employed within a certain period of time after graduation) is not a reliable measure of the effectiveness of a career center's programs because there are many factors outside the circle of influence of the career center that have an impact on whether graduates find employment. Such factors may include the economy, quality of and demand for the graduate's academic program, and the graduate's willingness to relocate to find employment.

As a result, more career centers are focusing on assessing student learning outcomes: what are students learning because of using the services and attending the programs offered through the career center? For example, to assess student learning in a career development course at Barry University, an instructor designed resume, cover letter, and interviewing rubrics, or "grids." The instructor used the rubrics to determine whether the students' level of knowledge and skill has improved by comparing resumes, cover letters, and interview quality before and after students have completed the career development course (NACE, 2006).

OTHER TRENDS

NACE (2005) provides further insight into the issues and trends identified by career center staff. These trends include strengthening the image of the career center within its institution, branding the institution and career center to employers, understanding risk management and legal issues related to the recruiting and hiring process, and working with faculty and other campus stakeholders (such as university development and alumni relations) to assist students, alumni, and employers with job search and recruitment.

According to career center respondents, collaborating with other groups to promote or facilitate the work of career services is increasingly important (NACE, 2009). Partner options, ranked in order of the number and percentage of respondents choosing a particular partner option, include:

- Alumni relations
- Faculty
- Academic Advising
- Development
- Multi-school consortium
- Professional or trade association
- Another college career center
- For-profit counseling center

Collaborating with employers, alumni, and parents to provide experiential education opportunities such as job shadowing, co-op, and internships is a trend that will continue to grow. Employers want employees who are fully trained and ready to work, and increasingly utilize experiential programs as a means for identifying and hiring candidates.

Career centers will continue to be seen as important partners in the hiring process if they are adaptable and if they work in conjunction with other stakeholders in the campus community to meet the needs of both recruiters and students (NACE, 2009).

KEY WORDS

Candidate: One likely or suited to undergo or be chosen for something specified such as a job.

Mission: A specific task with which a person or a group is charged.

Reflection: Consideration of some subject matter, idea, or purpose.

Undecided: Students who have not chosen a major, but are enrolled within a college or university.

Upperclassman: A member of the junior or senior class in a school or college.

REFERENCES

Bartsch, K., & Hackett, G. (1979). Effects of a decision making course on locus of control, conceptualization and career planning. *Journal of College Student Personnel, 20*, 230–235.

California University of Pennsylvania. (2010). *Career services.* Retrieved from http://www.calu.edu/current-students/career-services/career-services/index.htm

Council for the Advancement of Standards. (1986). *CAS standards and guidelines for student services/development programs.* Washington, DC: Council for the Advancement of Standards.

Garis, J. W., & Bowlsbey, J. H. (1984, December). DISCOVER and the counselor: Their effect upon college student career planning progress. *ACT Research Report.* (85).

Garis, J. W., & Niles, S. G. (1990). The separate and combined effects of SIGI or DISCOVER and a career planning course on undecided university students. *Career Development Quarterly, 38*(3), 261–274.

Giordani, P. (2006). *National Association of Colleges and Employers through the years: The history and origins of the association.* NACE Journal. Retrieved from http://www.naceweb.org/Journal/2005october/National_Association_of_Colleges_and_Employers_History_Origins/

Herr, E. L., Rayman, J. R., & Garis, J. W. (1993). *Handbook for the college and university career center.* Westport, CT: Greenwood Press.

National Association of Colleges and Employers. (2005). Into the future: Top issues and trends for career services and college recruiting. *NACE Journal, 66*(1), 27–32.

National Association of Colleges and Employers. (2006). *Rubrics cubed: Three rubrics to help you determine student learning outcomes in career development courses.* Retrieved from http://www.naceweb.org/Publications/Journal

National Association of Colleges and Employers. (2009). Looking ahead: Highlights from the future trends survey. *NACE Journal, 70*(1), 22–28.

National Association of Colleges and Employers. (2010a). *What does the typical career center offer?* Retrieved from http://www.naceweb.org/Publications/Spotlight_Online/2010/0120/What_Does_the_Typical_Career_Center_Offer_.aspx

National Association of Colleges and Employers. (2010b). *How to handle the increase in alumni seeking career services.* Retrieved from http://www.naceweb.org/spotlightonline/121008c/Alumni_Seeking_Career_Services/?referal=knowledgecenter&menuid=0

National Association of Colleges and Employers. (2010c). *Principles for professional practice.* Retrieved from http://www.naceweb.org/principles/

Oregon State University. (2010). *University exploratory studies program.* Retrieved from http://oregonstate.edu/uesp/

Sampson, J. P., & Stripling, R. O. (1979). Strategies for counselor intervention with a computer-assisted career guidance system. *Vocational Guidance Quarterly, 27*, 230–238.

DISCUSSION QUESTIONS

1   Many college students change their majors several times during their journey through college. Briefly describe the services available for college students to explore career options.

2   How can schools provide career services to students?

3   Do you remember talking with someone in high school about career options? Discuss possible pros and cons concerning career counseling in high schools.

CONCLUSION

Trying to decide what to do for a career can be a daunting task for high school students. Fortunately, many schools are making career exploration a priority and are providing career counseling to all students. Many people may feel in the dark about how they can explore career options. Without career counseling settings, people may pick the first job they find, not realizing how the job will impact their lives for years to come. Adults who find themselves looking for a new career need to know that there are local centers that can help them explore new career opportunities.

INDEX OF KEY TERMS

- adult career counseling
- career counseling settings
- career counseling in schools
- college counseling centers
- one-stop career center

SUGGESTED PUBLICATIONS FOR FURTHER READING

Career One Stop. (n.d.). *Career One Stop.* Retrieved from https://www.careeronestop.org

Matta, T. F., Matta, J. S., & Matta, D. S. (2014). The changing landscape of career development in higher education. In J. L. Samide, G. T. Eliason, & J. Patrick (Eds.), *Career development across the lifespan: Counseling for community, schools, higher education, and beyond* (pp. 825–841). Charlotte, NC: Information Age.

Williams, C. T., Barrett, B. B., & Graham, L. H. (2011). Career development in the military. In J. L. Samide, G. T. Eliason, & J. Patrick (Eds.), *Career development in higher education* (pp. 327–341). Charlotte, NC: Information Age.

CONCLUSION

N ow that you have finished your course and completed the readings in this book, we want to encourage you to reflect on what you have learned. As mentioned in the introduction, many people (including counselors) assume that career exploration is only a secondary task and that finding a career is as easy as looking on a job website. Our goal was to provide you with selected readings that will expand your thinking about career exploration as well as factors involved in helping someone with their career development.

Knowing and being able to use career theories is a critical component of career counseling. This book not only provided information on career theories, it expanded your knowledge on how internal and external factors play a role in career development. The book also covered critical topics such as ethics, career resources, addressing diversity, and career counseling settings. One of our favorite chapters is on how career professionals can use technology as a vital piece in career counseling. Technology has changed the way professionals perform career counseling, and we are just in the beginning phases of how technology will shape our future careers.

Again, we encourage you to take some time to reflect on what you have learned through this book and your course on career counseling. The skills and knowledge you have learned will be used throughout *your career* as a mental health professional.

CPSIA information can be obtained
at www.ICGtesting.com
Printed in the USA
BVHW092102100920
588455BV00002B/87

9 781516 531615